MW01633750

LESSONS LEARNED II

Using Case Studies and History to Improve Safety Education

SafetyEd: Safety Education for Outdoor
and Remote Work Environments

SafetyEd: Safety Education for Outdoor
and Remote Work Environments
Deb Ajango
32789 Cumulus Road
Eagle River, Alaska 99577
1-907-696-3490
debajango@att.net
Find us on the web: www.safetyed.net

Editor: Deb Ajango
Associate Editor: Kay Landis
Copy Editor: Becky Makool
Assistant Editor: Karen Cafmeyer
Typesetting: Deb Ajango and Becky Makool
Printing and Binding: Watchmaker Publishing,
Palm Springs, California
Photographs: James Larabee, Brian Okonek, and Deb Ajango

Printed in the United States of America

ISBN 1-929148-54-2

LESSONS LEARNED II:
Using Case Studies and History to Improve Safety Education

Deb Ajango's great book, *Lessons Learned II*, is an instrumental read for all outdoor educators, wilderness instructors, and the outdoor community as a whole. The various case studies, along with insights from a variety of experts in the outdoor industry, outline many ideas for preventing accidents as well as dealing with the aftermath of a tragedy. It is a significant learning tool for all of us involved in outdoor education.

Daryl R. Miller
South District Ranger
Denali National Park and Preserve

Lessons Learned II uses several interesting case studies, presented by some of the best and brightest in the field of outdoor education, to provide a framework for discussing, developing, and maintaining risk management strategies. Whether you are developing an outdoor organization from the ground up or want to implement changes in an existing program, LLII is an insightful and enlightening tool.

Henry Wood
Accreditation Coordinator
Association for Experiential Education

Deb Ajango's new edition of *Lessons Learned* provides an in-depth road map for outdoor program leaders. Through some key case studies and informative chapters written by leaders in the field, she presents the critical issues all echelons and institutions must focus upon if we are to manage the risks we face and treat people well in the wake of tragedy.

Deb shares her own story of tragedy that resulted from having inherited a flawed program both at the field and administrative levels. She was hired as the academic coordinator for the University of Alaska's outdoor program, and less than three weeks later, she had to cope with the aftermath of a mountaineering accident that included two fatalities and 11 serious injuries. Her reflections on this experience alone are reason enough to read the book.

As to why all administrators of both schools and programs need the information presented, I am reminded of the headmaster of the Oregon Episcopal School in Portland who told me, following the tragic fatalities of seven students and two faculty on Mt. Hood in 1987, "Frankly, I had no idea what was going on in the field."

Jed Williamson
President, Sterling College
Editor, *Accidents in North American Mountaineering*

ACKNOWLEDGMENTS

I owe tremendous thanks to the many friends, colleagues, and even strangers who helped make this publication possible.

First, I would like to thank all of the people who allowed me to use their stories. By examining our shared pasts, we stand a greater chance for changing our futures. Thank you so much for allowing others to learn from your experiences.

Thank you to all of the contributing authors. Each agreed to submit work simply because he or she believed in the cause.

Thank you to Kay Landis, associate editor, who once again helped shape ideas, provided encouragement, and kept me on track. I look forward to a third book together.

Thank you to Becky Makool and Karen Cafmeyer, whose professional expertise improved the writing and the presentation.

Thank you to James Larabee and Brian Okonek for the use of their photographs.

And last but not least, thank you to my parents for teaching me to persevere.

When I cowrote and edited *Lessons Learned: A Guide to Accident Prevention and Crisis Response* I knew we were exploring uncharted territory. The text broached a previously off-limits subject: It addressed the topic of program fatalities head on. By writing about my experience with a multi-fatality accident on Ptarmigan Peak in Alaska, I hoped to convince readers that it is okay to talk about tragic events. In hindsight, however, I think the book did not go far enough. Because the information was more factual than personal, it was interesting but not compelling.

There are myriad resources these days that explain what it takes to run a quality outdoor program, and a variety of authors offer excellent advice. In theory, any service provider should be able to create an effective risk management system by following these guidelines. By checking off the steps, program managers should be able to feel confident that they can avoid most incidents. They also may feel assured that they will know what to do if something does go wrong. But there is a significant difference between theory and reality.

Lessons Learned II is personal. It applies theories to real life, using case studies to demonstrate how and why accidents can happen, even in quality programs, under the watch of quality people. These intimate accounts of serious incidents, failed response plans, and chaotic accident scenes also reveal the true and potentially devastating effects an accident can have—on participants, on families, on employees, and on organizations themselves. Simply put, the stakes couldn't be higher. If our industry hopes to avoid repeating mistakes, it is not just "okay" to talk about them. It is, in fact, essential that we share our experiences and examine them in detail.

Chapters One and Two provide in-depth chronologies of two serious incidents. One group of participants was made up of inexperienced teens; the other of relatively experienced adults. The teens' program consisted of day trips with a single overnight campout; the other outing involved climbing to the top of North America's highest mountain. In the first case study, a young boy nearly drowned. In the second, a man experienced severe frostbite.

At first glance, the two stories might seem very different, but they actually share a number of similarities. In both cases, people were seriously injured. In neither case was there a single obvious mistake that led to the accident. In fact, it is possible to use both cases as examples of how injuries can result from inherent risks. That is, no matter how solid a program is, due to the nature of outdoor activities, sometimes people get hurt.

As you read these two stories, I ask you not to jump to early judgment. Instead, try to consider the events from the perspectives of the participants, their loved ones, of the trip leaders, and then of the program managers. Both programs did many things well; we can learn from that. Both also made mistakes, one program perhaps more than the other. Before these stories were "over" (which in reality they will never be), one service provider was alleged to be negligent. In the second incident, the participants accepted that the damage they endured was simply "part of the game" they had chosen to play.

Chapter Three assesses the accident prevention strategies used by the programs involved in the case studies. By comparing each outfitter's operating procedures to the 10 components of a risk management system, I identify some subtleties of risk management planning, some mistakes that service providers sometimes make, and several theories to explain why a claim of negligence was made in the first case but not in the second.

Chapter Four addresses emergency action plans. Case studies of real emergencies reveal a significant gap between planning and reality, as I experienced firsthand at the University of Alaska Anchorage. This analysis examines the element of surprise, considers the special cases of subcontractors and volunteers, and explains why some organizations seem to survive serious incidents intact while others are challenged to the core.

Chapter Five offers information that is new to the industry. *In the Path of the Ripple* describes the effects an accident can have on trip leaders and program managers who were in charge when participants were seriously injured or killed. Several outdoor professionals share their stories and experiences, revealing how seriously employees can be traumatized. The chapter also examines what helped or hindered their recoveries, how likely they are to stay in the industry after their experiences, and how the incidents continue to resonate throughout their lives.

In Chapter Six, attorney Charles "Reb" Gregg applies legal theory to the introductory case studies, moving from pre-trip preparations through post-incident actions. In discussing how a prosecuting and/or defense lawyer might view each case, Mr. Gregg shows how well-thought-out actions can guide an organization through even the worst kind of incident to a reasonable, if not positive, outcome.

Chapters Seven, Eight, and Nine include insights from Drew Leemon, a long-time risk manager; Blaine Smith, a veteran guide of 20 years; and Jerry Dzugan, a distinguished marine safety expert. Mr. Leemon offers an update of his work from *Lessons Learned I* on "How Accidents Happen." Mr. Smith, the lead guide on the trip described in Chapter Two, shares his views on what it means to be a leader. Mr. Dzugan examines why people engage in risky behaviors in the first place. If certain key questions can be answered, Mr. Dzugan believes, program and industry leaders will be better equipped to make positive changes in a safety culture.

Lessons Learned II concludes with some words from Vicki Cornish, an administrator with the National Oceanic and Atmospheric Administration. For several years, Ms. Cornish oversaw the National Observer Program (NOP)—a program that trains young, inexperienced men and women to spend days to weeks on marine vessels, often on the high seas, gathering data for the government. The NOP recently engaged in an aggressive effort to standardize and improve its safety training. Ms. Cornish highlights some of its actions and successes, and offers a message about learning across industries.

In all, this text provides a broad and relevant overview of accident prevention and crisis response. The case studies and historic accounts can help outdoor professionals from all walks of life improve their understanding of safety education. But my greatest hope is that, by reading *Lessons Learned II*, people will develop a willingness to talk about accidents, to share their successes and mistakes, and to accept that everyone within the outdoor industry has, and can learn from, a common past.

Deb Ajango
Eagle River, Alaska

Adam's Story

By Kay Landis, with assistance from Phil Dzialo © 2005

This case study describes a 1998 near-drowning incident on Massachusetts' Deerfield River involving 12-year-old Adam Dzialo, a participant in an adventure program run by Greenfield Community College (GCC). The account includes reviews of pre- and post-incident actions along with the perspective of the boy's parents on the years that stretched between the original incident and a final settlement with the state of Massachusetts.

The information provided here has been compiled from several sources, including a chronology by GCC, an incident/accident investigation by Charles Walbridge, a risk management evaluation by Ian Wade, and personal accounts by Adam's parents, Phil and Sharon Dzialo. This chapter is not intended to provide a judgment of actions, nor does the editor profess all information to be inarguable fact. Instead, it is included to help readers understand the effects that a serious accident and post-incident response can have on family members and loved ones. Further, it offers a good example of how different audiences can have different understandings of such concepts as negligence and inherent risk.

Adam. In the summer of 1998, Adam Dzialo was 12 years old. Blond haired, blue eyed, wiry, and athletic, he was a boy who loved sports and was good at everything he played. In baseball, he was an all-star. In hockey, he was the goalie who stopped five penalty shots in a row to lead his team to victory. He enjoyed soccer. He excelled at golf. His room was laden with sports memorabilia. When he wasn't playing a sport, he was at a sports camp. "He was in perpetual motion," says Phil, Adam's father. "He only crashed long enough to play video games."

Adam's family had a busy summer planned for him that year. He was signed up for six sports camps, including a hockey camp in Rhode Island that was to be his first week away from home and Team Adventure, an outdoor program run by the local community college. The Team Adventure brochure promised "five days of fun and excitement!" featuring a ropes course, rock climbing, canoeing, hiking, a river crossing, and one overnight camping trip. No previous experience was required; participants needed only to have an eagerness to learn new skills and an interest in having fun.

Adam was the 13th boy to sign up for the Team Adventure camp that week. The program was normally limited to 12 participants, as the brochures and advertising stated, but the director was willing to bend the rules and raise the cap to allow Adam and a 14th boy to enroll. The program had a new van, with greater capacity, and the director felt the leaders could handle the two extra youths.

Team Adventure. Team Adventure was an adventure program for kids (ages 12 to 15) run by Adventures Unlimited, a non-credit community education program of Greenfield Community College (GCC). Adventures Unlimited was well-established and had been successfully running custom outdoor courses for youths since 1991. Team Adventure was in its second season.

Team Adventure was managed by a part-time director and staffed largely by graduates of GCC's Outdoor Leadership Program (OLP). The OLP was a solid organization, accredited by the Association for Experiential Education. The two programs (OLP and Adventures Unlimited) maintained separate offices and reported upward to different college administrators, but they shared equipment and a certain symbiosis of purpose. The academically oriented OLP prepared graduates to lead entry-level adventure outings and services, and Adventures Unlimited offered OLP students and graduates employment opportunities as instructors and trip leaders. Adam's camp was run by two of these graduates, Patrick and Heather; the program director was also a graduate. Partly because these programs shared equipment, Adventures Unlimited was able to keep its costs down and offer its courses at substantially lower rates than most commercial programs.

The Team Adventure activities were designed to introduce participants to a different type of outdoor skill or experience each day. The kids had the opportunity to complete a ropes course, climb a rock face, canoe a river, and practice a river crossing, then finish up with a Thursday night campout and a Friday summit hike. On many of the earlier trips, however, participants complained about the Friday hike; it just wasn't exciting enough. Heather and Patrick had asked for permission to alter the itinerary for the group and try a river swimming and rescue drill instead. Permission was granted.

And so the itinerary for Adam's group was modified.

And so the itinerary for Adam's group was modified. The hike to the summit was scheduled for Thursday, and on Friday there would be a hike to Deerfield River where the group would engage in "river activities."

River Activities. Everything went fine on days one through four. The boys all did well on the ropes course, the rock climb, and the canoe trip. On Thursday night, they camped overnight at Mohawk State Forest. The trip leaders described the group as very strong and Adam as aggressive and athletic.

On Friday morning, the group broke camp and headed for the river, stopping briefly along the way to get the water release time. The Deerfield's flow is controlled by scheduled water releases from New England Power's Fife Brook dam, and Heather and Patrick wanted to time their activities so that they could be finished before the full force of water hit the group. Before the release, the Deerfield is only a shallow stream. Afterward, it rises gradually and progressively as a bubble of water makes its way down the riverbed. Boaters time their trips to coincide with the release, when the water is at its highest and fastest. Swimmers or waders, however, often want to avoid the increased flow.

Friday's release was set for 10 a.m. It would take a few hours for the bubble to reach the site where the day's activities were planned, so the instructors felt no need to rush. After obtaining the release time, the leaders stopped the group for lunch, discussed how to read water with the students, and fit them with life jackets. They tested each jacket by attempting to lift it over the boy's head. At just under 90 pounds, Adam was a little small for an adult-sized jacket, but it passed their test, and they decided it was an acceptable fit.

The site the leaders had chosen was a Class I rapid with a cobbled bed, a place where the river narrows, then drops gently, creating a two-foot wave. The Safety Code of American Whitewater determines that Class I rapids have "fast-moving water with riffles and small waves ... few obstructions, all obvious and easily missed with training. Risk to swimmers is slight; self-rescue is easy" (AWA 1998). It seemed like an excellent choice for a swimming and rescue drill, and indeed had been used for this kind of activity many times by multiple organizations.

On the bank, the group split into two teams. The swimmers went upstream with Patrick while the rescuers (i.e., rope throwers) went downstream with Heather. They stopped about 200 feet apart.

Upstream, Patrick provided a briefing for the swimmers, explaining where to swim (near the middle of the river), the proper position (feet up and pointing downstream), how to grab the throw bag, and what to do if the throw bag missed (swim to shore). It had been predetermined that before each boy went, Patrick would look both ways and give a thumbs-up sign to Heather to indicate he was ready. When Heather returned the sign, the swimmer would be free to go.

Downstream, Heather explained the proper use of throw bags to her group and positioned two rescuers near her side, along the bank. The plan was that if the first throw bag missed the swimmer, the second boy would throw his bag. After a swimmer finished his turn, he would join the rescuers. After a rescuer threw his line, he would hike upstream to join the swimmers; thus, every participant would have a chance to experience both roles.

The boys were not required to participate in the swim, and a few opted out. But all those who wanted to try it took a turn, and all completed the exercise without incident.

At 1:25 p.m., the leaders brought the group together again. Patrick had to drive one of the boys upstream to meet his mother at a prearranged pickup point. He would be gone about 10 minutes. A second boy volunteered to go with the two. Heather said she felt comfortable continuing the exercise in Patrick's absence, so some of the boys went back upstream to take another run at the river. Heather stayed downstream with the rescuers. The signaling system would be the same, but the boys would decide for themselves when to enter the water.

By this time, the full release from the dam had arrived. Commercial rafts began to appear, carrying guides and clients. Two boats had already gone by. A third came up just as Adam was preparing for his swim. The guide asked if the boys wanted to go first, and they said no, they would rather wait. The guide ran the drop, then spun his boat around to face upstream so his guests could watch.

What happened next was described by the guide and is summarized in the investigative report: "Adam was floating in a seated position, feet low and head up. He waved to his friends downstream, then appeared to stand up. His body flipped over and disappeared under water. His arm came up once or twice as he struggled … [and perhaps] the back of his head appeared for a split second" (Walbridge 1998).

Just before Adam went under water, one of the boys with Heather asked her a question about the timing of the throw-rope toss. She glanced away from Adam for a brief moment. When she looked back, Adam was gone. In his place was an orange and yellow object bobbing in place under the water at about midstream.

The Rescue. With the frantic cries from Adam's teammates ringing in her ears, Heather ran upstream along the shore and tried to swim out to the boy. The current forced her back downstream. A fourth raft came along momentarily, and the guide tried to grab Adam as he went by. But Adam was too deep, and the water was too strong. He missed.

During the next few minutes, 21 boats in two groups (running close together) all came upon the site. Assessing the situation quickly, several of the rafting guides pushed their boats to shore, discharged their passengers, and joined the rescue operation. Several attempted to wade out to Adam. All were swept away by the current. Some of the guides then tried to create a "human chain" to reach the boy, but the current was too strong. More than five minutes had passed since Adam went under.

Next the group created a "tag line." Several guides and dozens of raft customers were used as anchors, holding onto a rope that stretched from shore to shore. Rescuers moved hand-over-hand toward Adam, facing upstream. Several guides were able to reach Adam, and while maintaining a hold on the rope with one hand, they reached under the water with their free hands. One guide was able to get a firm grip on Adam's life jacket. He let go of the rope, pulling as hard as he could with both hands. He was able to pull the life jacket free, but Adam's foot remained lodged. Adam had now been under the water for 15 to 20 minutes.

Because there was too much slack in the tag line, which allowed rescuers to get dragged under the surface of the water, trees were added to the onshore anchor systems and additional ropes were used to pull the tag line taut. Finally, four men attached a raft to the line across the river and maneuvered it as close as they could to where Adam was trapped. A fifth man threw them a rescue bag and used it to pull the boat into a better position. One of the men in the raft reached down more than two feet into the water. With his own face submerged, he pulled Adam's head to the surface. He started rescue breathing while two others worked to pull Adam free. It took all their strength, but at last they were successful.

Meanwhile, Patrick had returned, several people had called 911, and emergency personnel had already arrived on the scene. Within minutes, Adam was transferred to an ambulance, carried to a nearby heliport, and flown by helicopter to Bay State Medical Center. He had been under the water for 25 minutes.

He had been under the water for 25 minutes.

At around 1:55 p.m., GCC's telephone operator received a call from the Shelburne Fire Department, asking for the outdoor program supervisor and saying that it was an emergency. It took some time to contact the director, Tashima, who was leading a ropes course on campus. When Tashima called back, she was told that there had been an accident with the student group at the river. The conversation was brief: no names, no details, just an order to get there as fast as she could. It was a 45-minute drive to the spot where the group had gathered, and Tashima didn't discover the magnitude of the tragedy until she arrived. The scene was still chaotic and intense. The instructors were answering questions from the State Troopers and were still trying to figure out for themselves the extent of the incident, all while trying to provide for the well-being of the remaining boys in their group.

Tashima called the Dzialos' home but no one answered. Not wanting to leave a message on a recorder, she hung up and called the hospital to find out more about Adam's condition. She was told that the situation was serious and that Adam's parents were already there. Tashima then turned her attention back to the Troopers, the trip leaders, and the rest of the boys.

Receiving Word of the Incident. Sharon Dzialo had spent part of her day packing Adam's things for the upcoming hockey camp. "My heart and mind were filled with Adam that day," she says. "I was missing him and wondering how tired and cranky he'd be after his adventure. And he had more adventures to go." She planned to pick him up from the community college in the late afternoon and take him straight to his all-star baseball tournament that evening. "Adam liked to keep busy," she says. That kind of schedule, she notes, was nothing unusual for him.

A little before 3:00 p.m., Sharon left the house to pick up their daughter, Aimee, from her summer job at the YMCA. While she was gone, Phil returned home from work. Phil, too, was thinking of Adam, looking forward to seeing his son in an hour or two and hearing how he'd enjoyed his first camping experience.

At 3:05 p.m., the phone rang. It was a social worker from Bay State Medical Center in Springfield, Massachusetts, 45 miles away. "Your son," she said, "has been involved in a swimming accident and is here at the Trauma Center."

A swimming accident? Phil was puzzled. That couldn't be right. Adam was supposed to be hiking a summit today. "There must be a mistake," Phil told her.

It was not a mistake, the woman replied. "It is Adam. And his condition is serious." The conversation was short, and the woman did not provide many details. But Adam's father clearly remembers the final words of advice the caller offered: "Don't come alone."

Phil would later write, "The trip from Greenfield to Springfield took 40 minutes, the longest 40-minute period of time that any parent could experience. Time to panic, time to cry, time to plan a son's funeral. Time to dwell in the hell of fear and desolation."

Sharon's state of mind at the time was slightly more hopeful. "I drove because I remember feeling that I was in better shape than Phil. He just kept repeating their words, 'Don't come alone.' I focused on driving and tried to ignore the sickening feeling in the pit of my stomach. I wasn't sure that I would make it to the hospital without getting sick. But then, minutes before we arrived, when I could actually see the hospital directly in front of us, I experienced an amazing feeling. My whole being was flooded with calm. I looked at Phil and said, 'Adam is still with us. I would know if he was not.'"

The Dzialos were met at the entrance by a social worker, who told them what she knew about the accident and Adam's condition. Adam had arrived without a pulse, but they had revived him in the Trauma Center and were trying to stabilize him now. For what seemed like many hours, Phil and Sharon waited together, in a closed room, alone with their fear. Sharon remembers feeling an intense, unassuageable cold. She could not warm herself and kept calling for blankets.

Finally, the social worker returned. Adam had been stabilized, she told them, and was being moved to Pediatric Intensive Care. He was on a ventilator and in a medically induced coma. Would they like to go with him in the elevator?

That first sight of Adam was "a scene I could never have imagined, even in my darkest moments," writes Sharon. "Adam was on a stretcher. His eyes were closed, and he looked puffy and gray. He was on oxygen, and two doctors were monitoring his transport. ... It was Adam, but it wasn't Adam. He bore little resemblance to the wiry, hyper, athletic boy we had said goodbye to the previous morning. He felt untouchable—too cold, too gray, too far away. Again, the cold—I was freezing."

Phil leaned against the wall of the elevator and began to cry. The tears continued for days. "I can't stop," he would tell Sharon. He felt the pain of Adam's trauma to the depths of his soul.

That night, the college president called and left a message for the Dzialos. The next day, the president and the dean visited them at the hospital. They offered their condolences and assured Phil and Sharon that they would answer all of the family's questions later, when the Dzialos were ready.

The First Three Months. After the first 72 hours, the doctors told Adam's parents that he would live. However, they held out very little hope for a full recovery. Adam had suffered from "anoxic encephalopathy" as a result of the near drowning; the neuromuscular system that controls movement had been damaged. Doctors, at that time, said that Adam would not walk—or talk—again.

The family received most of their initial information about the accident from the medical team, from Adam's friends, and from the parents of other campers who came to visit them in the hospital over the next few days. They heard that Adam's life jacket had been pulled off him; that many boats had floated by, right over Adam's head, yet had been unable to rescue him; that one counselor had left to run an errand, leaving only a single adult to supervise the activity; and that the remaining leader had been "hysterical" and done nothing to save the drowning boy. "Everything you didn't want to hear," Phil remembers.

> To Adam's father, it was clear that someone had done something wrong.

Devastated by these reports, Phil called the Team Adventures program director. Tashima told him that she had been advised not to talk to him, but she would confirm that, yes, one of the trip leaders had left the site briefly. She could not, unfortunately, say anything more.

Meanwhile, the college president had been heard referring to the incident as a freak accident. His assertion that the college had "complied with industry standards" sounded to

Phil like GCC was trying to say that it had done nothing wrong. Phil called the president and asked him to stop saying such things. To Adam's father, it was clear that someone had done something wrong. Shouldn't they work together to learn the facts before speculating to the media?

In the meantime, the college arranged for a psychologist and a minister to facilitate a Critical Incident Stress Debriefing for the remaining group participants. During the debriefing, the boys made cards for Adam and his family. The college had intended to deliver the cards to the hospital, but the parents asked that the college stay away for the time being. A second debriefing was arranged for the participants' parents and families. The Dzialos, who were holding vigil at the hospital, did not attend.

The Dzialos say that they tried to get answers to their questions from the college on numerous occasions during those early weeks, but they felt as if they were rebuffed every time. Finally in September, two months after the accident, the GCC president and Human Resources director agreed to meet with Phil and give him the instructors' statements about what had happened that day. The statements were a start, but Phil still felt the need to learn and do more. He asked to be a partner in the investigation and to sit on the committee that would evaluate the incident. "I wanted to be part of a solution that would preclude such a thing from ever happening again," says Phil. The president and the director promised to "look into it" and get back to him. "But they never did," Phil says today.

And so began the adversarial relationship between the Dzialos and the college administrators. Upon legal advice, GCC took the position that its employees could not, should not, and would not talk to the Dzialos. Its general counsel was quoted in the Boston Globe (2001) as saying that the college's "no-comment" stance was "not indicative of any lack of compassion or sympathy by the college community for this young boy." But to the Dzialos, it felt callous—not to mention evasive, insulting, and needlessly cruel. It felt like the college cared more for its image and reputation than it did for the truth.

Adam spent six weeks in Pediatric Intensive Care and several more at the Connecticut Children's Medical Center. His parents never left his side. He was finally able to return home in September—nearly two months after the incident—still unable to move or speak.

According to the Dzialos, there was still no definitive word from the college. Frustrated, Phil hired his own investigator in an attempt to understand what had happened. Finally, on October 7, the college engaged Charles Walbridge, noted water safety expert, to complete an external investigation. Mr. Walbridge was given "complete autonomy" to "discover all relevant information" that might prevent a similar accident from occurring again. Specifically, he was asked to detail "what factors contributed to the accident and how they can be avoided" (GCC 1998).

Phil read about the hiring in the newspaper. He found Walbridge's phone number on the Internet and called him up to learn more about his credentials. Phil was disturbed by what he considered to be a lack of experience with children on the investigator's part. How could someone who had never had kids himself or worked with them extensively judge the situation properly? Phil had a "premonition" that someone paid by the college could never be completely impartial, and he was particularly concerned that Walbridge had been engaged "in anticipation of litigation." To Phil, Walbridge sounded like a hired gun.

Walbridge reviewed program documents and materials; interviewed college personnel, course instructors, and other witnesses; and visited the site himself on several occasions. He delivered his report on November 2, 1998, a little more than three months after the accident.

Walbridge concluded that Adam's near-drowning was a case of foot entrapment, brought on by a combination of factors, including poor swimming technique and bad luck. The following excerpt from his report (1998) describes what can occur in this type of situation:

> *Foot entrapments result not from controlled wading, but from thrusting your foot blindly to the bottom when floating or swimming. You won't always catch your foot, but if you do you are going to be out of balance. Once your foot is caught in deep fast water no one is fast enough to pull their foot out or strong enough to stop the current from pushing their body under water.*

Visiting the site again when the water was low, Walbridge found a big rock in the middle of the river near the bottom of the rapid. Just downstream was a large flat rock, and next to that rock a crevice, roughly six inches in width. "The crevice was completely under water and quite invisible, even at low flows," he wrote. Placing a paddle in the crevice and looking back at it from where Patrick and Heather had stood on the bank, he guessed that this was the hazard in question. "We'll never know for sure," he admits. "Rocks and debris may have shifted since the accident. But I believe this is as close as we are going to get to knowing what held Adam under water."

Walbridge's report found no fault with the suitability of the activity, the site, or any of the equipment. It was "an excellent choice for a river swim and throw-bag drill … the last place any of us would have expected to encounter a foot entrapment," he wrote. The drills themselves were "an expected part of a well-designed whitewater training program" because they taught swimmers how life vests and proper body position could keep them safer in moving water. "In an area with many fast-flowing rivers, that's an important lesson in water safety that could save lives." Many outdoor programs, he noted, teach these skills successfully to students Adam's age.

The investigator also opined that a better-fitting life vest, a different kind of footwear, or a helmet would not have made much difference in the outcome. And once Adam was trapped, a wading rescue probably never had a chance. "The forces that pinned Adam Dzialo to the bottom of the river were enormous, probably hundreds of pounds. It took two adults, pulling with all their power, to release him." Walbridge himself found wading the river at full release to be extremely difficult. At 6'5" and 245 pounds, he could get close to the spot where Adam was trapped but was swept away whenever he tried to take the last step.

More effective instruction, he concluded, is the only thing that might have increased the odds for Adam. "Foot entrapments are catastrophic accidents," he wrote, "comparable to stepping in front of a moving car. The best policy is avoidance." Critical steps, he added, are to clearly warn participants of the dangers associated with foot entrapment and to make sure students are taught proper swimming techniques.

Although the Team Adventure instructors are confident that they warned the students not to stand up, adults who met with the students during a counseling session reported that the boys were not familiar with the term "foot entrapment" and did not understand what had happened to Adam, suggesting that the activity orientation regarding the risks and proper techniques was not as thorough or effective as it should have been. The split briefings, which likely made it difficult to ensure that each student had received proper instructions, might have contributed to missed communication. And it was "probably a mistake" to continue the drill after Patrick left the group, according to Walbridge's report (1998).

With Patrick gone, the student-to-staff ratio was 12:1, which is twice the commonly accepted industry standard of 6:1 (for supervision of this type of activity), and twice what the program had promised parents in its promotional materials.

With no instructor upstream to coach the swimmers, there could be no reminder of the hazards or proper swimming technique as they entered the water. "Many whitewater safety rules are counterintuitive," noted Walbridge, "and floating rather than standing up is one of these. Adults and kids who panic in current may attempt to stand despite instruction. ... The warning not to stand may need to be repeated several times to sink in."

The investigator was satisfied with the qualifications of the trip leaders and program director, but expressed some concern at the part-time status of the director. Walbridge recommended increasing the director's time commitment and hands-on involvement, developing a stronger staff training program, and developing a cadre of instructors so that more experienced leaders could be paired with novice instructors, at least during their first years.

Walbridge also recommended that the college prepare a disaster plan for the outdoor program that would include support for the friends and relatives of the victim, management of a thorough internal investigation, and communication with the media. College outdoor programs are particularly susceptible to post-accident communication problems, he wrote, because the key decision-makers are often several levels of separation from those running the programs and are frequently unfamiliar with the activities, issues, and disaster planning that goes along with the adventure programming territory.

In the end, Walbridge concluded that the accident had no single cause. Poor technique combined with inherent risk resulted in an entrapment. Admittedly, the activity could have been better organized, could have been better instructed, and could have had a better student-to-instructor ratio. But there is a "random element of uncontrolled risk" in all outdoor activities, and it was this risk that was to blame for Adam's injuries.

> *Although we warn against standing up in rapids, many people do so every year without injury. The odds are against a dangerous crevice being present in a Class I cobble rapid. That Adam's foot would find this crevice, which is smaller than a catcher's mitt, is also an incredible piece of bad luck. Had he touched bottom a few inches to either side there would have been no problem. This is an unfortunate example of the random element of uncontrolled risk that exists in all outdoor activities.* (Walbridge 1998)

Deteriorating Relationships. The Dzialo family was not allowed to see Walbridge's report before it was presented to GCC's Board of Trustees. Nor were they allowed to ask questions at the board meeting where the report was first made public. Adam's father agreed with the investigator's conclusions that instruction regarding proper swimming technique appeared inadequate and that the exercise should not have been attempted with one instructor absent. Phil disagreed vehemently, however, with any suggestion that the responsibility for the accident must be shared between the college and Adam. Even if Adam did panic in the rising water, even if he did put his foot down to try and slow himself, that instinctive reaction would hardly make it Adam's fault, Phil believed. Adam was only a boy, the Dzialos declared, and it would be ludicrous to expect him to perform a new skill without error. While Phil acknowledged that inherent risk played a role in the incident, he firmly believed that the college had been negligent in its actions.

Adam was only a boy ... it would be ludicrous to expect him to perform a new skill without error.

As a supplement to the Walbridge investigation, the college arranged for a program review to be conducted by Adventure Safety International Director Ian Wade. Wade's report, which was released on December 4, 1998, echoed earlier concerns about the time commitment of program leadership and recommended increasing the program director position to full time. Additional conclusions suggested that GCC keep better documentation of staff qualifications, adopt common standards for all of the college's outdoor programs, and improve its emergency response plans in the event of another incident. Wade also believed GCC should adopt a stronger review and approval process for any and all new program activities, such as river rescue drills.

Over the next few months, a task force was formed and public meetings were held to discuss possible changes to the Adventures Unlimited program. The Board of Trustees approved expanding the coordinator position to full time with defined responsibilities. It was a hollow victory, according to the Dzialos. The position was never filled, and the program—suspended after the accident—never reopened.

Around that time, the family contacted local lawmakers about creating regulations for summer or youth camps that might preclude an accident like Adam's from ever happening again. To their surprise, they discovered that this type of youth camp oversight already existed. State regulations note, for example, that campers may not participate in whitewater activities unless they first receive *Red Cross Level 4* swimming certification. Adam had taken swim lessons at the YMCA, and he had passed a swim test conducted by the Team Adventure instructors, but he was not Red Cross certified at any level.

And then in March 1999, eight months after the accident, the Dzialos learned of a letter that the Greenfield Health Director had sent to the college in early August 1998 (a few weeks after the incident). A state official, reading about Adam in the paper, had checked for the adventure program's license to run the camp and discovered that it had none. The letter ordered the college to immediately "cease and desist" offering Team Adventure activities. According to the Dzialos, the college never mentioned the letter's existence to the accident investigators, the media, or the family.

Adventures Unlimited was already closed, so the order itself was moot. Upon questioning, the college president said that he considered the licensing requirement to be an oversight, a technicality of day camp regulations that they hadn't known applied to them. GCC never mentioned the letter to anybody, he added, because no one ever asked about it. Phil believes, however, that this information was intentionally withheld in order to hide the fact that GCC was out of compliance with statewide camping regulations.

The relevance of the letter, and GCC's motive in withholding it, will likely always remain a point of contention. In fact, a number of other similar local programs acknowledged that they, too, did not consider the licensing requirement relevant. But from the Dzialos' point of view, the college had crossed the line of no return. "At that point, my anger shot from a two to a 10," Phil says. "As far as we were concerned, the college's actions—of withholding this type of information—were unforgivable." The incident cemented the family's belief that college officials were engaged in cover-ups and lies. Wanting others to know what had happened, Phil released the Health Director's cease-and-desist letter to the media (1998).

For the first six months after the incident, Adam lay ramrod straight in bed, his arms locked against his chest, in a state of "physiological terror" as his family puts it. Because the boy had gone so long without oxygen to his brain, there was significant long-term damage that required ongoing attention. Sharon quit her job to take care of him. The painkillers and tranquilizers prescribed by his doctors helped Adam's muscles to relax, but they did nothing to improve his condition over the long run. For that, the family turned to physical therapy, craniosacral therapy, Shiatzu massage, and other alternative therapies to release the blocked energy in Adam's body and start him on the road to recovery.

With Sharon out of work, the family struggled financially. Adam's care cost about $30,000 in out-of-pocket expenses annually. Further, the family lost money on an investment after a downturn in the real estate market. These losses, combined with the mounting expenses and a single income, forced the family into bankruptcy in April 1999. "Everything went," says Phil, including the piano and the boat and some rental property they had in Vermont. According to the Dzialos, a partial settlement might have helped ease their strain, but the college still had not met directly with them, nor, says Phil, had GCC taken steps to accept financial responsibility for Adam's care.

In December 1999, the Dzialos met with GCC officials for two days of mediation to discuss what the college could do to help. The family presented a long list of services and equipment that Adam needed, including a variety of physical therapies and a wheelchair van for transport. College representatives countered with an offer of their own. They would 1) hold a large, significant fund-raiser to help with Adam's medical expenses; 2) present a safety symposium for area camp directors and outdoor leaders; and 3) recommend that the Attorney General settle Adam's claim for a total of $100,000. [1]

The Dzialos accepted the fund-raiser and the safety symposium as gestures of good will, seeing them as hopeful signs that maybe the college and family could work together at last. But they would not accept the financial piece. One

---

[1] Under Chapter 258 of the Massachusetts Tort Claims Act, $100,000 is the legal limit of the amount a person can recover from an act of negligence committed by the state, regardless of the severity of the damage. While this act protects the state from bankruptcy, it does not necessarily provide adequate financial assistance to people who have been harmed. Because GCC is a state college, any claim or suit would be made against the Commonwealth.

hundred thousand dollars would not begin to pay for what Adam needed, they believed, at that time or in the future. "That last item was an insult," says Phil. "They knew that attorney fees and liens would eat up the whole amount, and there would be nothing at all left for Adam. But we shook hands on the other two pieces, and then we waited."

The college held an initial fund-raiser in the spring of 2000, which raised about $1,200. A second event, featuring hot air balloon rides, was canceled due to bad weather. The big fund-raiser was planned for November 2000. It would be a dinner/show format, with guest speaker Ian Wade and a raffle for a mountain climbing trip. The camp safety symposium was to be held one month later, in December. Phil, wanting to take part, asked if he could present a workshop on "Appropriate Institutional Responses to Critical Incidents." College officials agreed to his request.

The Lawsuit. With the statute of limitations running out, the Dzialos filed a civil lawsuit in federal court in October 2000. The college matched the move by canceling the November fund-raiser. Although the December safety symposium was held, GCC withdrew its agreement to have Phil present his workshop. Phil countered with an emotional and very public appeal to the Board of Trustees, accusing the college of lying and breaking promises to his 14-year-old son.

The lawsuit was moved to a state court in the summer of 2001. The family's argument, which was based on the State-Created Danger Doctrine, asserted that the state should have known Team Adventure was headed for danger. It cited inadequate staffing and the fact that the camp was unlicensed, and argued that there was no real "informed consent" because the parents had no idea their son would be participating in whitewater activities.

With the lawsuit came the depositions—many of them—which took place over several months. "Thousands of dollars were spent," Phil would later write, "and people's lives and integrity, including our own, were questioned." Memories of the incident had faded over time, and positions on both sides had become entrenched. The family found certain questions directed at them particularly painful. Had they read all the camp literature? Had they discussed it with others? Had they checked references? Wasn't that Adam's signature on the waiver of liability form? The Dzialos saw these questions as an attempt to blame the victim and reacted with both anguish and rage. "The effect on our family is indescribable; the feeling of inadequacy inexpressible. How responsible can the parents be for an accident that occurs under another's watch?"

By this time, the college and the family were so far apart that it seemed as if each side had lost the ability to empathize with the other's point of view, and emotion, in some instances, began to replace logic. In what he calls a "desperate attempt to get the college to understand my passion," Phil delivered to the college library a copy of *John Q*, a movie about a father trying to get his dying son on a heart transplant list. The father eventually takes the emergency room staff hostage and threatens to shoot himself unless the doctors comply. Phil saw the movie as an accurate portrayal of a father—like himself—who would never give up fighting for his child's well-being. The college considered it a threat and referred the matter to the District Attorney's office for investigation.

It seemed as if each side had lost the ability to empathize with the other's point of view.

In March 2004, the Dzialos reached a settlement with the state of Massachusetts that created an account of $936,000. Most of this amount was used to purchase an annuity for Adam that would help pay his expenses once he reaches 22. Attorney fees cost about $175,000. It took $25,000 to buy back claims against the lawsuit from bankruptcy court and another $15,000 to deal with the insurance companies that still have liens against the settlement. Phil and Sharon used some of the money to get a new hospital bed and a wheelchair van, and reserved a bit more for the nontraditional therapies Adam continues to receive.

Today, Adam is 19. The wiry, athletic boy in perpetual motion has grown into a young man who needs assistance with every aspect of daily living. The sports he used to play have been replaced by rehabilitation regimens, including physical therapy five times a week, speech therapy four times a week, and Advanced Biomechanical Rehabilitation exercises three hours a day. He communicates with his eyes. He laughs. He smiles. But he cannot walk or talk. Under a combination of therapies, his head control has strengthened, his mobility has increased, and he has grown more alert and responsive. Phil and Sharon strongly believe he will, one day, walk and talk again. And, they add, they love him as he is.

Phil's, Sharon's, and Aimee's lives also have changed dramatically over the past seven years. They have spent tremendous time and energy trying to heal, and learning what it means to be survivors.

Since that day in 1998, the Dzialos have sought what they believe is justice for Adam and closure for themselves. "From day one," Phil writes, "we wanted just a few basic things":

> *First, we wanted compassion and simple human kindness.*
>
> *Second, we wanted to know the truth and to be full partners in the investigation. When the college refused to talk to us, when they greeted our every query with "no comment," and especially when we discovered they had withheld information from us, our anger turned to rage.*

Third, we needed help with Adam's care, both immediately and over the long term. A few small gestures in the beginning would have made a world of difference to our healing. But ultimately we needed a fair financial settlement that would provide basic care for as long as Adam needs it, even if that means his whole life. The longer the institution delayed, the angrier we got and the greater our demands became.

And lastly, we needed to find meaning in the event, to know that the injury did not occur in vain. My intent in sharing Adam's story lies in my continued desire to find meaning in his devastating injuries. If I can help others understand what it feels like to experience a catastrophic event, perhaps I will be able to effect change. Perhaps a trip leader will think twice about all of the "what ifs," take an extra step in preparing for a worst-case scenario, and thereby prevent a tragedy. Perhaps program administrators or board members will recognize that no matter how bad they may feel or how fearful of litigation they may be, that the injured party and their families are experiencing far worse fear and pain. Maybe they will be more willing to let down their armor and to show the compassion that is so desperately needed.

Lessons to be Learned. Phil was never given the opportunity to present his ideas about an appropriate institutional response to a critical incident in any type of public workshop. However, he says he is thankful that, through this book, he is able to offer the following suggestions to program administrators and outdoor professionals who might one day find themselves in a similar situation. The following are lessons he hopes others can learn:

1. *Demonstrate compassion. Extended hospital stays produce major disruptions of family life and involve many out-of-pocket expenses. You could send the victim's family a gas card or phone card. Hold a fund-raiser. Organize a weekly supper and bring it to their home. Offer to cut their lawn, clean their house, run an errand, or provide a few moments of respite. These simple human kindnesses are the best way to demonstrate that you are genuine, compassionate, and caring.*

2. *Tell the truth—the whole truth—and add new details as they come to light. Omissions, cover-up attempts (even the perception of one), and lies can damage your credibility forever. A family that believes it's been lied to will search that much harder for the truth and is likely to seek compensation for both the injuries and the lies.*

3. *Partner with the victims and their families. Include them in the investigation and allow them to be the first to see the reports. Let them ask their questions. Include them in the development of new policies and procedures. They may have no technical expertise to offer, but they will appreciate being included and knowing that their contributions are important.*

4. *Take responsibility for the incident. You don't have to say, "It was our fault," but you do need to say, "It happened on our watch and we will take some responsibility." It's the basic "you break it, you buy it" principle. It's the decent thing to do.*

5. *Talk, talk, talk. Communicate with the victim's family as often and as long as they want. Don't become angry or defensive, and don't retreat behind a wall of "no*

comment" either. Think beyond protecting the institution, and approach the legal questions with compassion for the family and concern for the victim's welfare.

6. *Try to understand and respect what the family is going through. If possible, offer some immediate financial assistance to get them through the rough spots. Stay open, be responsive, and act like you would like to be treated if your roles were reversed.*

7. *Don't make promises you aren't going to keep. If you offer to hold a fund-raiser, then hold it. If you offer the family a chance to participate in the process, then give them that chance. Don't ignore or withdraw from offers previously made.*

8. *Never forget what happened or who it happened to. Call or visit the family on anniversaries, send cards on their birthdays, commemorate the event with an appropriate ceremony or gesture. Victims need to know that they are not forgotten and that their experience has meaning for others as well as themselves.*

In preparing this story for publication, Phil thought back over the seven years since that terrible day on the Deerfield River. "What did we lose?" he writes. "Nothing":

> *Adam is still Adam, albeit slowed down considerably. He is still happy, still filled with energy, still playful with his eyes. It was his energy and his passion for life that allowed both his body and his spirit to survive 25 minutes under water. He stayed with us to teach us something, and we continue to learn from him each and every day.*

I lost a golf partner and a weekend warrior. But I did not lose my dream, and I did not lose my hope. Adam is still with us, and we work daily for his recovery and return.

The settlement should allow our family to put many of our frustrations behind us, but we're not there yet. Most of our lingering pain comes from the way people disappeared from our lives after the first year. And we still carry anger from nearly seven years of confronting what appeared to us to be an unresponsive, inhuman institution that wouldn't even talk to us much less help us deal with what had happened to our son.

In the end, we wanted an apology and we wanted something good to come of this whole thing. We may never get the apology, but we hope that in telling our story we can help create the "something good."

Chuck's Story

By Deb Ajango, with assistance from Chuck Bonning © 2005

This case study follows Chuck Bonning, a full-time college professor and part-time adventurer, from the summit of Mount McKinley through a harrowing descent, high-altitude bivouac, and helicopter rescue to the hospital where he was treated for extensive frostbite. The story details Chuck's feelings toward the guiding service that led him up—and down—the mountain, and includes an account from his wife, Rachel, who received word of the incident while still at home in Michigan.

Chuck and Rachel provide survivors' insights into what it took to endure and ultimately find meaning in this experience. Throughout the narrative, they also reflect on what went wrong and what went right before, during, and after the storm that changed their lives.

Chuck. In 1997, Chuck Bonning was 47 years old, an auto mechanics professor at Ferris State University in Michigan, a husband, a father, and a part-time adventurer. His latest passion was High Pointing, and he had spent the last four years of his life on a personal quest to summit the highest points in each of the 50 states. He had already conquered California's Mount Whitney—at 14,494 feet, the second highest point on the list—as well as Britton Hill in Florida (345 feet), Timm's Hill in Wisconsin (1,951 feet), and 46 other summits of varying heights and difficulty.

On May 11, 1997, he started a journey to reach the highest point of them all. The high point of Alaska, the summit of Mount McKinley, is also the highest spot in all of North

America. It is a small platform of concrete-hard snow. The temperature rarely climbs above zero degrees Fahrenheit, even in summer. Getting there requires a vast expenditure of time, energy, and will power. On summit day, nearly every climber experiences headaches, fatigue, and nausea. At that altitude, everything takes tremendous effort, and everything happens in slow motion.

Chuck was an experienced camper who had spent many nights in a tent—on a mountain, near a stream, alongside northern lakes. But climbing Mount McKinley was in a whole other league for him, and he knew it. The cold, the high altitude, and the extreme conditions would be greater than anything he had ever faced before. "I certainly wasn't a professional mountaineer," he says, "but still, I was pretty sure I could do it."

Climbing Mount McKinley was in a whole other league for him.

By May 28, Chuck had spent three weeks of arduous work on the mountain itself. The original group of nine clients and three guides had started the ascent carrying 100 pounds of equipment each. At base camp, the clients had been given two days of hands-on training in knot tying, anchor systems, and crevasse rescue. As the group ascended to a colder, more extreme environment, evening lectures on frostbite, altitude illness, and hypothermia were conducted.

On May 29, after 20 days of winter camping, acclimatizing their bodies to the thin air, and shuttling loads ever higher up the mountain, five climbers, including Chuck, had finally made it to the top. Joining Chuck on the summit that day were two old friends, Steve and Andy, one new friend, Dave, and their guide, Blaine.

On the summit, Chuck felt that his hard work and preparation had paid off. Although he was suffering from the normal discomforts of "altitude," it was pretty much what he had expected. He was aching but warm, tired but healthy. He also realized that he and the others were only "halfway there"; the summit climb would not be considered a true success until everyone had descended safely back to camp at 17,200 feet. It was a moment Chuck had looked forward to for a very long time. But it was only the beginning of his story.

Alaska Denali Guiding. Given his limited big-mountain experience, Chuck decided that it would be best to join a guided team rather than attempt the summit on his own. He and his friends began by learning about and rating the guiding agencies that offered trips. They devised a spreadsheet. Then by using a point system, the men ranked each agency based on summit success, cost, strength of referrals, and safety record. Ultimately, Chuck decided on Alaska Denali Guiding (ADG), an outfitter based in Talkeetna, Alaska. "I was looking for an organization that seemed professional, one that I could trust," Chuck says. ADG had been around for 20 years and was known for providing educational workshops throughout a climb, which Chuck considered a plus. But more importantly, he adds, "They had a reputation for being safe."

Once he made his decision, which was the summer before the start of the trip, Chuck spent endless hours learning about the mountain, including the hazards it posed. He read everything he could get his hands on about what it would be like. He and his climbing friends shared fitness regimens, and the men talked often about what they were doing to get in shape. Chuck also learned about the experience of the people who would be his guides, which was provided through the guiding agency and the National Park Service.

Diane, one of ADG's owners, checked up on him—as well as the other clients—throughout this period. Through conversations, brochures, a Web site, and a recommended reading list, she tried to help the climbers understand what it would be like to ascend to 20,000 feet. She talked to Chuck about fitness requirements and sent a recommended training routine as well as a trip itinerary and a comprehensive equipment list. Further, all team members were required to have their physicians review information about the trip and mountain environment. The doctors were then asked to sign a form acknowledging that the client was healthy and fit enough to tackle the task ahead. It was apparent that, Chuck says, "ADG wanted to make sure we were taking it seriously."

The Summit Climb. The weather on May 29 was not perfect for a summit attempt. When the group left its high camp (17,200 feet) at around 10:00 a.m., a light wind was blowing out of the north, and a high cloud cover obscured the sun. The lead guide, Blaine, had considered not setting out at all, knowing that if they climbed all morning and then were forced to turn back because of weather, they would likely not have the energy to make a second attempt, even on a later day. But north winds, while cold, typically do not indicate an approaching storm. As long as it did not get any worse, Blaine thought they had a decent chance of making it to the top and back.

The weather on May 29 was not perfect for a summit attempt.

When they reached Denali Pass (18,200 feet), the group stopped to rest and to reevaluate the weather, which remained "iffy," according to Chuck. The winds and sky were not good but not bad. Blaine asked for each member's feedback. Everyone agreed to continue.

Over the next six hours or so, the group climbed an additional 1,500 feet. As they ascended, they seemed to climb out of the clouds, and by the time they reached 19,700 feet, the sky was a deep blue. The winds were light. A couple of the men took pictures during a break, and their photographs depict clear, "bluebird" skies.

At roughly 19,800 feet is a section of the mountain known fondly as Pig Hill. The hill earned its name as the result of the sound climbers make as they grunt their way to the top. Pig Hill is a trip-buster. Many people stop there, refusing to expend the energy it takes to make it to the summit. At the bottom of Pig Hill is a relatively flat area, protected from the wind, which can be a good place for climbers to hang out while others continue. One of the clients, Larry, decided this spot would be his summit. He was too tired to go farther, and he did not want to spend what little energy he had left knowing he still had to descend. He and the second guide, Willie, dug a little hole, sat on their insulated pads, and relaxed in the sun while the others went on.

At the top of Pig Hill is Summit Ridge. Here, climbers are exposed for the first time to the entire southeastern portion of Alaska, which stretches out before them. Summit Ridge is narrow, only a few feet wide in places, and it falls off dramatically on the south side. From Summit Ridge, climbers can see the Ruth Amphitheater, the entire southern Alaska Range, and on clear days, even Anchorage and Prince William Sound, 200 miles away. From the ridge, climbers are also completely exposed to the winds blowing out of the south.

Chuck's group noticed a change in wind direction as soon as it crested Pig Hill. The change was not extreme, however, and no one was overly concerned. The team traveled slowly and carefully along the ridge, covering the last 200 feet in about an hour. One by one, on belay, the group set foot on the summit.

They were only on the summit for a few minutes when Chuck sensed that something was wrong. Andy would say later that as they stepped onto the summit it was as if they had stepped on a wind button. As the clients congratulated each other and took a few pictures, Blaine grew seriously alarmed. In a matter of moments, the clear blue sky was gone, replaced by a deepening gray. The winds from the south were strong and coming in fast. The temperature was dropping, quickly and significantly, and the wind chill had plummeted to well below zero. Visibility was diminishing rapidly as well.

"Let's go!" Blaine shouted. The curt command, along with the tension in his voice, conveyed the urgency of the situation. The five quickly assembled their equipment and struck out along the disappearing tracks they had cut into the snow just minutes before.

As it descended along the narrow sections of Summit Ridge, the group was careful to stay on route in spite of the evolving rage of the storm. A wrong move to the north would lead to a 400-foot drop and serious injuries, but an errant boot step to the south would mean a fall of 3,000 feet. In good weather, the terrain is fairly easy to negotiate. On this day, it was horrific.

Chuck began having trouble right away. The low oxygen of high altitude combined with a rapidly accumulating coating of frost on his face mask made it difficult to breathe. He pulled off his ice-encrusted goggles for only a moment, but the slicing wind and snow burned his eyes. Several of the other climbers faced the same dilemma. They could not see at all with the goggles on, and only a little better without them. Chuck decided it was best without them, but from then on, he had to work hard just to keep his eyelids from freezing shut.

At the bottom of Pig Hill, the group reunited with Willie and Larry. About two hours had gone by since the group had separated, and in that short time, the conditions had changed completely.

As the team took stock of itself, everyone realized how grave the situation was. "I can imagine few places, on that mountain or throughout my travels, where a situation could be more serious," Chuck recalls. Their tents, food, and camping gear remained at 17,200 feet, approximately 2,600 feet below. A descent in good weather would take three to four hours; in the worsening conditions they faced, it would take much longer. The margin for error in that type of environment is slim. "Yet there we were," Chuck adds, "tired, dehydrated, and utterly alone in terms of getting help from the outside world."

The men struggled in vain to retrace their steps and return to camp, but the lack of visibility was too disorienting. Their wands (3-foot metal or bamboo markers placed in the snow to mark the route back to camp in case of whiteout conditions) had all blown away. Although their compasses reassured them that they were headed in the right direction, they also knew that aspects of the terrain were treacherous, and being even slightly off-route could be fatal.

The atmosphere was utter chaos, with winds so strong it was as if they were moving in a blender. Communication was next to impossible, and team members were forced to scream inches from a partner's ear to be heard above the howling gale.

Chuck remembers the scene as intense, but he was not about to give up. "I realized that we had somehow stepped into one of life's worst-case scenarios. I'm sure we all questioned our mortality and calculated the odds of survival."

When the group could no longer stand against the assault of the wind—after the smallest members of the group were literally blown off their feet—Blaine decided that they had no choice but to hunker down and wait out the storm. They carried survival equipment, yet digging in to the concrete-hard snow seemed nearly impossible. Nonetheless, descent was out of the question. "We knew that a night at 19,000 feet would be brutal, but we had reached a point where the alternative, to continue our descent, was worse," Chuck recalls.

Using their slim, steel shovels, the group chiseled out a square platform in the icy terrain. Blaine retrieved an 8-foot by 8-foot nylon sack—an all-purpose bag he carried as an emergency shelter—from his pack, and had three clients climb inside. The group carried four sleeping bags with them, and one was handed to the threesome for warmth. The fit was tight and claustrophobic, but it protected them at least a little from the frigid wind.

The guides then attempted to build an igloo with their snow saw. Using the sharp-toothed metal blade, they were able to cut 2-foot-square ice blocks out of the mountain slope. It took at least an hour, but with Andy's help, the guides were somehow able to construct a small shelter. Once it was complete, the clients were shuffled from the sack to the dome, and an attempt was made to hand a sleeping bag inside. The wind, however, ripped the bag from a climber's grip, and the men watched as the $700 flash-of-blue flew quickly out of sight. Meanwhile, blowing snow whipped through the door, filling the tiny house and burying those inside.

Blaine and Willie continued to work, chinking shut the cracks in the igloo before the wind blew it apart. They placed packs in front of the doorway to block the wind as the five men inside tried their best to stay warm and fight off hypothermia. Once the clients were somewhat protected, the guides tried to build a second protective wall of snow for themselves. As Blaine recalls, they would build a wall, and it would fall down. Then *they* would fall down. Then they would try again. "We were so rummy," Blaine says, "we just couldn't get anything to work. The whole night we were cutting blocks. We spent at least six hours doing nothing but trying." In the end, the effort proved fruitless. When the guides finally reached a point where they were too tired to move, they simply huddled together for warmth outside the igloo in the storm.

At times he wondered if he was going to die.

Chuck cannot remember many details from that night, but some images are indelible. "I will never forget sitting there in that igloo, looking over at Larry and Steve," he says. "They looked like frozen statues, covered with snow from head to toe. It was so incredible, so *weird*, like a scene from the movies. It was like seeing two frozen corpses, sitting there totally motionless, completely covered with ice."

Chuck also admits that at times he wondered if he was going to die. "At some point during the night I went blind, and I thought my body was shutting down. I thought that might be it." (*His blindness, he later learned, was due to frostbitten corneas.*)

Steve remembers the night as the longest of his life. "Each of us could have gone to sleep in 60 seconds or less if we had let our guards down and allowed ourselves to do so. I had never in my life been so exhausted!" But, he adds, he knew that if any of them fell asleep, they likely would never wake up again.

By 6:00 a.m., the men had been fighting the storm for roughly 12 hours. The winds were still strong, but they had let up enough that Blaine believed the group should try moving. Chuck did not think he could make it back to camp and, believing he would hinder his teammates' descent, pleaded with the guides to leave him behind. "Leave me with a sleeping bag!" he reasoned. "You can send a rescue team once the weather breaks." Neither Blaine nor Willie would hear of it and readied the group for the 2,000-foot descent to their tents.

Chuck emerged from the icy dome and straightened his stiff body for the first time in hours. His hands, however, remained frozen in a fisted position. Much of the team's equipment—including the group's radio—had been lost during the night, and some team members were forced to travel without crampons or ice axes. The beaten and exhausted men began to move, shuffling along on short-rope teams like drunkards, slipping and sliding toward camp.

Movement for Chuck was exceedingly difficult. "At one point, after a short tumble, I was totally gassed and couldn't get up. Before McKinley, I'd pushed my body by running marathons and climbing mountains, but I had never before reached a point where I could not move. After I fell, I lay exhausted, in total silence, and I prayed to God for the strength to continue."

It was not the first time Chuck had prayed that night. Looking back on the ordeal, he credits his Christian faith as a crucial element in his survival. Scripture verses came to him unbidden and gave him strength to continue.

Early that afternoon, after six hours of descent, the seven men staggered into the 17,200-foot camp and were greeted by climbers from other teams who offered support, guided them to their tents, and melted pots of snow to make hot drinks. Steve, Dave, and Andy also had suffered frostbite, and helpers warmed the climbers' frozen parts through skin-to-skin contact. Finally the men began relaxing, and one by one, they were able to drift off into a deep, hard sleep.

As the afternoon turned into evening, the winds increased in intensity, and the possibility for any type of immediate rescue vanished. Throughout the next 12 hours, the wind raged and snow fell in earnest. The clients knew that the guides were attempting to coordinate a rescue; however, until the winds died down, no helicopter pilot could consider landing. The violent snapping of the tent walls suggested that they might be stranded indefinitely.

After nearly 24 hours of waiting, Chuck finally heard the distant approach of rotors. He and Dave were helped outside and escorted to a makeshift landing site—an area in the snow that had been marked for the pilot. When the crewman threw open the cargo door, Chuck was covered by the blast from the rotors and felt, briefly, like he was back in the storm. As the helicopter lifted off, he remembers the stench of the exhaust burning his nostrils. But, he adds, the details mattered little: He was on board, and though he was damaged and blind, soon he would be safe.

The helicopter carried Chuck and Dave to Providence Alaska Medical Center in Anchorage, about 160 air miles south of the mountain. "After spending three weeks in the extreme cold and stark environment of McKinley, my senses were overwhelmed as I was wheeled into the emergency room," Chuck says. "I was acutely aware of all the sounds, voices, and smells that had been absent on the mountain."

A nurse covered him with a blanket, and a soothing voice said, "Chuck, you're going to be all right. They are going to take good care of you here." It was Diane, co-owner of ADG, who had driven down from Talkeetna and was waiting at the hospital for the helicopter to arrive. Although the hospital staff was wonderful, the reassurance Chuck felt from having her there buoyed his spirits. "I was so grateful that she took control of my care, immediately and thoroughly."

Meanwhile, Dave was treated in a nearby bed. His frostbite, it turned out, was not nearly as severe as Chuck's; yet he, too, was elated to be off the mountain and in the safe confines of the hospital.

The hospital staff made Chuck as comfortable as possible and then helped him call his family. He knew that his wife had been briefed on the incident by ADG, but he would be the one to fill her in on the details. It would be a tough call, and he was determined to sound as cheerful as possible. One of the nurses held the phone to his ear and dialed the number. Rachel answered on the first ring.

"I have good news," Chuck said. "I summitted McKinley." He waited a second and added, "But I have some bad news, too. I have some problems." He then explained the extent of his injuries. "I love you, Rachel, but I'm in a bad way here." Though he did not want her to worry unnecessarily, he wanted to be honest. "I might lose my hands." Rachel asked if she should come to Anchorage. "I think so," Chuck said, to which she replied, "I'll be on the next plane."

After the call, the doctors and staff went to work. Chuck remembers the IV lines being started. He was stripped naked and submerged in warm water in an attempt to raise his body temperature. Amid the cacophony of noise and confusion that seemed to swirl around him, he was able to pick out each separate conversation: a female voice with a southern drawl; a gruff, commanding man giving orders. Without sight, Chuck simply relied on his hearing and remained alone in his thoughts, replaying the last few days and trying to imagine what lay ahead.

Receiving Word of the Incident. Back in Michigan, Rachel had been feeling tired and anxious for several days. She had not been sleeping well, mainly, she says, because she knew that Chuck and his climbing team were near the summit. On the night of May 29, she woke disturbed and felt a sudden and urgent need to pray. "Although I was unaware of his predicament, something told me to ask for help." Restless, she was unable to sleep the rest of the night.

On May 30, Rachel was relieved when 5:00 p.m. finally arrived and her workday ended. "I had been invited to go to dinner with Chuck's parents, but I was tired, and I felt the need for some time alone." Consequently, she politely declined and headed home. She was ready to relax and looked forward to some sleep.

Diane got to the point quickly. Something had gone wrong.

The phone rang almost immediately as she walked in the front door. It was Diane from ADG. Rachel remembers feeling strong and conflicting emotions at the sound of Diane's voice. She was excited and relieved to finally receive an update on the team's progress, but concerned that the call was not from Chuck.

Diane got to the point quickly. Something had gone wrong. Chuck and his team had been stranded high on the mountain. They were all alive and the group was now relatively safe at their high camp. But it was possible that Chuck might be severely frostbitten. Diane added that as soon as the weather broke, a helicopter would attempt to transport the most-severely injured climbers—including Chuck—to an Anchorage hospital.

"During the call," Rachel says, "I remembered a conversation I had had earlier in the week when a girlfriend and I were talking about Chuck. 'Woman, I don't know how you do it,' my friend declared. 'What if he dies on one of his climbing expeditions?'" Rachel's response came easily. "I said, 'Then he's going to die doing what he loves to do. I refuse to live my life in fear of what *might* happen.'" Though Rachel's own words echoed in her head as Diane spoke, her heart sank as the seriousness of the situation set in.

That evening Rachel called their son, Bill; Chuck's parents; and a number of friends, filling them in on the day's events and asking for their emotional support and prayers. For the second straight night, Rachel slept poorly.

The following morning, Diane's husband, Brian (who was also with ADG), contacted Rachel to say that a rescue had been initiated. Brian had climbed Mount McKinley many times, and Rachel felt he must have known what it was like for the team still on the mountain. His voice was reassuring, and she found comfort in his words. Brian acknowledged, however, that a helicopter rescue at that altitude would be tricky—the pilot would not be able to land unless the weather and wind conditions were just right. He ended by saying that someone from ADG would call back as soon as they knew more.

Shortly after lunch, Rachel received another call from ADG. The wind conditions must have been perfect because the pilot was able to land on his first attempt. Chuck was on board and on his way to Anchorage.

Less than 36 hours later, near midnight, Rachel landed in Anchorage, where the northern sun was still shining. She had arranged to have Don, a friend of Chuck's, pick her up at the airport, and she was not expecting the soft, sweet voice she heard.

"Rachel?" someone called out. Somewhat surprised, Rachel looked around and saw a young woman looking directly at her. "My name is Deb, and I'm with ADG. Don is parking the car." A second later she added, "We're here to take you to see Chuck."

On the way to the hospital, Deb and Don filled Rachel in on Chuck's condition. "They told me that his attitude was positive, but they added that he was not going to look like he did the last time I saw him," Rachel says. "Deb was carrying a book written by Dr. William Mills, a frostbite specialist (1993). She didn't want me to be shocked by Chuck's physical appearance, so before she took me to his room, she took the time to go through some close-up views of frostbite injuries."

Although the gesture was well intended, Rachel was tempted to reject it. "I don't care what he looks like, I felt like telling her. I just want to see him!" Instead, Rachel says, she kept silent, listened to what Deb had to say, and studied the photographs as the young woman turned the pages. Rachel found the pictures horrifying. But she took a deep breath and, with resolve, told herself, "I can do this. Surely, it couldn't be that bad, could it?"

When Rachel entered Room 450, Don announced to Chuck, "We have a visitor for you." Before Rachel was able to rush to the bed, a nurse handed her a mask, which gave her time to quickly scan the nearby stranger's swollen face and black nose. "Wow!" Rachel remembers. "Is that my husband?" Her shock dissolved quickly, however, when Chuck spoke his first words. Although he looked awful, Rachel thought he was the most beautiful sight in the whole world. From that point on, she recalls, nothing mattered except that they were together again.

"Initially," Rachel admits, "when Deb showed me the frostbite photos, I was not interested. Yet as I sat with Chuck, I was so very thankful that she had taken the time to talk to me. While the hazards of mountaineering and the potential of frostbite were familiar to her—a McKinley guide—the reality and severity of the injury were foreign to me. Deb helped me understand what to expect, and she helped me realize what Chuck would be up against." As a result, Rachel knew that Chuck's and her future might be difficult, but she also knew that somehow the two of them would make it through the days, months, and years ahead.

The Long Road to Recovery. Before the couple knew it, life at the Providence Alaska Medical Center became routine. Chuck's eyesight began improving, and the days were filled with whirlpool baths, therapy, X-rays, doctors' rounds, phone calls, and visitors. Daily, the two were inundated with cards from friends and family back home. "They made us laugh and sometimes cry," Chuck says. "We felt so blessed to have such love and support from family and friends, and we needed that support desperately."

The guides, down from the mountain, came to see the two often. "Sensing our depressed spirits," Chuck notes, "they would have us laughing before too long. Even though we were on an emotional roller coaster, we shall never forget and can never thank them enough for what they did for us. They were like family, and we sensed that they were feeling our pain."

The guides, down from the mountain, came to see the two often.

Even strangers offered tremendous support. Friends of a friend invited Rachel to stay with them in Anchorage. A member of Chuck's climbing team loaned her a car. The nurses at the Thermal Unit took a special interest in their needs as well. They were all, the couple believes, very crucial in their emotional recovery.

Somehow, Chuck recalls, ADG's Diane had convinced Dr. Mills (the frostbite expert and author) to come out of retirement in order to help treat the climbers and their injuries. Mills is known throughout the world for his expertise and has treated hundreds of frostbitten patients.

A true Alaskan, Dr. Mills is something of a gruff character. He is also a straight shooter, according to Chuck. "He wouldn't pull any punches when Rachel or I had a question about my prognosis, yet he answered in a compassionate way that always left us with hope."

On their last day at Providence, the doctor sat Rachel and Chuck down and had a heart-to-heart talk about what they could expect next. As usual, Mills was clear and direct. "He said I would be able to keep both my thumbs," Chuck recalls, "plus my right little finger and maybe a part of my left ring finger. The rest would have to be amputated." But, Chuck says, the doctor left a ray of hope by adding, "You will have fully functional hands."

It was more than Chuck could believe right then. "Fully functional hands?" he remembers thinking. "Are you kidding? I'll be a freak!"

He was thankful to be alive and was acutely aware that he had come close to a far worse fate. But still, losing his fingers would be devastating. He needed them for their sense of touch, for getting dressed, for his work at the college. The news hit hard. To a great degree, he realized, the life he had known was over.

It was time for Chuck to go home to Michigan and take up the next phase of his recovery, but for some reason he dreaded the prospect. "The thought of returning made me sick," he says. "I was afraid to face my family and friends, and I couldn't bear the thought of the surgeries to come." Yet he knew he would need to face the inevitable. So with Rachel's encouragement and with his hands freshly skinned from debridement and completely bandaged, Chuck said good-bye to the Anchorage crew and turned to the airport and journey ahead.

Touching down in Grand Rapids, he was surprised by his sense of relief. He was even more surprised by what happened next. "As we headed toward baggage, we were suddenly engulfed by people—by family, coworkers, and friends, all cheering and carrying flowers and balloons. My dad led the pack, embracing me with a big bear hug. 'It's so great to have you home!' he said. And I agreed. When I looked at the crowd around me, my apprehensions melted away, and I realized my support team had suddenly increased tenfold."

With the amputation only days away, Chuck spent a good part of the time thinking nostalgically about his fingers. "It felt like I was saying good-bye to old friends," he says. "They had held my wife's hand at our wedding. They had helped me grip my bicycle handlebars as I rode around the world. I used them to make my living. How could I go on without them?"

The following months included surgeries and countless hours of grueling therapies as Chuck wavered between determination, denial, and depression. "I kept hoping it was all simply a nightmare. I so wanted to wake up and have it all end." Yet, as survivors are forced to do, Chuck endured. And with the help of his support team, he was somehow able to overcome the hardships.

"Rachel was with me day and night. She bathed me and helped me dress. She fed me, one spoonful at a time. She changed my bandages, and even wiped my behind. Her attitude made it clear that I wasn't a burden. Instead, amazingly, she truly believed it was a blessing to help."

Their son, Bill, was a constant cheerleader. Initially he had flown to Anchorage to be near his parents. "In Michigan," Chuck adds, "he would often drive two hours after work to come see me and to give his mom a break." Chuck's parents and five sisters each took turns as well.

But, Chuck says, he learned the true meaning of commitment when his sister, Darlene, spent hours teaching herself how to tie her shoes with her finger and thumbs. "Once she had mastered the skill, she proudly showed me what she had learned, and she reminded me that someday I would be able to perform life's everyday functions." Today Chuck ties his shoes just as his sister demonstrated.

Throughout Chuck's recovery, Rachel and he maintained their faith and used it to gain strength. "During my darkest days and nights," Chuck says, "my greatest solace came from the Bible." A passage in Matthew, in fact, changed his attitude and ultimately his future. "After reading it, I made the decision to turn my nightmare over to God, trusting that He would take care of me." Soon the couple found their spiritual life growing by leaps and bounds. Their church family came to their aid by praying, sending them food, and visiting constantly. Remembering what it meant to him, Chuck notes, "I am convinced that a person's spiritual beliefs can be crucial following a tragedy. May we never forget the importance of a survivor's faith during his or her recovery."

In August 1999, two years after his accident and with his son, Bill, at his side, Chuck climbed his 50th high point, Granite Peak in Montana. By reaching the summit of the technical rock route, he finally was able to complete his goal of standing on the highest point of all 50 states. "While some people may consider me crazy for continuing to climb after my experience on McKinley, it was an easy choice. Life is hard. But I've always believed that life is an adventure, and risk is simply part of the game."

Reflections. Eight years have passed since that fateful day on North America's highest peak. Much has been lost and much has been gained along the way. Chuck and Rachel have learned and grown tremendously as a result of their experience, and they are willing to share what they have learned with others.

Although the ordeal was challenging, and there were certainly dark times, Chuck says that not all aspects of being a "survivor" are bad. "I appreciate the small things in life much more now—the smell of fresh-cut hay, a bee buzzing from flower to flower. Things that went unnoticed before now occupy my daily life." In fact, he believes his prayers for a full recovery were answered: He has regained full eyesight, and he is able to do today everything that he could before the accident.

"I know we cannot remove all danger from our lives, and personally, I'm not sure we should try. When we choose to play life safe, we might be limiting the chance of harm, but I believe we also limit our ability to grow, learn, love, and enjoy many of life's pleasures. Even my son, who isn't thrilled that I still climb, was willing to admit, 'I would rather have a dad without fingers who has taken me on many adventures than a dad with fingers who just sits on the couch!'"

Asked to reflect on lessons learned from the climb itself, Chuck starts by talking about his selection of ADG. "Before our climb, when my buddies and I researched the guides and services on McKinley, ADG and Blaine were considered among the best." He learned this by talking to people who had been on the mountain and by asking for recommendations. He wanted to feel confident that he would be signing on with a company that took all aspects of the experience seriously. "Looking back, I'm glad I made a careful choice."

Is he angry? Does he believe mistakes were made? Chuck cannot bring himself to criticize the ADG guides for their decision to go to the summit. He believes their judgment was based on years of experience, and given the conditions that were present at the time, he thinks they made the right call.

"Our team stopped a couple times [on summit day] to assess the weather," Chuck notes. "It hadn't been perfect, but it wasn't bad, and we all agreed it was good enough to continue." Chuck also realizes that a guide's or an instructor's decisions—right or wrong—are an expected part of outdoor pursuits. Given Blaine's background and many years of experience, Chuck was comfortable following his lead.

The night on the mountain, Chuck says, was awful. But he believes their decision to hunker down was wise, particularly in light of what happened to two British climbers/soldiers who were also on the mountain that day.

The British team had passed Chuck and his partners in the storm, near the summit. Although the ADG team asked the two if they would like to join them, the men told the ADG group that they were unprepared to spend the night in the storm. Instead, the two pushed on toward the relative safety of their camp at 17,200 feet. Shortly after leaving the ADG team, however, at around 19,000 feet, they stepped off an unseen cliff and tumbled 4,000 feet. One of the men died, and the other suffered extreme frostbite.

According to the *International Express* (1998), the survivor later sued his commander and unit, claiming that he never should have been allowed to attempt the summit. He said that he was not properly equipped for the climb and that the team should not have been on the mountain when ferocious weather was imminent. The soldier, who had been on seven previous climbing expeditions, added, "The way the army handled this episode has made me rather bitter."

Chuck is aware of the lawsuit brought by the British climber, but he feels his experience was different in several key ways. He believes ADG did a good job helping him prepare for the climb and making sure its guides were prepared for a worst-case scenario. Further, he believes that the equipment his group carried was critical in their bivouac and that his guides' ability to deal with a crisis situation was integral in the group's survival that night. "Maybe he [the British climber] was trying to make things right by seeking litigation," Chuck suggests, "but in my case, it didn't make sense."

"At no time did I ever feel that ADG was trying to hide the facts or cover up anything."

Chuck is equally impressed with ADG's post-incident actions and follow-through. "Throughout my recovery in Anchorage, ADG did everything they could to help Rachel and me through the most difficult time of our lives. They approached the incident with total compassion and openness. At no time did I ever feel that ADG was trying to hide the facts or cover up anything about our accident. Instead, they took the approach of, 'Let's find out what went wrong so this will never happen again.'"

Asked if his response to the incident might have been different if ADG had not been so kind or upfront afterward, Chuck took a second to respond. "I think it would have triggered a response, fair or not, that maybe a mistake had been made. I guess it would have felt like they were trying to cover something up. It's kind of funny," he adds, "because I really don't think a mistake was made. But if they had taken a closed or defensive position, I don't think I would have trusted them."

Rachel shares Chuck's positive feelings toward the guiding company. "I felt such gratitude that ADG kept me informed. Not once did they try to make light of the situation. They did their best to answer my questions and kept me abreast of what was happening." She says she would have felt terrible, perhaps even angry, if she had not been notified of the situation, even when the group was still on the mountain and facts were unknown.

In fact, Rachel considers Diane a real "trouper" for coming to see the couple on a nearly daily basis and for providing support long after the climb had ended. She adds that Diane and Brian even called periodically after she and Chuck returned to Michigan.

When asked what aspects of his hospital stay helped or hindered his recovery, Chuck says, "We could never put into words how caring and compassionate the hospital staff was and how important they were in my recovery. They literally would do anything we asked."

There was one unpleasant doctor, however, who Chuck describes as cold. "I never expected everyone to become personally involved or take a direct interest in my care, but I found the man's hardened approach especially distasteful. I can easily see how a seemingly callous or indifferent 'no comment' or 'circle the wagons' strategy could lead to bad feelings."

In fact, Chuck is quick to conclude that kindness is a requirement for recovery. "Empathy and support should come first," he says. "That is a lesson I wish everyone could learn."

Lessons to be Learned. Chuck has a few words of wisdom for outdoor leaders and administrators:

1. *It is important to help a client comprehend the risks in advance. As experienced as I was, I really did not have an understanding of what life would be like at high altitude before the trip started. However, because I did my homework, and because of ADG's efforts, I think I*

started the trip with an appropriate grasp of the hazards associated with climbing a big mountain. As a result, I was more prepared to accept what happened. Novice adventurers, on the other hand, might have unrealistic expectations that a guide can keep them "safe."

2. *It is important for an organization to have a plan in the event that something goes wrong. I believe our group—clients and guides alike—was prepared for a worst-case scenario, not only due to the guides' training and experience, but as a result of evening classes, good role modeling and habits, and the safety equipment we carried to the summit.*

3. *An organization, just like a client, should be willing to accept that sometimes people get hurt, and consequently, leaders and managers need to be prepared to deal with the aftermath.*

Chuck was asked if he has any concluding remarks. Mainly, he says, he wants to make sure people do not let fear guide their actions. He thinks it is important for people to take risks in life, whether that means climbing a mountain or showing vulnerabilities. But because people who take risks sometimes get hurt, it is just as important to be prepared for the potential consequences.

Organizations need to be diligent in examining accidents—their own and those that happen to others—so that proper protocol can be established to keep injuries to a bare minimum. In our case, the uncontrollable weather on Denali [McKinley] bit us. The team that I climbed with prided itself on being the safest team on the mountain; yet, we suffered an accident.

Some people may be tempted to pity me, but I feel fortunate. Admittedly there were days when I questioned my ability to continue, and I doubted my capacity to endure and survive. It certainly wasn't easy. But the tragedy that struck me was met head-on by a constant and unshakable group of people who put truth, honesty, and compassion above all else. I was never a victim, and throughout my recovery, no one ever walked the other way or tried to hide behind a wall of self-interest.

If you or your organization is faced with an incident, don't let fear—even the fear of admitting fault—guide your actions. Don't be afraid to take a risk, to do the right thing, simply because you are uncertain of the consequences. Don't circle the wagons and shoot inward. Instead, remember the importance of being human, and offer a hand to someone in need. Isn't that the way life should be?

Epilogue: Chuck retired in 2004, at age 54, from his position as a full professor with Ferris State University. He recently purchased a BMW motorcycle he and Rachel enjoy riding together. They long to go back to Alaska to visit all the people who were instrumental in their healing.

Risk Management Planning: A Closer Look

By Deb Ajango © 2005

This chapter provides an assessment of the risk management strategies used by the programs involved in the Chapter One and Chapter Two accidents. By comparing Greenfield Community College's and Alaska Denali Guiding's operating procedures to the 10 components of a risk management system, the author is able to identify some of the less obvious aspects of risk management planning, including mistakes that service providers sometimes make.

In the summer of 1998, in Greenfield, Massachusetts, Team Adventure began a week of summer fun for teens. The kids looked forward to five days of outdoor activities and meeting new friends. Although the trip's leaders and the teens' parents probably accepted that one of the boys might suffer a few bumps or bruises, no one expected it to end like it did. A year earlier, thousands of miles away, a similar story unfolded on North America's tallest peak. A group of strangers gathered together to attempt a climb of Mount McKinley. Although the climbers knew there were risks, they looked forward to the expedition, accepting that the probability of serious injury or death was small.

On the surface, these two incidents probably appear night-and-day different. One group was made up of inexperienced teens; the other included relatively experienced adults. The former was based on day trips and a single overnight campout; the latter involved climbing to the top of a continent.

But in reality, the two groups and the incidents share a number of similarities. In both cases, the service providers (Greenfield Community College [GCC] and Alaska Denali Guiding [ADG]) sold adventure. Each program's marketing noted that there were risks associated with the activities, and both acknowledged that participants could be hurt or even killed.

Each service provider knew it was important that customers be adequately prepared for what lay ahead, and in both cases, that task was difficult. Both programs catered to participants who were trying something new and different; although the organizations tried to explain what the activities and environments would be like, there was no real point of relativity. As a result, some would argue that true assumptions of risk on the part of the customers were all but impossible.

In both instances, inherent risk played a significant role in the ensuing accidents.

Both agencies made attempts to manage the risks associated with their respective activities. Each hired skilled leaders, educated participants about proper procedures, and purchased and used appropriate equipment. The programs knew that the chance of a serious incident, though small, existed; as a result, ADG and GCC had emergency action plans in place.

And in both instances, inherent risk played a significant role in the ensuing accidents. In fact, it could be argued that the most striking similarity between the two incidents is the effect the forces of nature had on the outcomes.

Nonetheless, in the GCC case study, a claim of negligence was made. A number of the program's actions—prior to, during, and after the accident—were questioned, and painful litigation ensued. In contrast, no claims or suits were ever filed following the McKinley storm. The survivors did not feel "wronged," and they were willing to live with the fact that the injuries they suffered were simply "part of the game" that they had chosen to play.

Both the Deerfield River and Mount McKinley incidents changed a number of lives. Two sets of families are now considered survivors. Several of the participants endured emotional as well as physical scars. Employees in both cases were traumatized as well, and three of the four trip leaders never again worked in the outdoor industry. So why is it that one incident ended in a lawsuit and recrimination while the second seemingly was accepted as fate or bad luck? Does the greatest difference between the two cases lie within the clients' interpretations of inherent risk and negligence? Or did subtle distinctions exist between the programs' risk management systems—distinctions that might have affected the overall safety of the participants as well as the survivors' responses once they had been hurt?

This chapter will help the reader understand some of the more intricate components of risk management planning. The information provided here is not intended to find fault with or criticize actions of those involved; instead, it is meant to enlighten trip leaders and program managers. By taking a closer look at the case studies presented at the start of this book, I will identify some of the less obvious aspects associated with risk management, including mistakes that service providers sometimes make.

Overall, a risk management system should address six key features of an organization's identity: *why*, *what*, *who*, *where*, *when*, and *how*. Together, these components can be used to create a system that enhances a student's or client's experience, decreases the likelihood of an accident, and ultimately reduces an organization's exposure to legal liability. Although most risk management plans include at least some of these components, many either lack or are lax in one or more.

An effective system, on the other hand, pays careful attention to all of them.

KEY FEATURES OF A RISK MANAGEMENT SYSTEM

- Why – program philosophy, mission statement, risk management goals
- What – selection of course activities and curriculum
- Who – selection and training of staff and participants
- Where – venue selection
- When – course scheduling and resource considerations
- How – accepted field practices

Ideally, as each feature is discussed, decided upon, and formalized, it should be documented and organized into a policy and procedure manual or operational handbook. But even if an organization chooses not to craft a formal document, it is important that none of the components is forgotten or overlooked.

Further, the system should not be people-dependent. That is, although a particular person might be very skilled and able to complete a variety of tasks, the success of the system should not be dependent on any one individual. By making sure that the requisite expertise lies within an organization, and not within a single person, the success of the system is more likely to remain intact even after key people move on.

Finally, a risk management system should have various checks and balances in order to provide appropriate and ongoing assessment and oversight. An example of this might include, but would not be limited to, internal and external audits, the use of a risk management committee, and/or multiple evaluations that can help a program assess its risk management practices.

TEN COMPONENTS OF A QUALITY RISK MANAGEMENT SYSTEM

In order to address the *why*, *what*, *who, where*, *when,* and *how* of an outdoor or adventure program, or of any group that sends workers into remote environments for that matter, an organization should thoroughly examine its practices in the following areas:

1. Selection of program activities
2. Presentation of core material and assessment of participant progress
3. Field practices and field safety
4. Venue selection and appropriateness
5. Staff qualifications
6. Participant preparedness and readiness
7. Nutrition, hydration, and hygiene
8. Equipment
9. Transportation
10. Program oversight and system of ongoing evaluation

In combination, these 10 steps can be used to implement accident prevention strategies. The final product is often referred to as a risk management plan.

1. Selection of program activities

All organizations make choices about which activities to offer, from backpacking to rock climbing to international classes for credit. Before embarking on any new activity, a good question to ask is this: Is the activity worth the risk? Organizations concerned with risk management should select an activity because it supports their program's mission and not simply because it is marketable or because it sounds like fun. Fire walking may be a completely appropriate activity for an outfitter whose primary goal is to provide clients with a thrill or short-term adventure. However, the same activity seems incompatible with an organization whose goal is to provide environmental or outdoor education. Specifically, when selecting activities for inclusion, an organization might address the appropriateness of the activities based on each of the following:

- Mission
- Staff skills and experience (or lack of)
- Staff availability
- Students' backgrounds: skill levels, experience, etc.
- Inclusivity: the ability to adapt and modify activities for various learners
- Risks and hazards associated with a venue and activity
- Ability of staff to assess and manage the risks
- Ability of staff to handle foreseeable (even if unlikely) emergencies

Program managers can use a list like this to assess whether or not an activity makes sense and can be successfully administered in the safest manner possible.

Given the above bullet-point list, ADG appears to have selected reasonable activities for its customers. Although climbing Mount McKinley can expose people to fairly extreme hazards, the activity was within the program's mission. Further, the risks were known, safety measures were in place, the guides were well trained, and the activity was not beyond the level of the clients.

GCC's Team Adventure program, too, seems to have selected appropriate activities. Thc outings were fun yet educational (mission), involved relatively low risk, and were not beyond the reach of the average teen. Although GCC was criticized by some people for conducting the river activity, given the program's mission, it seems reasonable that it would provide water-safety training to youths in the area. In fact, Charles Walbridge, the accident investigator, concluded that the throw-bag drills and swimming exercise were part of a "well designed whitewater training program" that taught swimmers how life vests and proper body position could keep them safer in moving water (1998). "In an area with many fast-flowing rivers," Walbridge added, "that's an important lesson in water safety that could save lives."

On the other hand, while it is *not* reasonable to base a program's risk management plan on highly unlikely events and emergencies (such as a meteor strike), it *is* reasonable to plan for a foreseeable worst-case scenario. Given the potential hazards associated with the river activity (foot entrapment), the difficulty associated with a rescue, and the fact that foot entrapment is indeed a foreseeable (though unlikely) emergency, the selection of river rescue might be considered an appropriate but potentially dangerous outing for the young group and their leaders. In the end, GCC was left to decide: Was the activity worth the risk?

In the end, GCC was left to decide: Was the activity worth the risk?

Later in this section we will address other, perhaps more applicable, details of the river activity—i.e., how, where, and when the activity took place.

2. Presentation of core material and assessment of participant progress

Whether a program introduces novices to the outdoors, provides avalanche training to adults, or specializes in conducting high-risk activities, if and when student performance is required for the student's safety, it is essential that there is a system in place for presenting core material. It also is important to assess participant progress in a quality manner. Two steps that can help guide this process lie in creating a comprehensive curriculum and identifying expected outcomes. The benefits of developing solid curriculum are fourfold:

1. It helps instructors clarify which topics are "need to know" and which are considered "nice to know."

2. It assists instructors in structuring their classes around a proven sequence and provides them with a checklist (outline) so that they will not forget key and fundamental concepts.

3. It provides realistic timelines for each topic or activity.

4. It provides clear goals and measurable outcomes that can help students and instructors recognize and measure progress and success.

The basic rule is that key (need to know) concepts must be covered meticulously, each and every outing. Secondary (nice to know) topics can be included if and when there is time. This might sound easy, but it can be a surprisingly challenging task. For example, key information usually is presented in lecture format, whether it is in a classroom or on the edge of a river or pool. The lecture format is effective in providing a lot of information in a short amount of time, but it is not terribly effective for student understanding and assimilation of that information. Different instructors may tend to emphasize different points. Instructors who decide all subjects are important inevitably try to cover too much in too short a time. Consequently, students are not able to differentiate between need-to-know and nice-to-know concepts.

Further, when instructors feel pressed for time, they may omit or downgrade the quality of participant assessments. If performance tests are used, they may be conducted in large groups or in such a rushed manner that no true evaluation of student understanding or progress is actually achieved.

A well-crafted curriculum, on the other hand, avoids these pitfalls. It is organized so that key topics are covered first and thoroughly. Enough time is allowed so that student progress can be assessed. Topics are presented via logical sequencing, and creative methodologies are used. As a result, as a course progresses, students are prepared mentally and physically for increasingly difficult tasks.

If the foundational material is a prerequisite for safe operations, students should be tested individually before they are allowed to move to more advanced skills. Students should clearly understand what is expected of them, and they should be able to gauge their own progress according to these expectations.

In traditional education, student understanding of subject matter can be measured through written tests, papers, and/or projects. In outdoor education, similar but perhaps more imaginative appraisal methods will need to be employed. When evaluating performance, skill tests can be used.

Some instructors may complain that strict course curriculum guidelines feel stifling, but those employees should be encouraged to be creative in their methods of delivery. Ultimately, each instructor can develop his or her own style to present the material and measure success.

On the climb of Mount McKinley, Chuck's education began long before the team set foot on the mountain. Not only was he offered a recommended reading list, but the service provider contacted him on several occasions to help him become better prepared for the adventure ahead. Further, ADG offered a number of "classes" during the expedition. The clients were given hands-on training in knots, anchor systems, and crevasse rescue within the first two days of the climb, before they ever left base camp. As the group ascended to a colder, more extreme environment, evening lectures on frostbite, altitude, and hypothermia were included as well.

Given this progression, it appears that the ADG guides and managers covered appropriate topics in a logical sequence. Although it is not clear that the teaching had a direct effect on the group's survival, nor is it known what type (if any) of student assessment was conducted, the clients later stated that they felt well prepped and trained. They added that they believed they had received good directions and developed good habits over the course of the trip. And although the clients were expected to follow directions throughout the climb, at no time were the clients wholly responsible for their own safety.

GCC also appeared to have designed its curriculum with some care. The trip leaders based each day's outline on need-to-know topics. Each undertaking included stated educational goals and outcomes. On the day of the incident, the instructors followed a logical sequence when teaching the key concepts for the day. Students were fitted with life vests, the group discussed the attendant risks and hazards of the river activity, and the teens practiced using throw ropes on land. It is not clear, however, that students clearly understood the dangers associated with foot entrapment. Further, the method used by staff to teach "river swimming" appears to have been lecture based. And given the activity structure and timeline, it would have been very difficult to assess whether or not the students were sufficiently skilled to swim the river and avoid an emergency.

When student performance can make a difference in student safety, it is critical that information be presented in a highly effective manner.

Because the consequence of a foot entrapment is potentially so severe (investigator Walbridge compared it to stepping in front of a moving car), it is not clear that GCC and its instructors did enough to teach "river swimming" with the thoroughness it deserved. Walbridge concluded in his report that "more effective instruction is the only thing that might have increased the odds for Adam" (1998). When student performance can make a difference in student safety, it is critical that information be presented in a highly effective manner, and measures must be taken to ensure that students are ready for the next step.

Even though the teaching of this particular skill is in question, when compared to other similar programs, GCC seems to have taken reasonable steps in the development of its curriculum. In fact, many outdoor programs conduct their activities with far less structure and oversight in place. And tragically, over the past decade, a number of programs have experienced serious incidents because students assessed as "strong," "talented," and even "hot" by their instructors were not able to perform a particular skill without error.

3. Field practices and field safety

Many organizations choose to limit the number of policies field staff must follow, leaving it up to the instructor to decide exactly how a course is run. While this approach has its supporters, it is probably neither the safest nor the best way to run an operation. Policies and rules are not the enemy; they can be used to guide an instructor's decisions and minimize risk.

Identifying and following accepted field practices in the outdoors is no different than identifying and accepting safety practices in other professions, such as aviation or medicine. The goal is to ensure that appropriate decisions are made based on agreed-upon criteria rather than individual whim. By scripting the protocols and having them available for instructor and student reference, an organization can minimize assumptions, provide clarification, and create backup systems to make sure nothing important is forgotten.

If outdoor programs followed the lead of other industries in which human error can lead to injury or death, it is likely that a number of standards, or standard operating procedures, would become the norm rather than the exception.

According to decades of data, not only do human beings err, but they err frequently and in predictable ways. The aviation industry recognizes this fact and has taken countermeasures accordingly. As a result, the frequency of operational errors has been reduced to one in 100,000 flights.

The medical industry also has accepted that highly educated doctors make mistakes on a regular basis. Many of the mistakes, in fact, are made in fairly benign settings. Take the example of writing out a prescription—a rote procedure that relies on memory and attention, but a process that rarely takes place under dire or stressful circumstances. Consistently and perhaps inevitably, physicians write down the wrong drug or dose, labels are misread, or pharmacists do not provide backup checks. As it is, medication mix-ups currently are the most common type of medical error. And while it might be tempting to assume that complacent or inept professionals are the ones making all the mistakes, medical studies have shown that repeat offenders are not the problem. Instead, research suggests that virtually everyone who cares for hospital patients will, sooner or later, make a serious mistake.

By acknowledging that human error is inevitable, the medical industry—like the aviation industry—has focused on creating routines or systems that can help reduce the number of incidents. For example, equipment has been redesigned with infallible human beings in mind. Monitors are now used to detect commonly repeated errors. It has become standard procedure to initial, with a marker, the body part that will be operated on as well. And pilot-like checklists are used in the average operating room.

Unfortunately, the outdoor industry stubbornly refuses to standardize its equipment or its procedures. Instead, "industry standards" seem murky and ambiguous at best and even change from one part of the country to another. Even though outdoor leaders go through far less training than pilots or surgeons, many believe that rules, checklists, and policies are not necessary and can in fact decrease field safety. While it is true that outdoor programs cannot and should not create a rigid set of rules that governs all decisions or actions, it is foolish to think, conversely, that standardization and checklists have no place in the industry.

Examples of policy topics that should be reviewed and potentially adopted include, but should not be limited to, the following:

- Ratios and supervision
- Course preparation and pre-outing checks
- Safety practices (i.e., field practices) specific to various activities
- Transportation
- Equipment: selection, tracking, and maintenance
- Emergency action plans

Risk management policies should reflect the program's mission and philosophy. They should make sense to administrators, trip leaders, and participants. It usually is useful to get input from a variety of people, perhaps even a risk management committee, at the policy-writing stage. Once a policy has been adopted, it is important that people at all levels of the organization know it, accept it, and understand that they are expected to follow it.

A policy and procedure manual is a useful tool for storing a program's operating procedures, but simply asking new employees to read it might not be the best method for educating them. Instead, active and interactive training sessions that use experiential methodologies tend to be more effective in ensuring that information is understood and assimilated.

Both GCC and ADG did an adequate job of identifying standard operating procedures. In fact, in some ways, GCC's policies appear to have been a bit more rigid than ADG's (which would be reasonable given the backgrounds of staff and participants). For example, GCC's trip leaders were expected to call about water levels prior to the start of the activity, check PFD fit (by attempting to lift it over a student's head), and ask for permission before altering activities or an agenda. Although these actions might seem like common sense, instructors were not really given an option to follow or ignore them.

ADG, too, had some policies that were considered "musts." For example, although the trip leaders were allowed to make many field decisions, they were expected to carry survival equipment to the summit, including sleeping bags, a steel shovel, and a snow saw. The program's owners/managers did not leave this decision up to instructor discretion, even if the weather seemed perfect. As a result, the ADG group was well equipped during the storm. In fact, the heavy steel shovel and snow saw may even have contributed to their survival.

If something is important enough to be a policy (like ratios or carrying survival equipment), programs should ensure that trip leaders do not deviate from that policy (as the GCC trip leaders did) simply because the rule seems inconvenient or unimportant at the time. The student/instructor ratio in the Deerfield River case may or may not have directly contributed to the accident, but it certainly was brought into question afterward. Further, as Drew Leemon points out in Chapter Seven, it is worth remembering that seemingly small events, taken alone, can appear fairly innocuous; cumulatively, however, the hazards or actions increase the accident potential.

4. Venue selection and appropriateness

Venue selection is one of the most frequently overlooked aspects of a risk management plan. Too often organizations choose venues based on a particular site's popularity, proximity, or marketability instead of thoroughly assessing its attendant risks. At times, venues are used to satisfy an instructor's agenda. However, it is unacceptable for an instructor, bored with the "easy and familiar" routes, to take students or clients to a more challenging site simply for personal pleasure. Although he or she may convince himself or herself that the experience will benefit all, the choice may increase the level of risk to students unnecessarily.

Ideally, the choice in venue should be based on a number of considerations: the program's mission; the hazards associated with the area; the experience and expertise of the staff; the experience, skill level, and readiness of the participants; and the goals of the activity. Does the site provide the type of terrain necessary to meet course goals? Can the course goals be met by using another less hazardous site? Are there good teaching spots or enough water/shade in the area? Once details like these have been considered, an organization can feel confident knowing that the decision was made with course success and participant safety in mind.

Mount McKinley, admittedly, offers a number of objective hazards. However, given ADG's mission, the guides' abilities, the clients' backgrounds, and the program's marketing efforts, the high altitude venue was appropriate. ADG was quite honest about the risks and hazards associated with the trip, and required that participants be skilled and experienced winter campers in order to sign up. Because of these steps, Chuck was able to make an educated choice about joining the expedition.

GCC's venues, for the most part, also were appropriate given its mission, staff, and clientele. In fact, most outdoor educators would consider Class I water to be reasonable for river-rescue training, even if it involved a group of teens. Indeed, local groups used the exact spot regularly. However, because there were few opportunities for a quick and efficient rescue, especially after the upriver water release, the Deerfield River venue comes into question.

Program managers and trip leaders might consider using Figure 3.1 to help clarify risk-benefit analysis decisions.

The information in the chart, which was first introduced by an unknown source years ago, still applies today.

Probability of Consequences

High probability that something bad will happen. — Consequences will likely be minor.	High probability that something bad will happen. — Consequences could potentially be severe.
Low probability that something bad will happen. — Consequences will likely be minor.	Low probability that something bad will happen. — Consequences could potentially be severe.

Severity of Consequences

Figure 3.1 *The above chart can be used to help clarify risk-benefit analysis decisions. By modifying the activity, staff skill, clientele, or venue, one can alter where on the chart the risk might fall (source unknown).*

In Figure 3.1, the lower left square represents low-probability, low-consequence situations. That is, given the activity, venue, and participant profiles, there is a low probability for incident. In the event that an incident would occur, it would probably be minor in nature. As a case in point: If a group of healthy young adults decides to hike on a flat, well-marked trail (absent of storms, wild animals, moving water, snow slopes, etc.), it would be very unlikely that they would meet a disastrous end.

The upper right box, on the other hand, represents a very different scenario: i.e., high probability, high consequence. All things considered, there is a fairly good chance that there will be a highly undesirable outcome. An example of a high-risk, high-consequence setup might be an expedition on Mount Everest that targets unfit elders over 70. The chance for problems is high, and the consequences could be quite severe. This type of arrangement is nearly always avoided.

The upper left and lower right boxes are more ambiguous. These two squares involve either a high-probability, low-consequence arrangement (upper left), or a low-probability, high-consequence scenario (lower right). A number of traditional sports tend to fall into the former category. In football, gymnastics, and hockey, for instance, there is a good chance that, sooner or later, a participant will be injured, but the odds are that the injury will not be debilitating or fatal. Certain outdoor activities (including the Team Adventure river rescue exercise), on the other hand, tend to fall into the latter category. Although the odds of Adam becoming trapped were quite small, the consequence was catastrophic.

Program managers and trip leaders should be careful to remember that by modifying even a single element (such as staff skill sets, student preparedness, or venue), a program might end up pushing a low-risk, low-consequence activity into a low-risk, high-consequence one. If GCC had used a (theoretically) sandy-bottom river for its rescue activity, or if it had conducted the activity when there was less flow, it might have been able to reduce the odds of an accident as well as the severity of consequences considerably.

The questions, then, are these: Is it (or when is it) appropriate to expose participants to activities if there is a small chance that they will be seriously injured or killed? And, does the answer change according to the program's mission, staff, and/or clientele?

Given that GCC had an educational mission and was trying to teach teens about the hazards associated with moving water—especially given that these local teens likely would partake in some sort of water-based activity later in life—some people would argue that the risk and venue were appropriate.

Given the extreme nature of potential consequences and given that the clientele were children, others would conclude otherwise.

In the end, programs are left to carefully consider how the hazards associated with a venue might affect the risk-benefit analysis according to their unique circumstances. Unless there is a compelling reason to seek out hazards, the risk should be kept to a minimum.

5. Staff qualifications

The "who" of an outdoor service provider includes up to three kinds of people: staff, volunteers/interns, and students/clients. Each of these categories has a unique relationship to the organization that is worth examining. Instructor and volunteer considerations are identified here; student/client considerations are addressed later in this chapter.

Staff. Even if all aspects of a risk management system have been considered and properly addressed, the system will be jeopardized if poorly qualified leaders are hired to take groups into the field. Further, each organization needs qualified managers who can assess the risk to students, leaders, and even the institution. But how does a program recognize a good instructor or manager? Which qualities are most important? And what should an organization look for when selecting and hiring staff?

The following list identifies a number of core competencies that an outdoor leader should possess to some degree. The level of mastery a person has in each of these areas should increase as that person's level of responsibility increases. Further, the level of competency required will be dependent on the activities conducted.

- Technical skills
- Rescue skills (i.e., technical rescue)

- Emergency response (medical skills, communication, group management, etc.)
- The ability to assess and manage risks to self and others
- Instructional and facilitation skills; group and time management skills
- Problem-solving and decision-making skills; experience-based judgment
- Effective speaking and listening skills
- Strong professional (and environmental) ethics
- Leadership skills and a flexible leadership style

Unfortunately, laymen sometimes confuse recreational outdoor users with experts. Just because someone is an ardent bird watcher with years of experience does not make him or her an ornithologist. And just because someone is an experienced camper does not qualify him or her to lead others in the same activity. In fact, many of the skills identified in the above list will not be developed without formal training, instruction, and/or mentoring.

The following definitions can be used to help illustrate how students progress to become competent outdoor leaders.

A *beginning student* has not yet learned to recognize, assess, and manage risk for himself or herself. This student has little to no background in the selected activity, and performance mistakes should be anticipated. Many students are at the novice or beginning level when they sign up for a trip with a service provider.

An *advanced student* has not only learned to anticipate, recognize, assess, and manage risk for himself or herself, but he or she can now start to do so for his or her peers. This person will make fewer "beginner" mistakes, and on the surface, it will appear that he or she is competent in many areas. Once a student has mastered a variety of skills, he or she should have the minimum background to be considered for an assistant instructor position.

It should be noted that many low-budget and volunteer groups—as well as research-based groups and educational institutes—often use advanced students to lead trips and facilitate activities. Though the trip leaders might be considered experts in certain topics, they are not experts in leading or managing risk for others. In these cases, the programs should be careful to choose low-probability, low-consequence activeities and venues whenever possible.

B*eginning instructors* should be competent in the skill areas or activities they will be supervising. Because these people have fairly extensive field experience, they should be able to recognize, assess, and manage risk for themselves as well as for others. They should have a basic but unpolished ability to anticipate the mistakes that students will make. They also should have a solid understanding of the differences between personal, group, and institutional risk management. Beginning instructors should have some training in first aid and should be skilled in carrying out an organization's crisis response plan.

Supervisors should realize that beginning instructors, like beginning students, will make mistakes.

Supervisors should realize that beginning instructors, like beginning students, will make mistakes. Because the role is new to them, they will likely have gaps in certain competency areas, and supervision—as well as training—should be provided accordingly.

A *lead instructor* should be skilled in recognizing, assessing, and managing risk for himself or herself and others, in a given environment, and over an extended period of time. Not only should this person be extremely competent in the activity, but he or she should be adept at recognizing and minimizing inherent risks of the activity and the environment. Further, because this person has extensive personal as well as professional field experience, he or she should be able to anticipate student errors and should be skilled at problem solving and improvising.

The lead instructor should have the ability to successfully disseminate information and, in many cases, to challenge students intellectually and provide educational guidance. This person also should be trained in crisis response (i.e., emergency protocol, technical rescue skills, and wilderness medicine).

The program's *risk manager* should be able to provide a big-picture view of the outfitter's risk management system. He or she also should have a good grasp of the following: trends in the industry; relevance of close calls; common mistakes that students make prior to a course start and while in the field; common mistakes that instructors make prior to a course start and while in the field; and potential hazards that can harm the institution.

An error that programs sometimes make is to place a traditional "safety officer" in this role. That is, the position is filled by someone who has a strong background in worker safety, OSHA requirements, or workers' compensation. Unfortunately, traditional safety officers have little expertise in field activities or the unique challenges posed by remote environments.

Outdoor risk managers, on the other hand, have unique skill sets. They typically are able to use accident statistics to improve system-wide risk management practices. They are able to guide the "right" students and employees through the door so that there is a proper "fit" between student, instructor, and program mission. They know how to create training plans to help students and instructors become well prepared, even before they enter the field. Outdoor risk managers know what technology exists to improve program safety; which activities are appropriate, according to mission and student/instructor backgrounds; and which local venues can be used to meet course objectives while at the same time posing the fewest environmental hazards possible.

By all accounts, both GCC and ADG hired qualified, competent field staff. According to program representatives, all four trip leaders were skilled in most, if not all, of the areas identified. Further, all were qualified to work as lead and assistant instructors, based on their experience levels and credentials.

Although the GCC accident investigator (Walbridge 1998) questioned some of the GCC instructors' decisions and methods, those actions could only, at most, be considered human error, not incompetence. Walbridge acknowledged that the teaching system and sequence used up to the point of the river activity seemed quite good. What he questioned was whether or not the instructors taught the skill of river swimming well or effectively. The decision to allow a 12:1 ratio might have been a mistake, but it was not the primary cause of the accident. In the end, the investigator concluded that the incident was the result of a combination of factors, including facilitation of the activity and inherent risk.

In the ADG case study, some readers might believe the guides made a mistake by allowing the group to go to the summit in less than perfect weather. (As a reminder, a member of a nearby team made a similar claim against his leader.) But again, human beings err, and even if one considers the decision to ascend a mistake, it would be far-fetched to claim that the trip leaders were incompetent.

Perhaps the greatest recognizable error in the Deerfield River incident was that the instructors were unable to deal with the emergency once Adam was trapped. While this might be an unfair criticism in this particular instance—a quick and efficient response would have been difficult for anyone given the circumstances—it does appear that the instructors mistakenly relied on accident prevention measures and were inadequately prepared for crisis response. Although the primary goal for instructors is to prevent serious problems from occurring in the first place, it is also essential that they are trained to deal with the "what ifs" or worst-case scenarios than can and sometimes do occur.

One could hardly argue, for example, that it would be acceptable for a backcountry ski instructor to lead students into avalanche terrain unless he or she has the ability (knowledge and equipment) to quickly find and dig out a burial. Even if everyone agreed that the instructor was quite good at avoiding avalanches, it would be exceedingly difficult to justify to a widow or parent why beacons, shovels, and probes were left behind. In the event that a quick response is unrealistic, it is up to the program to modify the venue or activity, or to at least honestly disclose to participants that their own survival might hinge on their (or an instructor's) ability to perform certain skills.

Unfortunately, it seems that many of today's leaders are not truly ready to deal with worst-case scenarios. A number of outfitters require only that their employees have a certification in wilderness medicine. While this training can be invaluable in assisting with a medical emergency, it is insufficient when a technical rescue is in order.

Some organizations do require that trip leaders be exposed to technical rescue trainings, but these same companies often accept that, as long as employees can carry out simulated rescues at base camp, under the guidance of senior instructors, under no particular time constraint, they have met the criteria of "rescue skills." A prudent service provider, on the other hand, will include rescue scenarios as an ongoing part of staff training. By making sure staff skills are honed in this important but rarely used area, they are minimizing the probability that a minor emergency may become a serious if not fatal event.

Volunteers. The use of unpaid (volunteer) staff is fairly common in outdoor agencies. In fact, some programs run exclusively on volunteers or use a limited number of paid staff to supervise and support the volunteer crew. Examples include nature programs, scouting groups, or even college outing clubs.

Volunteers can effectively minimize costs, but the strategy is not without risk. A volunteer, who is rarely held to the same hiring and training standards as an employee, cannot be expected to provide the same level of leadership, competence, or commitment as a paid instructor. Yet these leaders are often put into positions in which they are required to make difficult decisions. In the event of an accident, the practice is almost sure to be questioned, especially if a volunteer is being used in place of a paid instructor.

To address these concerns, an organization might decide to create minimum "hiring" standards and clarify the roles of and expectations for volunteers. If volunteers are used as trip leaders, they should have strong technical skills and crisis response training, and they should have significant personal experience in the activity itself. Whenever possible, they should "work" under the direct supervision of a lead or qualified instructor. Finally, volunteers should be required to attend an orientation similar to that of a new paid employee. At that time, expectations can be clarified, questions can be asked and answered, and assumptions can be annulled.

6. Participant preparedness and readiness

Selecting the "right" participants for a course or trip is far more challenging than simply creating a flashy brochure for clients and then collecting registration forms as they come in. Instead, the goal is to get a good fit between customer and activity, which means matching expectations to reality and physical ability to the demands of the field experience. When the fit is good, everyone is more likely to achieve his or her goals and walk away satisfied. When the fit is bad, it can lead to disaster.

Consider this analogy: Imagine that it were possible for you to own and manage a racetrack for people who want to experience the thrill of auto racing in a "safe" environment. The venue and cars would be modified to minimize the danger. There would be no immovable objects anywhere near the speedway, and the walls of the track would be designed specifically to nudge errant race cars back onto the track. The cars would only go 100 mph. Air bags, seat belts, and side beams would be installed in all vehicles. You would require that customers have a valid driver's license. You assume that as long as people are able to drive and understand the risks, you would have done all that you could do in the name of safety; the choice (to participate or not) was now theirs.

What you didn't mention in your brochure (you thought it was unimportant), however, was that you had removed the side mirrors from your race cars because of the hazard they present to passing drivers. The rear-view mirror, instead, has been enlarged. The side windows have also been modified for improved over-the-shoulder viewing. As long as drivers do mirror and shoulder checks for the presence of other vehicles, there should be virtually no blind spots.

A customer with a clean driving record signs up and is quite excited to get going. Unknown to you, he had neck surgery years ago and is unable to look over his shoulder. He does not notice the lack of side mirrors as he gets in the car, but within seconds, he realizes that they are missing. He must now decide if he should continue with an activity that he feels uncomfortable doing or park the race car and try to get his money back. Fearing confrontation and inconvenience, he drives on, only to cause an accident on his fifth lap.

If you had only known of his condition (which he didn't think to tell you about), you could have offered portable side mirrors! You also had lights to attach to the top of the car so that other drivers would know to avoid his blind spot. In other words, had an appropriate *information exchange* taken place ahead of time, you might have been able to prevent the accident in the first place.

As silly as this scenario may seem, programs and clients experience similar interactions all the time. Assumptions are made by the service provider about client knowledge, fitness, and abilities; and assumptions are made by potential clients in regard to what the activity and environment will be like. In the end, the assumptions can come back to haunt everyone.

An information exchange is simply making sure that key information is offered and received prior to an outing start. Participants should receive the lowdown about an activity, environment, gear needs, or fitness requirements, and the service providers should find out whether or not there is any reason potential customers might be endangering themselves (or others) by participating. Often, once this exchange takes place, slight modifications (such as applying portable side mirrors or, more realistically, modifying venues or perhaps menus) can ultimately reduce the accident potential.

An information exchange is simply making sure that key information is offered and received prior to an outing start.

Because promotional literature usually is designed to sell a course and attract new clients, the natural tendency is to pick the most exciting language and spectacular photographs, and use the most enthusiastic endorsements from previous clients or students. But ironically, as Reb Gregg points out in Chapter Six, there is risk in presenting oneself in too good a light. In fact, an organization should be cautioned against using only pictures of smiling students in spectacular settings. This kind of advertising can convey a false image of what the environment may be like and create unrealistic expectations regarding the participants' comfort and well-being. All adventure education involves at least some level of risk, and not all trips end in success.

At the opposite extreme is advertising that is too negative. Literature that focuses only on the potential of injury is not likely to attract any customers at all. Further, while an organization may be tempted to overrate the difficulty of a course to ensure that only suitable clients apply, it may be setting itself up for trouble if it is too quick to judge those individuals who might appear unfit.

A more appropriate approach to marketing is one that uses promotional literature to educate and inform. Brochures, catalogs, and Web sites can help prepare participants for the experiences they will encounter in the field. When an organization takes the time to inform potential customers about what they can expect, what to wear, what challenges and risks they are likely to face, and what minimum skill and fitness levels are required for each activity, it does two important things: It increases the odds that there will be a good fit between customer and activity, and it reduces the number of ill-prepared and unqualified people who end up in the field.

This idea of educating potential customers so that they can make knowledgeable decisions regarding participation is known as *informed consent* (see Chapter Six). Informed and educated participants are better equipped to recognize hazards and, thus, help point out potential dangers. Further, when an instructor does a good job of educating group members about risks and rules, participants are often more engaged and apt to accept some responsibility for their own and others' well-being.

The second half of the information exchange includes gathering relevant information from participants. The questions asked should not be random and invasive; instead, they should be purposeful, and they should be asked in the name of safety. For example, trip leaders need to know which participants have certain preexisting medical conditions, such as anaphylaxis, diabetes, or seizure disorders. These conditions, specifically, can be influenced by the environment or activity. They also can lead to sudden emergencies under certain circumstances.

When medical needs or conditions are identified in advance, an organization has time to consider and plan for "what ifs" and to take whatever precautionary measures are necessary. Further, if a client or student identifies potential concerns or special needs, the program can modify the activity to promote inclusion and greater group success.

Some programs choose to deal with this issue by asking a single, generic question: Do you have any conditions that might affect your ability to participate safely in this activity? But this question does little to prevent problems. Participants will be familiar with their own bodies, for sure, but if they have never experienced the activity or environment, how can they possibly know if or how they might be affected?

If a program chooses to ask about medical backgrounds, it should know what to do with the information once it is received. Program managers and trip leaders should have a good understanding of how certain activities and environments can and often do affect relatively common medical conditions, and they should have an action plan in place in the event that a crisis occurs. This information can then be shared with the potential customer, who can then make a better informed decision about whether or not to participate. Some conditions may be of such concern that a physician's advice will be needed. In those cases, the doctor(s) can ultimately decide if participation is recommended. But typically, the medical information does not prevent a student from engaging in an outing.

ADG did an exceptional job of preparing its clients for their trip up McKinley. It took great effort to help each participant make an educated choice about enrolling. The outfitter required a doctor's verification of health. And it followed up by checking on clients on a regular basis prior to the trip start, offering training tips, and recommending reading that might help them better understand the high-altitude environment.

GCC also took steps to solicit qualified customers. Due to the nature of the activities, the college believed that participants did not need to be exceptionally fit or experienced, and GCC thus marketed to novice teens who were of decent health. The school did not require that students have any type of swimming certification, but it did check to see that the boys were able to swim. Parents and kids were given an itinerary of activities, and a list of the risks associated with those activities was included in the program's literature.

GCC slipped up in its information exchange, however, when the itinerary changed without prior notice. As Reb Gregg points out in Chapter Six, the college had an obligation to honestly and accurately let the participants (and their families) know what to expect. Because Friday's itinerary was altered to include the river rescue instead of a hike, it could be argued that GCC unfairly changed the contract—and risks—without informing the families. Readers would be wise to consider how something like this might happen within their own programs.

It could be argued that GCC unfairly changed the contract without informing the families.

In the past several years, a number of outdoor-related incidents have been associated with what might be called *non-sanctioned* activities or after-hour events. That is, participants have been injured during evening hikes or games, or during activities that were not explicitly described in any brochure. Although it is probably unrealistic to eliminate all activities of this sort, it is possible to manage them rather than to simply let them happen. It also seems fair to inform participants and their families of changes in schedules, or to let them know if after-hour or unsupervised activities will be allowed. Steps like these won't necessarily prevent accidents from happening, but they can eliminate most surprises, like the one the Dzialos experienced.

7. Nutrition, hydration, and hygiene

Although this topic might seem quite basic, there are countless cases of experienced trip leaders who have forgotten key items (such as dinner bags!) or assumed too much when it came to their clients' understanding of food, drink, and bodily functions. In the event that an activity extends beyond a few hours, especially if the activity involves strenuous exercise or an unfamiliar environment, nutrition and hydration needs should be viewed in a whole new context. Caloric needs in the field might differ significantly from what a participant is used to at home. Some foods might spoil more quickly than expected while others might freeze. Drinkable water might be hard to come by. Ultimately, bathroom needs come into play. In all, the newness of the experience can have an effect on the person's well-being, as well as his or her ability to eat or drink on demand. The more the process can be streamlined and standardized, the less chance there is that an item—or teaching point—will be forgotten or overlooked.

With practice, even beginners can come to understand the direct correlation between how they are feeling and what they consume. In order to become more effective stewards of their own health, however, students need to be taught these concepts from the trip's outset. It also is essential that bodily functions are addressed early and openly. This is especially important given that embarrassed students might be apt to intentionally dehydrate or starve themselves in order to avoid having to "go" too often. In short, trip leaders should remember that students new to the outdoors often require constant supervision to ensure that they are practicing good self-care, regardless of their personal or professional status back home.

GCC and ADG both did well in addressing the nutrition and hydration needs of their clients. Each recognized the importance of making sure that their participants were well fed and watered, and checklists were used to make sure that nothing essential to the trip was left behind.

The ADG group, however, was faced with a particularly difficult situation. Due to the dry air high on the mountain, dehydration was of utmost concern, even prior to the storm. There is a direct correlation between frostbite and dehydration; thus, the need to push clients to drink becomes essential. Unfortunately, water bottles routinely freeze at those temperatures unless they are kept close to the body. As it was, all of the clients' water bottles froze on summit day, and most of the clients reported that they did not drink enough.

A lesson to be learned from the ADG case study, perhaps, is that even when the guides are competent and the consequences of dehydration are made clear in advance (as they were to the clients), problems can still occur. Further, just because trip leaders *tell* participants to eat or drink, they cannot assume that it will happen. When Chuck was admitted to the hospital, he was very dehydrated—a condition that almost certainly contributed to the severity of his injuries. Although it is possible that some of the climbers might have suffered frostbite regardless of their water intake, it also is telling that the guides—more diligent in making sure that they ate and drank throughout the ordeal—went frostbite free.

Further, trip leaders should keep in mind that, even though dehydration might not be the cause of an accident, if an emergency does occur, like it did on McKinley, people whose bodies are low on food and water will not be able to deal with the challenge as ably as their fed and watered counterparts.

8. Equipment

Selecting, acquiring, and maintaining camping, boating, and/or climbing equipment are huge tasks that require time, expertise, and considerable financial resources. When assessing what equipment is needed, a program might start by reviewing these four areas: personal, group, safety/rescue, and communication needs. There definitely is overlap in these categories, but each plays a unique role in accident prevention and crisis response.

Personal gear. Personal equipment includes items that each participant will be expected to supply for himself or herself. If a service provider is simply offering short day hikes or raft trips, the list might be as basic as a water bottle, appropriate footwear, sunglasses, and sunscreen. However, if the trip involves a climb of Mount McKinley, the list also will include items such as warm clothing, boots, hats, gloves, gaiters, goggles, ice axe, crampons, thermos, sleeping bag, and pad (among others). Regardless of the extent of the list, if an organization expects or requires the customer to supply some of the equipment, the list should be clear and available to everyone who walks through the door.

Group gear. Group gear includes items that will be supplied by the outfitter but that will be used and shared by all. Equipment in this category might include, but would not be limited to, tents, stoves, fuel, and repair kits. Items that are essential to the conduct of the activity, such as backpacks, bikes, or boats, also might be listed under this category. Group gear lists usually are not handed out to participants but, instead, might be posted in the service provider's office or warehouse. In the event that an outfitter has an educational mission, the participants might actually be given the list as a learning resource.

Safety and rescue equipment. Some outfitters might include safety and rescue items in with gear group (or even personal gear), but this equipment is important enough that it deserves its own category. Examples of safety and rescue equipment might include a first aid kit; bear spray; an extra paddle or a throw rope; and/or beacons, shovels, and probes. While an experienced trip leader might be able to improvise forgotten or damaged items in the personal or group lists, missing safety/rescue items would be difficult to improvise and could result in a serious emergency.

Communication devices. Communication devices, in a nutshell, can attract attention and/or send a message. Examples might include, but would not be limited to, satellite phones, cell phones, flares, smoke, mirrors, walkie-talkies, EPIRBs, and/or radios. Communication equipment could be listed under safety gear in that it has the potential to affect a group's well-being in an emergency. However, given today's technology, items within this category are not always used only in emergency situations.

Equipment questions came into play in both incidents.

Although equipment lists were not reviewed in detail in the ADG and GCC case studies, it appears that for both organizations, equipment choices had been discussed and had been well thought out long before their respective activities began. As it turned out, equipment questions came into play in both incidents.

During the GCC activity, for example, students were fitted for PFDs. Although there is some debate over the sizing of Adam's PFD, most water-sport professionals likely would agree that someone who falls between two sizes would be better off wearing a cinched down larger size (that has greater buoyancy) compared to one that is obviously too tight. The fact that GCC had sizing options actually speaks well of the organization. Further, although questions were raised about the appropriateness of Adam's footwear, the investigator found nothing wrong with the equipment selected and used that day.

ADG's equipment selection probably served to minimize the injuries to participants. Because the ADG guides carried a steel shovel and a snow saw to the summit, for instance, the group was able to build a shelter so that clients could hide from the brutal wind. (Readers might be interested to know that most groups on McKinley do *not* carry these items on summit day.)

A good program manager does not only make sure that proper equipment is taken into the field, but he or she should be up to date on changing technology. Whenever new equipment is purchased, the program should make sure that proper training takes place so that trip leaders are comfortable and adept at using it.

Further, programs should take steps to standardize equipment whenever possible. Consider the following as a case in point: A water bottle that closely resembles a white gas fuel canister has fairly recently been introduced in the United States market. Not surprisingly, the number of accidental poisonings has risen. Equipment-related problems also have occurred due to inappropriate use of climbing software, hardware, and beacons. In most of these cases, the mistakes were due to a lack of familiarity with the gear. Rather than tempt fate, one should try to minimize the probability for confusion and error. Programs should seriously consider using only one type of climbing harness or belay device, for instance, especially if beginners are involved.

Finally, a system should be in place for making sure that equipment is appropriately distributed, adequately maintained, and properly stored. Field breakdowns are common, and a well-stocked repair kit should be carried on every trip. At trip's end, gear in need of maintenance should be tagged and separated so that it does not inadvertently reappear in the field, and time should be allotted to perform the repair.

9. Transportation

In the summer of 2005, the National Highway and Transportation Safety Administration (NHTSA) released a study of rollovers involving 15-passenger vans. At that time, the agency reissued—for the third time in four years—a customer service warning about using the popular vehicles. Specifically, the 2005 study found that three out of four vans had at least one improperly inflated tire, which increased the chance of a rollover. The agency went on to note that between the years 1990 and 2002, more than 1,576 of these vans were involved in serious crashes. There were 1,111 deaths. Six hundred and fifty-seven of the fatal incidents were single-vehicle crashes, and 349 involved rollovers.

A major vehicle accident would have serious consequences for nearly any service provider, and organizations that use these vans likely should take note: A number of ramifications have occurred following the NHTSA studies and warnings, from changes in laws, to modifications in insurer requirements, to improvements in driver training programs. If nonprofessional drivers are used to transport a service provider's customers, extreme care should be taken to make sure that they are well trained and are prepared to handle an unexpected event (such as a breakdown, a flat tire, or an accident). Ideally, drivers should be at least 21 years of age and should have three to five years of experience driving the type of vehicle that they will be asked to use to transport students. Drivers should be mature individuals who are ready to take their responsibilities seriously.

Whenever possible, driving records should be obtained and examined, or at the very least drivers should be asked to attest to their driving history for the past several years. Standards should be established for disqualifying or eliminating people who have unacceptable records.

In the event that trailers or other specialty equipment is used, additional training and education should be provided, such as the basics of backing up, hitching, and/or loading.

A detailed manual should be available to all drivers. Preferably, a copy should be stored in each vehicle. It should include a pre-trip checklist and should cover driver responsibilities and expectations, and it should let people know what to do in the event of an accident.

If the organization is expected to transport large numbers of passengers on a regular basis, it might consider subcontracting through a reputable organization (such as a bus company). Not only does this practice (of using an outside vendor that specializes in transport) tend to minimize risk to passengers, but it also greatly reduces the risk to an organization.

Transportation policies and practices were not assessed for GCC or ADG, and transportation issues had no bearing on either of these case studies. However, it might be worth a quick look at how similar small programs often operate.

Around the country, many service providers continue to use the vans in question. Though many managers are aware of the concerns posed by these vehicles, the programs cannot afford to purchase new vehicles and do not have the time or money to implement formal training programs. In cases like these, mangers should at least take some basic and prudent steps to minimize their exposure to incidents and lawsuits.

For example, the NHTSA study (2005) noted that not only was tire inflation an issue, but it found that 74 percent of all 15-passenger vans had *significantly* misinflated tires. (By contrast, 39 percent of passenger vehicles were found to have the same problem.) The NHTSA research has shown that improperly inflated tires can change handling characteristics and increase the potential for a rollover. The NHTSA also found that nearly 80 percent of those killed in van accidents were not wearing seat belts. Prior NHTSA research (2005) has shown that van rollover risk increases dramatically as the number of occupants increases from fewer than five to more than 10. In fact, when the vans are loaded with more than 10 occupants, the rollover rate is nearly three times the rollover rate for vans that are loaded lightly (i.e., with fewer than five occupants).

To reduce the risks associated with the vans, the NHTSA recommends that drivers *insist* that all occupants wear seat belts at all times; tires are checked at least once a week, using the manufacturer's recommended pressure levels; and no loads are placed on the roofs of the vehicles.

Even if service providers cannot afford to implement or send their drivers through formal training programs, they should follow the above advice. They also should take steps to make sure that all drivers transporting students or other participants undergo some sort of schooling and annual review. Not only should the education include a hands-on component, but it also should include a written test to ensure comprehension.

Finally, in the event that a service provider transports customers via boat or plane, it should check with its insurance company to make sure that no clause exists that forbids this action. In two recent cases, outfitters found out that their insurance companies would not allow this type of transport. In one case, the organization found out before an accident happened. In the second case, however, the outfitter did not learn of the clause until after there had been an accident. In the latter case (which involved a fatality), the service provider spent endless hours arguing with its insurance representatives and those of the air taxi operator over who would pay expenses.

10. Program oversight and system of ongoing evaluation

Each organization should have a system in place so that there is continuous and successful implementation of all risk management planning steps identified above. Such a system typically includes the following: a "risk manager" who is in charge of safety as well as changes to the system; an objective body that is charged with system oversight (a risk management committee works well); feedback loops to encourage open and honest communication on all levels; reviews of all incident and close call reports; and occasional safety audits to ensure that the system is really working as intended. Each of these components is described in more detail below:

Risk manager. It is often worthwhile for an organization to designate one employee as a "risk manager" or safety officer. While this title often refers to an employee who is responsible for monitoring worker safety and health, in an outdoor program, it refers to the employee who is given the time, resources, and authority to develop and oversee the organization's risk management system.

As noted earlier in this chapter, this person should have expertise in overseeing system-wide risk management practices. Not only should he or she be familiar with all of the various field activities and associated hazards, but the risk manager also should be able to recognize and mitigate risk to the employees and organization.

Risk management committee. Safety committees commonly are used in programs in which risk is inherent. In essence, a risk management committee can help provide input into all aspects of a risk management plan.

This diverse group of professionals from within as well as outside of an organization can help identify issues of concern and provide creative solutions. It also can help track incidents, and it can investigate or facilitate an investigation in the event of a serious incident or fatality. The committee can be used to review feedback (from staff and students), provide suggestions for change, and help identify safety guidelines that might be needed if/when new activities are proposed. Although this group is not typically given authority to make changes, it can serve as an excellent resource for the organization's risk manager and can help strengthen the organization's plan for ongoing oversight.

Feedback loops. While good communication is important in any organization or business, it is especially important that employees are able to communicate openly and honestly with one another when the customers' safety is involved. A risk management system rarely will work to its fullest potential unless all employees embrace the system, embrace the safety culture, and work to see that all aspects of the system are being addressed.

Specifically, it is important for all employees to be honest if/when they lack knowledge or training in an area, and it is important for supervisors to help all employees meet their training needs. Key administrators should be familiar with the risks as well as the benefits of program activities.

Incident and close call reports. All incidents and close calls should be recorded, and this information should be freely shared at all levels of the organization. If/when instructors fear that they will be reprimanded for their field errors or close calls, an atmosphere of secrecy and distrust almost always results. Instead, trip leaders should feel free to share and learn from their own and others' mistakes. It is only when mistakes are extreme, disregarded, and/or repeated that discipline or termination is in order.

Program review and evaluation. Once program modifications are implemented, it is essential that steps are taken to verify that any and all changes actually have resulted in improvements. Site visits and/or safety audits, for example, can be used to help employees and managers gain a better understanding of a program's strengths and weaknesses. Although this type of review or audit can be conducted in-house, it often requires the aid of an external or objective party.

In this regard, risk management committee members and/or qualified local professionals can help. Although paid consultants can be very beneficial, an organization does not necessarily need to hire an outside expert to review its programming. Instead, with a little guidance, a variety of professionals can conduct an assessment of the organization's functions. By using prepared safety-audit checklists, for instance, field observers can provide feedback on student understanding of inherent risks, student readiness, and instructor field practices.

The GCC system of oversight was marginal. It relied mainly on the expertise of a part-time coordinator who was in charge of the adventure program. Although Adventures Unlimited received peripheral supervision and expertise from the college's academic outdoor department, the two units were administered separately. The adventure program did not use a risk management committee, nor were formal safety audits conducted. Following the accident, both investigator Walbridge (1998) and Ian Wade (1998), the second reviewer, recommended that the coordinator position be increased to full time.

ADG, too, did not use a formal system of oversight. However, ADG's two owners were involved in virtually all risk management decisions, and only a handful of staff—carefully selected—were employed. The owners happened to embrace high safety standards and had extensive knowledge and experience. They interacted with colleagues on an ongoing basis. They also were expected to follow certain risk management guidelines set up by the National Park Service, which included having a formal emergency action plan in place. ADG did not, however, have a risk management committee, and the program had never conducted an official safety audit.

When a program does not use a formal system to oversee operations, owners/operators can only assume that their decisions and operating procedures compare well with other similar programs. Unfortunately, small-business owners and managers are often exceedingly busy just trying to make ends meet. Unless they are able to somehow stay abreast of emerging issues, changing technology, and/or incident trends, they commonly are behind the times when it comes to the industry's risk management practices.

The ADG system worked, it seems, because two very experienced owners/managers valued customer safety above all else. While this is not to suggest that GCC was callous in any way, GCC seems to have been affected by the same challenge that hampers many outdoor programs. That is, the college did not have or did not put the necessary resources into program oversight and evaluation. Instead, a single employee was expected to fulfill the roles of many.

Adventures Unlimited was a quality program that had been in existence for years. It had considered and addressed many, if not most, of the risk management components identified in this chapter. ADG, too, was a quality program that had not experienced a serious incident for two decades. Yet serious accidents occurred within both organizations.

Had the Deerfield River incident not occurred, GCC's program almost certainly would have passed the "sniff test" in anyone's book. On paper, it would have stacked up well against other outfitters. Even where flaws existed, they were not huge or obvious.

In spite of Chuck's experience and injuries, ADG seems to have had few flaws in its risk management system. ADG was a hair's breadth from suffering seven fatalities on the mountain; however, the outfitter had created a system that gave the guides and clients alike the best chance possible to endure a crisis. As a result, the outfitter and its participants survived, even when things went terribly wrong.

Good programs suffer accidents, and sometimes bad programs get away with never harming anyone.

Good programs suffer accidents, and sometimes bad programs get away with never harming anyone. The quality of a program should not be based solely on its accident rate. On the contrary, all programs should be built and assessed based on the components of a risk management system, as presented here.

It is nearly always a combination of small things that lead to tragedy. Taken alone, each might seem harmless. It often seems inconsequential to bend the rules once—to allow a student to take along marginally adequate equipment, to enroll that one extra participant, or to rush while teaching a topic. But together, the little things can add up to disaster. It is only through diligent review of a risk management system that employees can identify if and where these "little" problems exist. And it is only through ongoing effort that the little problems can continually be addressed and corrected.

There likely will always be injuries and fatalities associated with outdoor activities, but serious incidents should never become an accepted part of our industry. When they do occur, we have an obligation to discuss them openly, to remain free of judgment, to learn from them, and to use them as teaching vehicles.

Epilogue: A special thanks goes to GCC and ADG for allowing me to examine their actions and systems. By thoroughly analyzing risk management systems, we can learn to identify where some of the not-always-obvious problems lie. It is through efforts like this that the industry as a whole might improve.

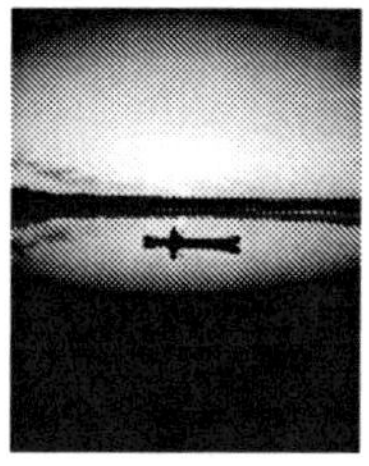

Creating a Workable Emergency Action Plan

By Deb Ajango © 2005

This chapter examines the key components of an emergency action plan (EAP), from the philosophical concepts that will be used to drive the plan to the detailed steps included in its implementation. By using a variety of case studies—starting with the University of Alaska Anchorage's response following a 1997 mountaineering accident—the author not only identifies measures unique to a quality EAP, but she also offers ideas on why seemingly well-crafted EAPs sometimes fail.

By 1996, I had already worked in the outdoor profession for a decade. Having spent nearly 2,000 days in the field, teaching and guiding others in a variety of environments and terrains, I decided it was time to take "the next step." So in the spring of 1997, I applied for, and was hired as, coordinator of the University of Alaska Anchorage's (UAA's) academic outdoor program. I knew that switching from trip leader to administrator would be a big change, but I thought I was ready for it. I had worked occasionally for the university in an adjunct capacity. I was familiar with the school. I figured what I didn't know up front, I could learn on the job.

My position officially started June 6, 1997. Not knowing that I would be offered the job, however, I had previously agreed to lead UAA's annual weeklong Eklutna Glacier Traverse that began three weeks later, on June 28. At around midnight on June 29, eight students, a co-instructor, and I were camped on the ice after a long day of travel. Everyone was fed, watered, safe, and looking forward to sleep. Just as we were about to retire for the night, the second instructor and I watched quizzically as a helicopter slowly made its way up the valley to hover above our camp. We were in a fairly remote area and, given the time of day, the sight seemed odd. We concluded that those on board must be searching for someone who was lost or injured.

It was only after the helicopter touched down and a passenger hopped out and headed straight for me that I knew the pilot was looking for us specifically. Without salutations the man said, "There's been an accident." My first thought was, "Which of my loved ones has been hurt or killed, my parents or my husband?" Then he added, "On Ptarmigan Peak." The information didn't register, and I thought there had been a mistake. "My husband wasn't on Ptarmigan Peak. Why was he telling me this?"

The man continued to add detail—two, maybe three people had died, many others were hurt—until it finally dawned on me that he was discussing a university mountaineering class, one from the program I now directed. Being so new to the coordinator position, it had slipped my mind that not only was I responsible for the welfare of the small group on the glacier, but I also was now entrusted with the well-being of an entire department worth of people, many of whom I had never met.

The situation seemed surreal. Within minutes I had packed my belongings and climbed into the helicopter, leaving the students and instructor alone on the ice. As we lifted off, I asked for more information, but the pilot and messenger had little to add—they didn't know the names of the victims, they didn't know how the accident had happened—so we rode to Anchorage in silence. Back at the office at 3:00 a.m., a small group of friends and colleagues filled me in on what facts were known. A group of beginning climbing students had fallen hundreds of feet down a steep, snow-filled gully. Two people had died; several others—as well as both instructors—were hurt. Over 100 people had helped with the rescue. The fall had been the lead story on all three local television stations that evening, and it was going to be the lead story in the next day's statewide newspaper. Some of the university's top people would be meeting in the morning to decide what to do next.

I took a shower, and with no sleep, I returned to the university for the 8:00 a.m. gathering. As the meeting began, I looked around the room in bewilderment at the 20 or so top administrators and their legal counsel, almost all of whom were strangers to me. They discussed their plan of action, with significant direction from the lawyers, never stopping to ask me a question or request my input. I felt as if I was looking into a fishbowl, watching the action from the outside, but not participating as a member of the team.

During the meeting, I had my own ideas about what should or shouldn't be done, but being the newcomer in the group, I felt hesitant to express them. Nevertheless, I had a "gut feeling" that we should not try to hide or minimize what had happened. Instead, I felt that we should be open and honest about the accident. We should reach out to the families, initiate an investigation, and discuss as well as learn from the tragedy.

The directive I received was clear: "You are not to talk about the accident. To anyone."

For the most part, however, the people in the room told me that my instincts were wrong. The directive I received was clear: "You are not to talk about the accident. To anyone. Do you understand?"

The meeting ended, and although things felt chaotic, I was confident that life would settle down in the near future. I knew that the university had a response plan on paper, and during those first 24 hours, it seemed as if the accident was handled with sensitivity and compassion. Administrators visited survivors and their families at the hospital, and a spokesperson stated, "Our first priority is the welfare of our students and staff." The community was told that answers were not immediately available but would be forthcoming. A "complete review" would be undertaken, the university promised, and people were asked to be patient until more was known (UAA 1997).

Unfortunately, the long-term goals were not as clear to UAA's decision-makers, and what was meant by a "complete review" was debated by everyone who had a stake in the outcome. Some of the employees and I, for instance, pushed hard for a review to take place as soon as possible. The outdoor program had its own EAP in place, and the department's instructors pointed out that the EAP clearly indicated that any serious incident would be investigated. Not only did we think a review would help answer the families' questions, but we did not see how the program could continue if we were not allowed to find out why things had gone so terribly wrong. A second group (made up of a mixture of lawyers and administrators) disagreed vehemently. Because it was beginning to look like mistakes had been made on the mountain, they believed that an investigation would only hurt, not help, the institution. In the interim, UAA released few details about the accident or about its plan.

As the months dragged on, the situation continued to deteriorate. I regularly received calls and visits from furious departmental instructors as well as community members. They demanded to know why things were taking so long. Why weren't the answers "forthcoming," as promised? At the same time, a group within the institution held firm that the "no comment" strategy was sound and defensible. They reasoned that most of the negativity was coming from a biased media anyway. This group was certain that everything would be okay in the long run.

While all of this was happening, the outdoor program fell into shambles. A moratorium had been placed on all climbing classes, and attendance in non-climbing classes plummeted. Employee morale reached an all-time low.

The institution's decision-makers were mired in indecision. Even from the outside, the leaders appeared unsure of themselves, and the community-at-large became suspicious of UAA's actions and intent. Public pressure grew for the university to change course, and in a widely circulated Anchorage Daily News editorial released in the fall, the university's Board of Regents was called on to rethink its priorities (1997b). The editorial asked, "Are the regents satisfied with the campus leaders' apparent emphasis on spin control and a general unwillingness among UAA officials to face the disaster's aftermath head-on? They shouldn't be."

The column continued, "Granted, it is the job of regents, the president, chancellors, and their minions to recognize the financial dangers posed by potential lawsuits. But when those costs are measured against getting to the bottom of a disaster and restoring public confidence, the university must err on the side of finding answers the public can trust."

Finally, after five months of turmoil, the university succumbed to the pressure and hired Jed Williamson to lead a review. Mr. Williamson had conducted 25 accident investigations and his credentials were unrivaled. Unfortunately, by then, there had been so much speculation and so many rumors that a number of theories existed about what had happened on the mountain that day. Nonetheless, when the review was completed, the employees of the outdoor program were not terribly surprised by the findings: Mistakes had been made (Williamson, Ratz, and Miller 1997).

The review team went over the report with the university's leaders and legal counsel in private. The findings stated that four roped teams were attempting to descend a steep snow gully when a member of the top team lost his footing. The improvised anchor system that his ropemates used to try to stop his fall failed, and his two stationary teammates were jerked from their stances. The team of three began to slide. Unable to self-arrest, they hit the four roped climbers below, who in turn fell and pulled out their anchor system. The seven climbers were now in an uncontrolled tumble. After sliding an additional 200 to 300 feet, the group hit two more rope teams, which were swept downslope by the impact. By the time the group came to a stop, the tangle of climbers, ropes, and gear had fallen nearly 1,000 feet.

The reviewers then went over their conclusions. They determined that the venue was too dangerous for the experience level of the students. The accident had occurred late on a Sunday afternoon, which meant that the class was probably in a hurry to get back to the trailhead. This, they believed, more than likely contributed to the instructors' decision to descend the slope using an untested system rather than take a longer, safer route down. Further, the trip leaders had misassessed the group's abilities and thus inappropriately allowed the students to rely on their own anchor systems and self-arrest skills.

UAA's administrators, it seemed, had not been expecting such a critical report, and they were unsure how to proceed. The attorney in the room advised the institution to accept the findings only as "one opinion," which would be considered along with others; however, she added, the report should not be accepted as "the final truth." Others disagreed with her, noting that the university had initiated the investigation and therefore was obligated to accept the findings. Besides, this group argued, how could they discard the report given the credentials of the investigators?

Finally, it was agreed that the university would accept the report's conclusions as stated. Investigator Williamson explained to the administrators that the next step would be to share the report with the families that night. The meeting would be behind closed doors, and after the attendees had had a chance to ask questions, Williamson and the rest of the review team would address the media.

The review team encouraged the university to send a representative to the gathering, but UAA's legal counsel recommended against it. She did not see how the institution would benefit by having someone in attendance, and she feared that whoever was present would be bombarded with difficult questions. The room grew quiet when there were no volunteers. Believing strongly that someone from the university should be there, I said I would go.

The meeting was held in a large banquet room at a downtown Anchorage hotel. The students, as well as their friends, families, and lawyers, sat around a dozen or so tables. I sat by myself. Everyone there had been given a copy of the report, and after Mr. Williamson made brief introductions, his team went over the findings carefully, letting the audience know what the investigators believed were the main contributing factors to the catastrophic fall (Williamson, Ratz, and Miller 1997).

I vaguely remember people asking a few follow-up questions when the reviewers finished. The attendees came across as polite and contained, and the review team members were very supportive and sensitive when responding. What I remember in detail was when the attendees turned their questions—and their outrage—to me. "Why couldn't you figure this out?" they asked. The weeks and months of pent-up anger seemed to pique. After being rebuffed time and again, the students and their loved ones finally got what they wanted—answers to their questions—and they were going to take the opportunity to let "the university" know how they felt about the delays. "Why did it take you so long to answer our questions?" they demanded to know. I was stunned and horrified: not only by the depth of their anger, but by my inability to answer their queries and because I had personally contributed to their pain. All I could do was tell them how truly sorry I was. I was sorry that the accident happened at all, and I

After being rebuffed time and again, the students and their loved ones finally got what they wanted—answers to their questions.

was sorry that we were not able to help them through such a difficult time.

Over the next 24 months, the outdoor department initiated a comprehensive examination, not just of its mountaineering courses, but of all aspects of its programming. At the same time, additional lawsuits and claims (a half dozen total) were filed. By the year 2000, all litigation had been settled and the program emerged, new and improved. Substantial changes had been made: Not only was the department re-named, but nearly all of its classes were redesigned. Policies and procedures were modified, and the program renewed and strengthened its commitment to safety. The moratorium against the climbing classes had been lifted, and students and instructors were back in the mountains around Anchorage. As a result of the process, the program had learned a great deal, not only about the accident itself, but also about how accidents generally tend to happen. It learned how to be better prepared in the event of a serious incident and what to do to move beyond such a tragedy.

Although the university's outdoor program was back on track, I was still recovering. It took years for me to be able to effectively evaluate my role in and response to the Ptarmigan Peak accident. Ultimately, by taking a close look at my own behaviors, and by talking with others who had experienced similar crises, not only was I able to identify mistakes I had made, but I was able to recognize how seriously I had been affected by all that had happened. The experience and pressure were intense and traumatic. I compounded the challenge by remaining silent. It was easily the most difficult time of my life.

Looking back, I have tried repeatedly to assess why things progressed from bad to worse over time. At first glance, UAA seemed prepared to handle a crisis: It had an EAP in place, representatives had arrived on the accident scene quickly, and professional spokespersons had answered reporters' questions. Yet over time, the plan seemed to fall apart as the institution's decision-makers faced one unanticipated challenge after another. In the end, we were judged harshly and critically, not only by the participants and their families, but by the student body and community as well.

So what was it about UAA's EAP that didn't work? And why is it that seemingly well-prepared organizations sometimes find themselves suffering the aftereffects of an incident for years on end?

All organizations are vulnerable to experiencing a crisis at some point, whether it is financial in nature or the result of a devastating accident. According to Rene A. Henry, risk management and public relations (PR) specialist, the most catastrophic "corporate" crisis occurs when someone dies after using a company's product (2000). For an outdoor service provider, or any organization that offers outdoor activities, that "product" is likely the activity or adventure itself. And while a serious incident or fatality can be difficult to overcome, if mismanaged, the experience can devastate an organization and all involved.

Most EAPs are formulated according to three basic goals: 1) Help the organization get back to its daily routine as soon as possible, 2) get the company's name out of the headlines, and 3) avoid litigation. But a quality EAP does not stop there. The health and welfare of all those connected to the incident are just as crucial to a company's survival. Because UAA's attorneys concentrated on the basics and refused to address the needs of the people, the university's EAP failed on several counts. In the end, employees spent countless hours dealing with post-incident tasks, UAA suffered a loss of credibility, the institution remained in the news for months, and it got sued anyway.

There are myriad considerations involved in creating a high-quality EAP, and effective crisis management is not a function of how well a group does on one part in isolation from the others. Instead, an organization's ability to handle all aspects of a crisis will determine whether or not the response is judged appropriate and effective. And in order for an organization to avoid the problems UAA faced, its decision-makers must first address some of the fundamental issues, or basic philosophies, that will ultimately drive the plan. Inevitably, when core values are not clear, a service provider may learn that it is not prepared to make the kinds of difficult choices that arise during difficult times.

FUNDAMENTAL CONCEPTS OF EMERGENCY ACTION PLANNING

Identifying Core Values. An increasing number of service providers have a basic EAP in place and feel confident that they are prepared to deal with a crisis. But the long-term strategy a company should embrace is not always obvious, nor are decisions typically unanimous among key employees. Is the goal to protect the organization from financial harm, or is care of the injured parties placed first, regardless of cost? Is the service provider willing to investigate the accident and share what it learns, or will it keep these secrets to itself? The answers to these questions are not black and white, and different voices will often give conflicting advice.

A link that is often missing or overlooked in the development of an EAP is the relationship between the organization's post-accident strategy and its core values. In fact, the mores of an organization and its managers will dictate its crisis-response policy. Whether a business wants to set and present a post-accident tone of open communication and compassion or one of tight-lipped toughness, its step-by-step approach will be a reflection of the company's (and its leaders') values. And although an agency's EAP tends to reflect a top-down approach, if employees at all levels are not in agreement with—or at the very least aware of—the philosophy behind the plan, there is a good chance things will not progress smoothly once it is put to the test.

Long before an accident occurs, an outfitter should consider how it will handle numerous worst-case scenarios, and various opinions (from program directors, attorneys, insurance carriers, and perhaps even the community or family members) should be sought out and considered. The decision-makers should weigh how contrasting actions will be viewed by different publics, and they should make sure their EAP fits well with the organization's mission and vision. A service provider that waits until after an accident to grapple with these issues should not be surprised to find dissension and infighting within the employee ranks, which will only intensify the situation.

Show You Care. One of the most critical steps in crisis response is to show you care. While this might sound basic, it is sometimes easier said than done. An organization that is perceived to lack compassion or to place legal considerations above ethical and human concerns can quickly earn the "villain" label, which will likely result in long-term damage to the organization's credibility and reputation.

> Following an outdoor accident, an outfitter should plan to provide a prompt, effective, and humane response.

Exxon's response to the 1989 *Exxon Valdez* oil spill provides a good example of how misassessing public reaction can lead to trouble. After the company's tanker spilled 11 million gallons of oil into Alaska's Prince William Sound, the company chairman responded by saying, "We're sorry. We're doing all we can" (Mitroff, Pearson, and Harrington 1996). Unfortunately, he also verbally minimized the damage caused by the spill and ridiculed people who declared the area devastated. The public was outraged. Despite the fact that Exxon ultimately spent more than *two billion* dollars on cleanup costs, many people considered the company's response callous and appalling.

Following an outdoor accident, an outfitter's priority should not be only to ascertain the number and extent of injuries, but it also should plan to provide a prompt, effective, and humane response—something more than a simple statement of sympathy or remorse. Consider the differences between Greenfield Community College's (GCC's) and Alaska Denali Guiding's (ADG's) actions described in Chapters One and Two. Although GCC offered condolences to the Dzialos, the family felt that the college's response lacked compassion. This fact soured all future interactions between the two parties. ADG, on the other hand, made it clear that Chuck was not simply a statistic or potential lawsuit. Once the storm on Mount McKinley abated, the owners and guides met Chuck at the hospital and visited him daily. ADG employees offered to help however they could, and their intentions and actions came across as sincere. Consequently, Chuck and his wife believed that the company truly cared about his well-being, and the couple maintained a positive relationship with the organization over the next several years.

According to PR specialist Henry, "In a crisis, perception is stronger than reality, and emotion stronger than fact" (2000). He adds, "As much as 50 percent of an institution's or organization's credibility can be lost by displaying a lack of caring." In Exxon's case, the public perception—that Exxon was not doing enough, and that it did not care enough—damaged the company's reputation for years. And although GCC representatives, in fact, might have cared deeply about Adam's condition and the Dzialos' circumstance, their response did not effectively convey that message.

There is nothing illegal about expressing compassion and sympathy to survivors and their families when people are injured or killed in an accident. Compassion does not imply that the organization will be a pushover or will accept responsibility for everything; rather, it shows that a service provider's concern for students, clients, families, and employees is valued over profits and reputations.

Accident Response When Someone Is to Blame. The advice to show compassion is easiest to follow when an incident is seen as "an act of God" or it is clear that a service provider was not at fault. Sometimes, however, an organization—or an employee of that organization—makes a mistake that results in an injury or fatality. When this happens, the company will be faced with a difficult dilemma. How can the program appear to care when its own actions contributed to the accident? And how can an outfitter apologize in the face of possible litigation?

The temptation in such a case can be to offer "no comment" and hope that the early criticism will diminish over time. Not surprisingly, this response often invokes anger and animosity. And though some businesses are willing to tough out negative media attention, the long-term consequence of inaction and silence can be prolonged problems with an organization's public relations, credibility, and employee morale.

Going back to the UAA case study, the institution, by all accounts, was faced with a truly difficult situation: A tragic accident occurred, two students died, and it appeared that mistakes had been made. The organization had to weigh all sides and decide on a "right" plan of action—that is, it wanted to balance the fiduciary responsibility of the institution with the needs (compassion, medical care, and a desire for answers) of the affected parties. It was not clear if choosing one route prohibited or diminished meeting the needs of the others. The university finally decided to conduct an external investigation, but only after five months of unanswered questions had passed. The prolonged struggle to find the right path did not go unnoticed.

Six months after the accident the university was still in the news. Many of the students, family members, and people in the community were unhappy with UAA's response, and a number of observers believed the institution had refused to accept responsibility for its actions.

"The university's behavior since the accident has been deplorable," one editorialist wrote in an Anchorage newspaper half a year after the fact (1997c). Around the same time, a second writer commented, "Accident prevention isn't about covering up mistakes; it's about understanding them so they don't get repeated. More than that though, common, human decency dictates that you deal honestly with people in a situation like this" (1997a).

If these opinions were any indication of the public's view at large, the local community seemed to allow that mistakes had been made during the outing. Accidents happen in mountaineering and the outdoors, they acknowledged. But people were not nearly as forgiving when it came to judging the university's long-term response.

Understand Why People Get Angry. An organization can take a number of missteps after an accident that can make an already difficult situation worse. Withholding information, for instance, tends to fuel distrust, which will almost certainly escalate the challenges. Coming across as callous, as noted above, can also lead to problems. In order to avoid this dilemma, it may be helpful to try to understand why people become angry after someone gets hurt.

> The reasons injured people sue are varied and often have little to do with money.

According to a Porter/Novelli public opinion poll, people get angry 75 percent of the time when an organization refuses to accept responsibility for its role in an accident, 72 percent of the time when they believe a crisis could have been prevented, 71 percent of the time when they perceive incomplete or inaccurate information has been provided by the organization, and 70 percent of the time when a business seems to place profit/money ahead of public interest (Henry 2000). Further, many people believe an organization has a responsibility to help the injured, to figure out what went wrong, and to make sure a similar crisis does not happen again.

Although cynics might believe that injured parties seek retribution out of spite or greed, statistics seem to suggest that the reasons injured people sue are varied and often have little to do with money. Information from the Vanderbilt Medical Center's Web site, for instance, suggests that many families file suits to obtain information (2005). One in five plaintiffs, in fact, indicated that they filed only after deciding there was no other way to find out "what really happened." Other families decided to file claims or suits based on the belief that their doctors had not listened to them, had not answered their questions, or had failed to warn them adequately about the risks. Finally, some families sued to protect other patients from someone they judged to be incompetent.

In other words, whether or not an injury or fatality leads to litigation might well depend on how the survivors are treated (or believe they have been treated) following an incident, and the long-term effects of the accident can and often will be influenced by an organization's response. And while not all events will be within an organization's control, it is unrealistic to expect a best-case outcome if an outfitter has not clarified where its priorities and philosophies lie.

Public Relations versus Legal Advice. It is common for both lawyers and PR representatives to provide post-accident input, and each position serves a useful role. PR experts generally will focus on maintaining or enhancing the image, credibility, and trustworthiness of the service provider. Attorneys are there to provide advice regarding the legal ramifications of potential decisions and actions; their priority is to protect the company's legal position.

A problem can arise if either of these professionals attempts to become involved in the other's discipline. Lawyers should not take the lead in public relations or crisis communication just as PR representatives should not practice law—rarely is one person thoroughly educated in both specialty areas. This lack of cross-training can be especially problematic if a lawyer wants to stonewall the media and minimize the release of information while, at the same time, a PR person is recommending full and immediate disclosure of known facts. Both opinions are valid, and ultimately an organization's leaders will need to decide: Is it better to risk potential financial damages in the court of law or long-term reputation and credibility damages in the court of public opinion?

As attorney Reb Gregg notes in Chapter Six, when dealing with the various parties, it is often best to work in an atmosphere of cooperation and openness. In fact, he believes post-event mismanagement—including refusal to share information with clients or families—can potentially enlarge a plaintiff's demands. Gregg, who has defended a number of cases involving outdoor accidents (including fatalities), adds, "The greatest need of the injured party (and family) is to understand what happened and why; that is, to attempt to make sense of the loss. Deprived of satisfaction in that regard, the plaintiff will often seek not just compensation, but vengeance."

The hope is not simply for an organization to protect its assets and come out looking good, but for it to find a win-win situation for all involved. By meeting the needs of the injured, their families, the community, and its employees, the organization might not only help people heal, but it also might be able to minimize legal expenses in the long run.

Be Willing to Change Course. It is not uncommon for an organization to find that—despite its best efforts—people are critical of its response following an accident. Every manager recognizes that he or she will not be able to please everyone. However, if the swell of opinion suggests that the service provider is starting to be seen as a villain, the company should reevaluate its strategy.

Let's return one last time to the UAA case study. The university's on-site response was appropriate and seemed sincere. But after the initial crisis stabilized, the survivors and public grew angry when they believed the organization's leaders were stonewalling.

The university was forced to rethink its strategy. Regardless of UAA's intent, the ongoing backlash was unexpected, so the institution took steps to change its course of action, counter the criticism, and learn from its mistakes. Not only did it finally initiate a review, but it reached out to the injured students and their loved ones, it sought public input on its revised risk management plan, and it asked for help from some of its worst critics. The organization thus acknowledged its mistakes and presented them publicly so that others could learn from them as well.

The university was forced to rethink its strategy.

Although the change in course was not easy, the long-term effect—in enhanced reputation and image, as well as toward overall healing—was significant. Outdoor professionals from around the country supported the university's willingness to share its learning, the media began reporting on the improvements that had been made within UAA's outdoor program, and, perhaps most importantly, the victims voiced relief and appreciation for the efforts.

EMERGENCY ACTION PLANNING SPECIFICS

Once an organization has clearly identified its core values and has dealt with key philosophical questions, it is ready to address specific steps of its EAP. The remainder of this chapter outlines the following sequence in detail: 1) managing the incident, 2) crisis communication, and 3) long-term considerations.

1. MANAGING THE INCIDENT

The initial goals in crisis response are to extract participants from a dangerous setting, provide care or assistance as needed, and minimize the chance that the event or injury could become an out-of-control situation. Specifically, the following steps are important to ensure that an incident is contained as quickly and effectively as possible:

- Provide immediate aid to the threatened or injured party.
- Clarify leadership roles.
- Identify means for initiating a rescue.
- Address miscellaneous responsibilities.

Provide Immediate Aid to the Threatened or Injured Party. As noted in Chapter Three, instructors should be trained and ready to deal with foreseeable emergencies, such as helping a student who has fallen into water, rescuing someone who has been buried in an avalanche, or assisting a climber who has become stuck on rappel.

Further, given that trip leaders have some duty to provide care to an injured participant, they should be trained in first aid. Specifically, trip leaders should have some sort of wilderness medicine education so that they are able to assess and manage *injuries* (such as cuts, sprains, and breaks) and *medical emergencies* (such as asthma and anaphylaxis). This does not mean that trip leaders need to be paramedics; however, they should be able to manage most non-life-threatening situations and they should be able to tell when someone needs a higher level of professional medical care.

In the event that trip leaders have emergency equipment on scene (such as beacons, throw ropes, or first aid kits), steps should be taken to ensure that the equipment is in good working order and that instructors/guides can use it correctly. For example, if a group takes an oxygen tank to a pool or a lake, everyone should be confident that the tank is full, is functional, and that the trip leaders know how to use it. Further, organizations should create systems whereby first aid kits are fully stocked when they are taken into the field, and all trip leaders should be familiar with the kits' contents.

Clarify Leadership Roles. Although leadership roles are often obvious during emergencies, this is not always the case. In fact, given the increase in the use of subcontractors by service providers (e.g., hiring an "expert" to lead a specific technical activity, to transport groups, or to share teaching responsibilities), it is not surprising that confusion, at times, reigns following an accident. Questions of leadership will likely arise, for instance, if an employee of an organization is given the role of chaperone while the subcontractor is considered *in charge.* Would the employee be expected to take control in an emergency, or would the subcontractor maintain that position?

Another difficult scenario is one in which a trip leader, trained in first aid, has the option of handing over the care of an injured participant to a good Samaritan (i.e., another client or a bystander) who has a higher level of training, even though the person is not a paid employee of the organization, and even though the person's training has little to do with the specific injury. This latter situation arose, in fact, on Mount McKinley during the storm described in Chapter Two. A physician from a nearby team offered help to Chuck's group once they returned to their tents at 17,200 feet. Unfortunately, the doctor rubbed a frostbitten part to warm it—which is contrary to protocol—and his actions likely exacerbated the damage.

Regardless of the details, and prior to any emergency, if and when more than one potential *chief* exists, credentials should be checked and roles should be clarified. Program managers should talk with subcontractors, if applicable. Ultimately, realistic "what if" scenarios should be considered, and roles should be agreed upon before the trip starts.

Identify Means for Initiating a Rescue. In some instances, a trip leader might need (and be able) to initiate a rapid response by using Emergency Medical Services (EMS). To assist the process, trip leaders should have quick and easy access to a working communication device. In the event that an outing takes place in a semi-urban environment, the outfitter should know when its groups are (and are not) within cell phone range. Program employees should also contact 911 prior to an accident—from all field sites—to find out if the cell calls reach the most appropriate dispatchers.

If and when a group travels outside of cell phone range, the service provider should have a system in place so that the trip leaders can somehow initiate a rescue when necessary. This might be via a satellite phone, a locator beacon, a radio, or some other means. No matter which method is adopted, the service provider should make sure that trip leaders are very familiar with the communication devices and have had practice using them. Further, if a group expects to travel to a particularly remote area, participants should be warned that rapid transport will be impossible, and this acknowledgment should likely be included in the *participant agreement* (see Chapter Six for more about this).

Once assistance is deemed necessary, the trip leaders should be able to pass along the group's exact location to an emergency dispatcher. If a beacon is used, this happens automatically. If a phone or radio is used, trip leaders should make sure to have accurate information, such as GPS coordinates, in order to expedite the rescue effort. Further, trip leaders should know which details are critical to convey so that if communication is difficult, extraneous information is kept to a minimum.

Address Miscellaneous Responsibilities. Following an emergency, some decisions are fairly straightforward. In other instances, knowing what to do is not really apparent. For example, what should a leader of a semi-urban trip do if a participant is injured—though not seriously—and refuses EMS care or transport? If the organization has no protocol or provides no guidelines, the instructor/guide might decide to continue with the outing, he or she might decide to transport the student/client to the emergency room directly, or the leader(s) might have the group return to its base or office. While any of these options could seem reasonable, it is worthwhile for an outfitter to review a variety of "what if" scenarios and help clarify if/when certain actions are expected or are not allowed.

Similarly, program managers should consider providing concrete guidelines in the event that a participant is fatally injured during an outing (or during transport). Given that many states have specific legal requirements following a death, an outfitter should research whether or not certain actions are required or forbidden. Further, if an organization wants or expects its trip leaders to collect and secure all relevant equipment (which some insurance companies request), it should educate its employees on the process.

Service providers should make sure that employees are not expected to be super-human throughout an ordeal.

Trip leaders should know how to manage *un*injured group members following a serious incident, and program managers would be wise to make sure that employees know how to de-escalate any growing chaos.

Finally, service providers should make sure that employees are not expected—or allowed—to be super-human throughout an ordeal. As a case in point, imagine Blaine Smith's—the lead guide in Chuck's Story—experience on Mount McKinley. After surviving the initial storm and reaching the "safety" of their camp, all members of the ADG team, including Blaine, were exhausted, hungry, dehydrated, and somewhat hypothermic. Yet Blaine continued to play the role of leader. After contacting the National Park Service (NPS) by radio to update rangers on the team's status, the guide was told to put on his snowshoes and stomp out a large area nearby so that a helicopter could land. Blaine spent more than an hour stumbling in the deep snow—"punch drunk" with fatigue as he describes it—making little to no progress on the task. When he radioed NPS again later with an update, he was told to try it again. After several attempts, Blaine was more exhausted than ever, the landing site was never completed, and due to the ceaseless high winds, the helicopter was not able to arrive until the following day. When asked recently why he didn't simply reject the rangers' orders, Blaine admitted that it never occurred to him. As the trip leader, he did what he thought he was supposed to do.

Blaine's account is not unusual. Several of the trip leaders and program managers interviewed for this book noted that they were "open to suggestions," "shell-shocked," and/or "emotionally fragile" immediately following their crises. This is not to say they had any type of a breakdown. But after experiencing a critical incident, it is not uncommon to have difficulty thinking clearly or making sound decisions.

A few of the trip leaders interviewed for this book reported feeling a lack of control over what was happening around them. In cases like those, it would be important for a service provider to include the leaders in at least some of the post-incident decision-making. The instructors might be allowed to remain with a group, for example, and continue to serve as the team leaders in some capacity. But someone should take care to see that these employees are given support, and are eating, drinking, and sleeping as necessary.

Liz Tuohy, a trip leader whose story is shared in Chapter Five, provides what some might consider an optimal solution to this potential dilemma. She says that after experiencing a serious incident when she was the trip leader, her company flew two high-level employees to the remote site. Liz was given the option of remaining in charge as the team made its way out of the field. The two new employees were there to provide support as well as to step in if/when needed.

Although it might not be feasible for a company to send an employee to assist with a rescue, all organizations should consider what it might be like for the leaders in the field. Not only is it important to care for the injured and uninjured parties, but it is also critical to make sure that employees are given the guidance and support they need.

2. CRISIS COMMUNICATION

Crisis communication starts when trip leaders first notify the office or home base of an emergency and ends only after the injured parties are secure, team members are out of the field, and next-of-kin as well as constituents have been advised of the situation. To make sure that none of these steps is overlooked, a service provider should have a plan for all of the following:

- Communicate from the field to the office.
- Notify the next-of-kin.
- Notify key constituents.
- Notify the media.
- Clarify the subcontractor's role.
- Provide information to uninjured employees and participants.
- Keep records.

Communicate from the Field to the Office. Once the accident scene is under control and appropriate care has been provided, a trip leader should immediately notify a supervisor and/or his or her office of the situation. While this step seems obvious, it is not always easy. At some organizations, such as universities, outings tend to occur over a weekend or even overseas. On those occasions, immediate communication with key personnel is difficult at best.

Further, it is not uncommon for only partial messages to be relayed from the field to administrators. For example, in one case study, a team called in to its base to say that an accident had occurred high on a mountain, but details were sketchy. Though they intended to call back with additional information, the satellite phone battery was low, and a follow-up call was never made. Consequently, office personnel were forced to guess what to do next.

In another case, an instructor decided to stay with an injured client while two fit runners (participants) were sent for help. Although the incident was not a life-threatening emergency, the team was hoping to arrange an assisted evacuation. When the runners reached a phone, they were not able to get hold of anyone from the organization (they left a message). Feeling the need to talk to a real person, they then called 911 as well as a local volunteer rescue group. Within an hour, and much to the instructor's (and program manager's) surprise, three separate rescues had been initiated.

> Much to the instructor's surprise, three separate rescues had been initiated.

In order to avoid these types of situations, outfitters should clarify exactly *whom* employees are supposed to call (and in what order) when attempting to initiate a rescue. If the trip leaders contact the office via a cell or satellite phone, they should make sure that the connection is clear and that the transfer of information is complete and accurate. Asking the person on the receiving end of the line to repeat key pieces of the conversation, for example, is a good practice.

The main consideration is that critical information is error free and relayed efficiently. The person who receives the call should make sure to write down all key points so that facts are not changed or forgotten as information is passed along the chain of communication.

Notify the Next-of-Kin. Long before a serious incident occurs, an organization should have procedures established for contacting a victim's loved one(s) in the event of an emergency. Consequently, emergency contact information, for trip leaders as well as participants, should be accurate, up-to-date, and easily accessible.

In the event that a potential emergency is still unfolding, some outfitters choose to wait to make a call, but these organizations should heed this warning: Families rarely like hearing of an accident via the media, or via law enforcement or hospital representatives. Recall the Dzialo case study. Even though GCC attempted to contact the family as soon as possible after Adam had been injured, the parents first heard of their son's accident from a medical center employee. The caller was not able to provide any details about Adam's condition or about the situation that led up to the accident. Ultimately, Adam's father reported being haunted by the messenger's words, "Don't come alone," during the drive to the hospital.

As an alternative, consider the approach ADG took. Although the guiding service initially did not know the extent of Chuck's injuries and although information was still incomplete, ADG's manager called Chuck's wife, Rachel, to let her know what was happening. The decision to call paid off. Not only was Rachel thankful for the call, but she admits she would have felt terrible, perhaps even angry, had she *not* been notified of the situation as it was developing.

When dealing with a fatality, an organization should use a liaison or trained spokesperson to contact family members, if at all possible. If a spokesperson is not available, the outfitter should make sure that whoever makes the call has clear guidelines to follow. Typically a person in an executive or high-level position is considered most appropriate to deliver the news. If lower-level employees know the deceased and/or their loved ones, however, it might be better for them to make the initial contact.

Once a family member is reached, information should be presented carefully, and statements should be clear and factual. The caller (or visitor) should be direct, avoid "beating around the bush," and yet use tact. To achieve this, the messenger might want to practice by role-playing with coworkers and colleagues and rehearsing what he or she would like to say. It is important to come across as sincere, and rehearsing a statement can help with one's presentation.

Once the news has been delivered, the messenger should offer whatever assistance is available (or has been deemed appropriate). He or she should let the family members know that they can expect updates, and steps should be taken to ensure that follow-up calls are made. The organization should also find out if the family member has access to a support network, and if possible, the messenger should encourage the loved one to contact a friend.

Notify Key Constituents. A key to successful crisis communication lies in an organization's ability to pass information along to key constituents in a timely manner. To be successful in achieving this goal, an outfitter must first identify all parties that would fall in the "need to know" category.

A trip leader's immediate supervisor, for example, will most likely be involved in post-incident actions and/or decisions. An organization might also want to establish contact with an attorney and/or an insurance representative. While a lawyer can be used to explain the legal ramifications of various decisions, an insurance representative can often let decision-makers know what benefits are available to an injured participant and/or his family. An insurance representative also might let the service provider know what post-incident actions are required or forbidden.

Some programs will want to include additional constituents in their chains of communication as well. For instance, multitiered organizations might require that representatives from their regional or national headquarters receive a call.

Further, many large organizations have access to professional media spokespersons. This person (or persons) should be notified of the event quickly, and he or she should be brought up to date on all applicable details. (Additional media guidelines are provided in the next section.)

What is most important is that a service provider decides early who falls in the "need to know" category. Names and contact phone numbers for all parties should be documented and updated regularly, and this information should be easily accessible. Once the need-to-know list is completed, the service provider should designate who, specifically, is responsible for contacting each of the constituents following an event.

What is most important is that a service provider decides early who falls in the "need to know" category.

Notify the Media. In the aftermath of a tragic accident, an EAP will be put to its ultimate test, and even the best-laid plan cannot guarantee affable interactions with the media. The UAA case study provides a good example of how strained relationships with the media can make an already difficult situation even worse. Following Adam Dzialo's near-drown accident, GCC experienced a similar challenge. Not only were local reporters critical of the college's post-incident actions, but a disparaging Web site was created to call attention to the school's long-term response.

While one might assume that negative news coverage is typical, consider what happened following a National Outdoor Leadership School (NOLS) fatality two years after the UAA incident. In 1999, the Alaska branch of NOLS found itself facing the same Anchorage-based media personnel on the Matanuska Glacier. A student was missing and presumed dead, and reporters went looking for answers. NOLS's reaction to their questions was very different from UAA's two years earlier. The NOLS spokesperson appeared knowledgeable and prepared, and set an immediate tone of cooperation with the media representatives.

While film and rescue crews gathered at the scene, the NOLS director fielded questions from several reporters. The media quickly learned that 11 students, descending the glacier following a climb of Mount Marcus Baker, had been several miles ahead of their instructors. One night at camp, the victim went off on his own to collect water, apparently slipped into a moulin (a hole in the glacier), and vanished.

Many of the reporters' questions and concerns were similar to those surrounding the UAA incident: Had the organization been through a similar accident in the past? Who was the student? What was his personal level of climbing experience? Inevitably, the interviewers wanted to know why the students were not supervised. Why was a 17-year-old allowed to travel on the glacier unroped?

The NOLS spokesperson was able to appease the media by answering many of the questions that the UAA spokesperson could not. He was able to provide background information about the program's mission and accident history in general, and the mountaineering course specifically. He explained that the students were in a "safe" area the night the tragedy occurred and therefore did not need to be roped. He also was able to defend the practice of allowing students to guide themselves out of an expedition by saying, "It allows the students to really test their leadership skills."

The media was told that an investigation would be conducted in order to learn more about the accident, and the spokesperson reported that additional information would be provided as it became available. An external review followed, and the findings—released to local news sources—recommended very little change to the program. Local and East Coast media seemed satisfied, and the reporters went away.

The key learning points are that a media plan should be in place, up to date, and readily available *before* an accident occurs. The plan should be clear and concise, and all employees should be familiar with it. A trained spokesperson should be available, if at all possible, and the person should be a compassionate and excellent communicator. Reporters covering an accident will want answers to the Journalists' Five W's: *Who* was hurt and *who* was in charge? *What* exactly happened? *When* did it happen? *Where* did it happen? And *why* did it happen? The media plan should instruct the spokesperson to anticipate this type of questioning and to be forthright and accurate about the descriptive facts, subject only to legal constraint.

In recognition of that restraint, the plan should clearly outline legal and institutional restrictions that might govern the release of information. For example, in most, if not all, states, it is illegal to disclose an injured person's medical records without consent. Release of information at public institutions also may be governed by state laws. Statements should avoid finding fault; assessing blame; or criticizing the conduct, policies, or equipment of any party until the incident has been fully investigated. And in order to avoid these types of mistakes, the spokesperson should consult with an attorney, if possible, prior to speaking to the media.

To support this process, a service provider might create a "working paper" that can help answer reporters' general questions. The working paper might include, but would not be limited to, information on the program's background, its safety policies, and its accident history. In the event that a program subcontracts out certain services, it also might include information on the relationship between the program and the subcontractor. Within larger organizations, the PR representative might not be intimately familiar with the outdoor program, especially if the company offers a variety of services. A working paper can be particularly helpful in these instances.

Finally, a spokesperson should remember to maintain an open mind and a good attitude when dealing with the media. This is especially important if an employee other than a professionally trained PR representative is used as the spokesperson. The media should not be considered the enemy: Reporters simply want to get a story. And a spokesperson's disposition or attitude could ultimately influence the treatment received.

Clarify the Subcontractor's Role. As part of its crisis communication plan, a service provider should clarify what role (if any) a subcontractor might have in the EAP following an incident. For example, if a participant is seriously injured while under the supervision of a subcontractor, will the subcontractor contact the participant's family, or will the service provider? Details about ongoing communication and long-term considerations (still to come) should be discussed as well. Finally, the provider and subcontractor might wish to compare media response strategies, simply to make sure their plans are compatible.

> Will the subcontractor contact the participant's family, or will the service provider?

A key purpose for engaging in this type of discussion is to confront assumptions and clarify roles. The goal is to help minimize confusion and eliminate inaccurate expectations at a time when quick, well-planned action is important.

Provide Information to Uninjured Employees and Participants. Serious incidents take a toll on everyone, including people who were not physically injured. And any employee or co-participant who knows the victim or who has been associated with the program likely will want updates or details following an accident. Consequently, as part of its crisis communication plan, an outfitter should consider which facts it will pass along and what information will remain confidential.

Although a service provider might choose to keep some information from its workers, it rarely is acceptable to keep all information private. Every staff member will want to know if or how events will affect him or her. As already noted, total silence or "no comment" type answers tend to create distrust and anxiety, even within the employee ranks. Education, on the other hand, often reduces stress, and if workers are given at least some information, especially in regard to how an incident might affect their day-to-day lives, office routines are likely to return to normal more quickly.

An organization should also consider providing information to uninjured students/clients, including those in the field as well as those who will be taking part in an upcoming trip. Potential customers likely will have heard about a serious incident or fatality, and service providers can minimize rumors by providing accurate details and being as open and honest as possible.

Finally, an organization should consider *how* it will provide information to employees and participants. It might choose to present the information in person, for instance, or in writing, via a newsletter, or even over the Internet. Regardless of the method used, the information should be factual and speculation should be avoided.

Keep Records. A final step in crisis communication is keeping track of what has been said and done. An organization should have a system in place for documenting information that comes into, as well as goes out of, the office. A supervisor or site manager should be able to see, in writing, exactly which constituents have or have not been contacted following an incident. Further, a record keeper should keep track of all incoming phone calls and requests from the media, and he or she should keep a copy of all news articles, film clips, press releases, and public memorandums about the incident. If an accident receives significant media attention, a service provider might consider fielding questions and/or providing up-to-date information via an 800-line or a Web site.

Finally, the record keeper might be expected to maintain any and all evidence associated with an incident, especially if there is a chance of future litigation. In the event that a participant or employee is seriously or fatally injured, an outfitter might consider taking the following steps:

- ✓ Compile and preserve all relevant paperwork, consents, and medical history documents that were disseminated to or signed by the participant.
- ✓ Locate and preserve records of the purchase, maintenance, and condition of relevant equipment that was being used at the time of the incident.
- ✓ Compile and document information on the training regimen that was used to educate participants and/or employees.
- ✓ Compile and document information on the instructor's or guide's background and credentials.

3. LONG-TERM CONSIDERATIONS

A number of EAPs are written to help an organization through the first few days of an accident's aftermath. A quality EAP, however, does not stop there. Instead, it also addresses myriad long-term decisions that will need to be made.

After the EAP is finalized, the organization should take steps to make sure its employees are familiar with the plan. If possible, the EAP should be tested periodically. And, each time the plan is used, the site should evaluate its overall effectiveness.

Specifically, before an EAP is considered "complete," an organization should contemplate how it will address each of the following areas:

- Provide ongoing and long-term support to the injured party and family members.

- Provide ongoing support to uninjured employees and participants.
- Conduct an investigation.
- Educate key personnel and test the EAP.
- Evaluate the EAP.

Provide Ongoing and Long-Term Support to the Injured Party and Family Members. In 2004, a northern service provider suffered multiple casualties during a scheduled outing. One client was killed and a second was seriously injured in a freak accident; a traveling rope team was struck by a landslide that had originated 1,000 feet above it. The guides and outfitter appeared to have done little wrong. And though the program managers could have said, "We're really sorry, but it wasn't our fault," they instead provided ongoing support to all who were affected.

They could have said, "We're really sorry, but it wasn't our fault." Instead they provided ongoing support to all who were affected.

To start, the outfitter sent its director to the hospital to visit the injured client. She stayed with him for days and served as his advocate. The provider also offered a Critical Incident Stress Debriefing (CISD) for the guides and office staff. It held a memorial. And it invited the deceased person's widow to come to its office and stay for several days. During her visit, the managers offered to have her flown over the site of the accident. "By offering her the choice," the director says in explaining the company's logic, "we felt like we were giving her some sense of control. She didn't have to say yes. But we decided that if she did, we would do whatever we could to facilitate the process." The outfitter's actions seemed to help. The widow took the flight. She also expressed appreciation for the program's ongoing support. And, according to the management team, the guides developed a tighter bond as a result of the experience.

So that a service provider does not need to make difficult choices during difficult times, it should address these types of issues in its EAP. Following a death, for example, a service provider might coordinate a memorial, help pay for a funeral, and/or send a condolence letter and flowers. While there is a chance that the family will reject the gestures, they are rarely seen as harmful.

Because workers' compensation can be used to help cover an employee's medical expenses, medical decisions regarding employees are often straightforward. But if the victim is a student, volunteer, intern, or contracted worker, the decisions can be gray. While an outfitter could simply point to the paperwork when a nonemployee is hurt (i.e., the part that says "you are on your own"), the strategy is sometimes easier said than done, especially if there is a chance that the organization could be considered liable. Decision-makers should keep in mind that a significant number of claims and suits are filed only after it becomes clear that patients cannot afford their mounting hospital bills. At the very least, a service provider might consider requiring nonemployees to carry their own insurance in order to avoid this type of predicament.

Not surprisingly, family members often will want to be with their injured loved ones following an accident. Consequently, an organization should consider whether or not it will help pay for travel and/or accommodations. An outfitter might also offer to make arrangements so that a family member can see the site where the accident occurred.

Regardless of which actions an organization decides to take, it should be careful not to make promises it cannot keep. An applicable case study can be used to reinforce this point. Following an accident in which several participants were injured, a service provider suggested to the injured and their family members that they (i.e., the provider's insurance company) would take care of hospital charges. Months later, the bills remained unpaid and the relationship between the parties deteriorated. Although the outfitter maintains that it fully intended to cover the costs, the accounts were not paid until after several of the families filed claims/suits. The father of one of the injured participants said later that his original intent was not to sue, but because the medical bills were adding up, he believed he had no choice.

Survivors and their loved ones have often noted that even the smallest gestures—such as an offering of flowers, phone cards, or anniversary letters—are greatly appreciated. But perhaps more importantly, survivors repeatedly have expressed the need to be treated with decency and kindness. In the GCC and ADG case studies, both the Dzialos and Bonnings emphasized the importance of showing compassion, telling the truth, and offering condolences following an incident. The hospital visits and support meant a great deal to Chuck and his wife. The lack of them created resentment in Phil and his family.

Survivors repeatedly have expressed the need to be treated with decency and kindness.

While there are no black-and-white answers when it comes to knowing what to say, do, or pay following a tragedy, a service provider should never forget that the ramifications of the incident will be tremendous and widespread. Even if the outfitter was not at fault, kindness costs little and can go a long way.

Provide Ongoing Support to Uninjured Employees and Participants. It is not easy for an employee or student/client to continue with a daily routine after watching a fellow class member or colleague become disabled or die. Consequently, it is important that uninjured employees and participants have a channel for releasing the emotional distress that might be caused by a catastrophic incident, and supervisors should make sure that some sort of support is available, free of charge. An outfitter might contact a local mental health agency, for instance, and arrange to have a counselor available on site for a few days, and supervisors should have a basic understanding of what services are available nearby.

Outfitters also should consider offering a CISD to employees and customers, especially those who witnessed the incident. CISD is not therapy, but it is a formalized process for allowing individuals to share experiences and become educated about the common effects that a crisis can have on a person. Because CISD often is more appropriate than counseling, managers should become familiar with the CISD process or at least become familiar with CISD resources that exist in the area.

Although CISD is not meant to be an end-all, many outdoor professionals have gone through one and found it to be highly beneficial. Consider Laurie Gullion's experience. Laurie was an employee for GCC at the time of Adam's near drowning, and though she felt highly distressed, frustrated, and powerless following the incident, the college did not allow a CISD until four years after the accident. Even though the debriefing was significantly delayed, Laurie still found it worthwhile.

"A big surprise for me was the critical incident debriefing. I was initially cynical going into it, but I found the directed exercises to be extremely beneficial in helping me to understand my own responses and those of other personnel. I learned how to create better boundaries between work and my personal life," she says.

A key to successful CISDs, it seems, is in the skill and experience of the facilitators. If a service provider decides to arrange a CISD, it should request that at least one of the leaders has a background in the outdoors, if possible. Following the UAA accident, the students attended a CISD run by university professionals—a police officer, the dean of students, and a mental health worker. Afterward, most of the participants noted that it was not terribly helpful. When questioned for details, they said that it was apparent that the debriefing team really could not relate to what the group had been through. The participants added that had the CISD leaders known what an ice axe was or had they been able to relate to what it was like to plunge step down a snowy slope, they would have been more credible empathizers. Instead, during the session, there seemed to be a gap between the facilitators and participants in empathy and understanding.

As part of its support, an outfitter also might offer time off to workers, which could include paid or unpaid leave. An organization might allow an employee to visit a colleague or participant in the hospital or attend a memorial service without having to take time off from work.

> An organization will need to decide if it will continue to employ a worker whose actions contributed to an accident.

Occasionally, an outfitter will need to decide whether or not a class or outing should continue following an accident. While one's instinct might be to end the course immediately out of respect for the victim(s), oftentimes those involved prefer some sort of closure. A final decision likely should include input from trip leaders as well as participants. If the trip resumes, team members generally are given the opportunity to take part in a CISD first.

Finally, an organization will need to consider whether or not it will continue to employ a worker whose actions contributed to an accident. Though the temptation might be to fire the employee without question, this is not always the best course of action. For example, any perception of unfair or excessive punishment can keep other trip leaders from talking about their incidents and close calls, which, in turn, can keep systemic problems hidden and prevent potential learning. And while it might be appropriate to rid the industry of someone who commits an overly egregious mistake, chances are good that the incident was the result of several minor errors, some of which likely were rooted in the risk management system.

Further, it is worthwhile to note that of the few outdoor instructors and managers who have remained in the profession following a serious incident (see Chapter Five), most report having developed a much deeper appreciation of the risks associated with the industry. The majority also have become more engaged in their programs' operating systems. Several have even shared what they have learned from their experiences, for the betterment of their programs.

No matter which decision is made, it is helpful to remember that the employee is hurting, too. Rather than adding to a leader's turmoil, it is hoped that the outfitter will find a way to help its colleague heal.

Conduct an Investigation. Long before it is ever faced with a real-life incident, a service provider should identify if and when an accident will be investigated and how the investigation will be conducted. Although some attorneys will argue against any type of review, program managers would be wise to remember that two of the most basic needs of a survivor and/or his family are to 1) find out what happened, and 2) find meaning in the event.

To aid in this process, any outdoor service provider that experiences an incident should be willing to critically evaluate its actions as well as its risk management practices. It then should use the findings to make improvements, if possible. In the event that a service provider opts to investigate a serious accident, information from Jed Williamson's *The Serious Incident (Accident) Review Process* can be used to guide the process (2000).

The first step of the review process is to choose a review team. Once a team is selected, certain ground rules will need to be established. For example, even though the service provider might be paying for the review, the investigators should be allowed to operate independently. The team's findings will be based on facts discovered.

The program will need to assure the team that it will have access to records and people, and the organization will be expected to provide support, as needed. The specific steps involved in the review process will be up to the investigators, but they generally include the following type of sequence: A work agreement will be created; team member assignments will be distributed; a visit to the incident site will be conducted; pertinent documents will be reviewed; and interviews will be completed.

After the review team comes to an initial conclusion, a draft report will be written. The report (or findings) will be shared with program representatives for feedback. If any errors are discovered, modifications can be made.

Finally, the service provider will need to decide if it is going to share information with the victims and/or their families. If the program wishes to keep the findings confidential, it should say so; if the findings will be released to the family (and perhaps the media), a plan should be in place so that the release of information is handled with care. Before a final decision is made, however, the provider should find out if its insurance company will allow this type of disclosure. (Some insurers will not even allow a review.)

Educate Key Personnel and Test the EAP. Catastrophic incidents rarely occur within an organization. As a result, most programs invest minimal time and money planning for a worst-case scenario, and when things finally do go wrong, there is a good chance that the EAP will fail in some regard. If an organization wants to avoid the pitfalls that can and often do occur following a disaster, and if it wants its employees to follow certain procedures, it should attempt to ensure that all personnel are familiar with the EAP, understand the roles they will be expected to play, and are given the opportunity to practice their roles during mock exercises.

A growing list of literature and research suggests that people's behaviors in a crisis can be modified (for the better) if they receive relevant training ahead of time. Jerry Dzugan points out in Chapter Nine, for example, that when marine safety and survival workshops include applicable hands-on techniques and practical methodologies, mariners respond more appropriately in emergencies. Further, although flight school testing has always been quite rigid, experts recently concluded that the past trainings for commercial pilots were insufficient when it came to crisis response. As a result, commercial pilots now are required to undergo crisis simulations on an annual basis, and this change seems to have effectively improved performance. Thus, one might extrapolate that EAP trainings could improve a worker's response as well.

A service provider also should consider revisiting, testing, and updating its EAP periodically. This might include staging an emergency and attempting to contact all applicable parties within a short, designated time frame. It also might include locating and revising working papers. In the event that any part of the EAP appears weak or flawed, modifications should be made.

Evaluate the EAP. While mock scenarios can provide useful information about a plan's workability, an outfitter will not get a true indication of an EAP's value or weaknesses until after a real-life crisis occurs. As a result, if an organization ever has to use its EAP in a true emergency, once all is said and done, it should follow up by conducting an evaluation of the effectiveness of the plan and of worker performance. The evaluation should be conducted by an objective person or group, and it should include input from employees, participants, family members, and the media.

The steps it takes to create a workable EAP are in many ways similar to the steps outdoor professionals take prior to, during, and immediately after an outing or voyage. That is, good risk managers—whether they work in the field or in the office—constantly will review as many "what if" scenarios as possible. Not only will they identify potential hazards, but they will know how to avoid those that are unnecessary, and they will know how to manage the risks that are part of doing business. And because they are trained and practiced in dealing with crises, if a worst-case scenario does happen—whether it is a broken bone, a breakdown in critical gear, or a fatality in the field—they will have their response plans in place, ready to assist them through the process. The keys to success in any emergency, they realize, lie in thinking ahead, anticipating consequences, and relying on one's principles to do the right thing.

As a final thought, it is worthwhile to remember that although a crisis, by definition, forces a change in behavior, it does not have to be a wholly negative experience. Two Chinese symbols—meaning challenge and opportunity—have been used to denote crises, and the Chinese believe that an opportunity for improvement exists in every critical event. The experience, they believe, can provide an opportunity to show competency and leadership, as well as learning and growth. The trick, of course, is in knowing how to best handle—and perhaps even find something good in—a worst-case event.

In the Path of the Ripple: The Effects of a Tragedy on a Program's Employees

By Deb Ajango © 2005

This chapter includes accounts and insights from trip leaders and program managers who have lived through incidents that resulted in serious injury or death to a participant or client. Starting with Kate Douglas's experience at Greenfield Community College, the chapter outlines some of the many challenging, frustrating, surprising, and healing aspects of their experiences. The author, who formerly worked as a therapist and an outdoor program director, also shares learning points from her own experience (described in Chapter Four) and provides information from the counseling profession on what it takes to survive a tragedy of this type.

At 5:00 on Friday afternoon, July 28, 1998, Kate Douglas left her office on the Greenfield Community College (GCC) campus. It was the end of her third week in her new position as associate dean of Behavioral Sciences and the beginning of a normal summer weekend. She had no particular plans. Other than spending the next couple days with her family, she didn't know what she would do.

Kate's life was changed that day by a phone call. It came in at 7:00 p.m. from Tashima Wildrose, the director of Adventures Unlimited. It was not an official phone call; Kate had no administrative authority over the youth program. Tashima was calling as a colleague and a friend. And she was calling in obvious distress.

"I want to tell you about something that happened," Tashima told Kate. There had been an accident during a day outing at the Deerfield River. The group had been floating the river, doing a rescue exercise. A boy named Adam Dzialo got his foot trapped in rocks and was under the water a long time. He was now in the hospital, in critical condition. His parents and the college's administrators had been notified, and all the other kids had gone home to their families.

As Kate heard these basic details, she felt concern not only for Adam, but also for Tashima, as well as the trip leaders, Patrick and Heather. The Adventures Unlimited program was run by GCC's Community Services division, so none of its staff reported to her. But Kate had more than 20 years' experience in outdoor education, and she knew how to handle an emergency. Tashima was obviously shaken. Nonetheless, she seemed to be doing all the right things. She also seemed to have the immediate support she needed. So after a short conversation, Kate felt comfortable hanging up.

Kate was still concerned for the traumatized trip leaders, however, so she then phoned each of them separately. As she talked to Heather about what happened, they focused on the foot entrapment. "How did he get his foot caught?" Kate wanted to know. "Did he try to stand?"

"I don't know," Heather replied. "I didn't see it. I looked away for just a moment, and I didn't see what happened."

"What about Patrick? Did he see it?"

"No, Patrick didn't see it, either."

Kate gave each trip leader the same advice. "Stay with family and friends this weekend," she said. "And write down everything that happened. Do it tonight, before you forget anything." Heather and Patrick both assured her that they had already given full accounts to the State Troopers. But Kate insisted: "Write it all down before you go to bed."

Early the next morning, Kate met with the college president, the head of the Community Services division, and a public relations specialist from GCC. Although Kate's role as associate dean did not require that she be there, she was not surprised to be included in the meeting. At GCC, her skill set was a rarity: She was an administrator with outdoor education experience. Only three weeks before, she had been in charge of the Outdoor Leadership Program through which Tashima, Heather, and Patrick had gotten their training.

Two of the four administrators in attendance at the meeting had been out of town when the river incident took place. They knew what had happened the day before, but none of them had all the details. The president wanted to proceed carefully, but he wasn't sure where to start. He asked the others, "What do we need to do first?"

Kate knew what the outdoor industry would expect.

Kate knew what the outdoor industry would expect. "Reach out to the Dzialo family," she said. "Make sure the instructors are okay. And do something for the other children who witnessed the accident." She added, "We should set up meetings with the boys and their parents as soon as possible. We need to tell them what happened and let them discuss their feelings." The others listened respectfully, accepted her advice, and agreed to hold debriefing sessions with the boys as well as their parents on Monday evening.

After the meeting, the president and Kate headed to the hospital. Although Kate acknowledges that she felt a certain loyalty toward her employer, she says, "My main concern was for Adam and his family. When I walked into an intensive care unit and saw a mom and dad clearly distraught, my heart just ached for them." Kate had not yet received any details regarding Adam's injuries, and she was shocked by the boy's serious condition. "I didn't really know how bad it was. I didn't know what to expect."

As Kate, the president, and the two anguished parents sat talking, Kate gravitated toward Sharon. She remembers the mother's pain with a special clarity. "We have so many questions about what happened," Sharon said. "We do too;

we'll find the answers," Kate told her, fully believing that at some point they would.

That afternoon, back at home, Kate wept. "I said to my husband, 'I don't know if I could ever do that again.' All I could do was put myself in their shoes. Especially Sharon's. If that had been my son, I thought, how could I possibly go on?"

Kate didn't talk to Heather and Patrick again until just before the Monday evening debriefing sessions. When the two instructors handed Kate their written reports, Kate passed them on to the head of the college's security team without reading them. The trip leaders joined the assembly for the boys; Kate moved to a different room and facilitated the gathering for the adults.

As Kate worked with the parents, she was as candid as she could be with the information she had. "I felt pretty good about the Monday evening sessions," she says. "The boys requested a follow-up meeting with the river guides who conducted the rescue, and we were able to arrange that. When I went to bed that night, I was confident that the college was moving in the right direction."

One critical detail had escaped her attention, however. Kate still didn't realize that Patrick had not been present at the time of the accident. Neither Patrick nor Heather had tried to hide this fact; it was in the reports they had made to the State Troopers on Friday. It also was in the report Patrick handed Kate on Monday evening. But Kate had not read the reports yet, and somehow this detail got lost.

It wasn't until Thursday afternoon when, in a conversation with Tashima, Kate realized that Heather was alone when the accident took place. She was stunned. Kate immediately called the college president to fill him in. She knew it would be important to pass this information on to the Dzialos. But Kate was too late. Adam's father had already learned this detail from others who had been at the scene and had received confirmation from Tashima. He was furious that college employees had not offered this news themselves. "Why would they keep that from me?" he was forced to wonder. He came to the conclusion that the college was trying to cover things up.

From that day on, Kate says, nothing was the same. Not only did the relationship between GCC and the Dzialos start to deteriorate, the college seemed to become fearful that the family might sue. That same week, Kate and two other college employees met with the GCC counsel for the first time. The lawyer made it clear that from that point forward no one should talk to the Dzialos. Nobody should talk to the press. Nobody should talk about the accident at all.

It didn't seem like such a bad idea at the time, Kate says. After what had just happened, she realized that maybe she didn't have the whole picture yet. Her training told her that there should be only one voice speaking for the college. Her thinking was, "Let's get all the information and use one spokesperson to share what happened." She assumed that the one voice would come from the president's office. She never imagined that no one from GCC would ever talk openly to the family or the media again.

Over time, Kate became frustrated with some of the college's choices. She believed that GCC needed to be more open and compassionate, and she told people so. "I was called into the president's office almost daily those first few weeks. I remember feeling as though people were listening to me, but they didn't act on my recommendations. I know I'm only one member of the team so I didn't expect to have everything go my way. But as things began to spiral out of control, I became more and more concerned."

As her frustrations grew, Kate became more vocal and more direct in her recommendations. "I felt that we needed advice from a lawyer who specialized in this area. I gave them Reb Gregg's name and asked the college to call him." Kate spoke with Reb herself on at least two occasions. The Texas attorney only reinforced Kate's belief that her views on how to proceed were sound.

Several times Kate tried to convince the president that the current strategy was not working. "He would nod his head, as if he was listening to and even considering my advice. But nothing changed." No matter what she said or did, the college continued on a route that seemed to create even more angst and animosity. The experience was not only exasperating, Kate says, but it was humiliating.

"I wasn't used to that kind of treatment. Normally, there's a lot of autonomy in faculty life. I'd had a lot of freedom to help create the (Outdoor Leadership) program. We had developed our own curriculum, protocols, policies, etc. And I expected to have a say in how this incident would be handled. But no matter how hard I tried, how direct I was, how many allies I led to the table, or which outside experts I suggested we bring in, my opinion just didn't matter. I have never had my professional judgment so utterly disregarded."

As the gap between the college and the family grew, the interactions between GCC and the Dzialos became harsh and bitter. The Dzialos' pain was inarguably the deepest, the most obvious, and the most undeniable. But many of the staff at GCC, including Kate, suffered as well. What had initially started as concern for others turned into an inner struggle that would have a fundamental effect on Kate's career and her life.

"Maybe if people read this [book], they'll make the change ahead of time."

Kate considered quitting on a number of occasions, but she stayed the course, hoping that she would make a positive impact somewhere along the way.

When asked what she would change if she had to do it again, Kate replies, "I don't know what I could have done to make things different. Could I have spoken louder? Could I have screamed louder? Would walking away have made a louder statement?" She thinks a moment and adds, "I don't think anything I could have done at that point would have changed a thing. That's why I've agreed to help with this book. Unless an organization addresses some of these [response] issues *before* the fact, it will likely run into the same challenges my college faced." Not only will participants' families suffer more for it, she believes, but employees will be negatively affected as well. Kate has hopes for the best. "Maybe if people read this, they'll make the change ahead of time."

When asked if she has any final words for other program managers, she thinks a moment and then says quietly, "I hope they never have to go through what we went through."

Liz Tuohy's life was changed on a different summer evening: June 26, 1996. The National Outdoor Leadership School (NOLS) course she was leading had been deep in the Absaroka Mountains of Wyoming for 24 days. They had five days left to go. As the trip's leader, Liz was in charge of supervising two co-instructors and a group of 15 students as they learned to travel independently in the mountains. The participants ranged in age from 16 to 33 years old, most of them novices to camping or backpacking. Liz herself was experienced; she had worked for NOLS for two years and had logged 44 weeks in the field as an instructor. It was her second time in the lead role. She was 25 years old.

The NOLS mission is to teach leadership and wilderness skills. The curriculum is designed to teach students outdoor living and travel skills, and to help them develop competency in a variety of areas. During the first 25 days of a trip, the instructors lead, coach, and assess the students continually in preparation for the culminating experience—the *student expedition*. On that final expedition, students break into small groups, choose a leader, plan an itinerary, and travel on their own for up to four days without direct supervision from the instructors. During that time, the participants are responsible for making real decisions. The lessons they learn not only serve them in the wilderness but are applicable to their daily lives at home or at work. In essence, the expedition is the culmination of NOLS's student-centered experiential approach to teaching leadership.

On June 26, Liz's students were traveling without their instructors in small teams of five each. Although the teams saw each other occasionally, they traveled independently and were allowed to make their own decisions. That evening, they all planned to rendezvous several miles away, on the north side of the South Buffalo Fork River. Groups One and Three chose to remain on the north side of the river for the day, opting not to cross to the opposite side. Group Two crossed to the south side that morning; the winter snowpack lingered long into June that year, and the students were looking for easier hiking.

About mid-afternoon, the members of Group Two arrived at an area where, according to the map, they had thought they would be able to recross the river. The water was high and fast at that location, however, so they retraced their steps upstream. For about an hour, they scouted for an easier place to cross.

Ultimately, Group Two found a spot where the river split into two channels. It appeared to be a challenging but reasonable crossing site. Three members of the group formed a human chain—it was a technique they had been taught and had practiced before. Jaime and Rick were on the ends; Katy was in the middle. The other two members of their team watched as spotters a little way downstream.

The chain faced upstream and moved across the river perpendicular to the current. The water was about knee deep. About halfway into a braid, Katy lost her footing and fell to her knees. She was short enough that, in that position, the water began pushing her forcefully downstream. The students on each side of her held her hands tightly, but as Jaime reached down to unbuckle Katie's hip belt, she slipped, too. Suddenly both of them were in the water.

The current carried Jaime into shallow water about 200 yards downstream where she was helped out by the two spotters. Katy was able to get her backpack off, but because she was in a deeper and stronger part of the river, she was out of reach of the others. Within seconds, Katy was swept downriver and around a bend. It is not clear exactly when she hit her head; no one saw it happen. But her unconscious body was carried a quarter of a mile downstream and onto a gravel bar.

In an attempt to get to Katy, Rick tried to cross the water. After a few failed attempts, he realized how dangerous it was and retreated. Perhaps 20 minutes later, Group Three came upon the scene and was flagged down by Group Two. The students from Group Three easily made it out to Katy. When they realized that she did not have a pulse, two of them, Jack and Molly, initiated CPR. Within minutes, however, they stopped; from the condition of her body, it was apparent that Katy was dead.

After the initial chaos subsided, a few students worked to warm Jamie and help her into dry clothes while others made camp. In the meantime, Jack and his teammates went to get the instructors.

Liz had just finished cooking dinner when Jack's team arrived to tell her what had happened. In those first few moments, Liz was stunned; the situation seemed surreal. She remembers putting a few items away as the reality sunk in. She had to decide quickly what to do next. According to what the students had told her, Liz knew the situation was no longer a rescue. She called a get-together of the students who were nearby and discussed the immediate priorities. Along with one of her co-instructors and two of the students, Liz then went back to the river and pulled Katy's body onto the bank. Afterward, she went upstream to talk to the group that was still on the opposite side.

Communication with the separated students was difficult. Liz went over to the riverbank and wrote notes on a file folder, holding it up for the students to read by binoculars. "Meet here at 6:30 a.m. Keep eating, drinking, try to sleep. We are not in a hurry. We will group up tomorrow. Thank you for being strong." She decided that two people would stay with Katy's body at all times, to protect it from bears and other scavengers. She and a student would take the first shift.

For the next several hours, Liz sat by Katy's side, reading the NOLS fatality protocol by firelight. By 3:00 a.m., when another group came to relieve her, she had a plan.

The morning after Katy's death, Liz's first priority was to have all of the students regroup. It took until 11:00 a.m. to get everyone—and their gear—safely across the river, but it was a relief to be together again. Next, Liz dispatched a runner team of four, led by an instructor, to hike 12 miles to the nearest road. From there, the team would notify NOLS's administration of the fatality.

Liz's group had a ground-to-air radio (cell and satellite phones were not commonly used at the time), so Liz stayed behind and worked the radio all afternoon. Because the airspace over Yellowstone is restricted, there was very little airplane traffic. Finally around 5:00 p.m., Liz was able to reach a commercial airliner, which forwarded a message to NOLS.

That evening, a NOLS representative flew over their camp in a fixed-wing plane. Liz was able to speak to him via radio, confirming that Katy was dead. She let him know that the others were okay, and the situation was under control. A helicopter flew in and took Katy's body away at 9:30 p.m.

The next morning, two NOLS representatives flew in with a deputy sheriff. The NOLS employees told Liz, "You're still the course leader. We're here to do whatever we can to help." The deputy looked at the site where Katy had died and interviewed all the students. Around noon, the entire group loaded its extra gear (and the deputy) onto the helicopter. The instructors and students started walking out. They reached the road the following afternoon. It was Day 27, and their course was over.

Liz had considered the possibility that someone might get hurt, or even killed, during one of her courses someday. But the experience was more intense than she had ever imagined. "When Katy died, I found myself in a situation that I really had no direct training for—I don't think any of us is prepared for something like that."

As the trip leader, she had been responsible for managing the risks of an outing, and now someone was dead. It was hard to put those two pieces together and hard to come to terms with it. "Katy's death was definitely the most traumatic event that had occurred in my life. It is difficult in some ways to sort it out: simply experiencing death, and experiencing the death of someone who I was responsible for, and then being responsible for the welfare of 16 people in a remote place in a traumatic situation. Each of the factors has had a profound effect on my life." But while the experience was heartbreaking and difficult, not all aspects of it were bad.

The experience was more intense than she had ever imagined.

In 1997, I, too, dealt with a professional tragedy (described in Chapter Four). As a result of our shared experiences, Kate, Liz, and I now belong to a dubious club of sorts: We know what it is like to have a serious injury or death happen on our watch.

Fortunately, the club is small. Outdoor programs do not routinely suffer disabling or fatal injuries, so few of their employees can relate to what we have been through. I compare the misfortune of membership to what it might be like to be the victim of a crime. I imagine that it must be terribly hard. But until I experience it for myself, I will never truly know how it feels.

Like most outdoor professionals, I always understood that an accident could happen to me. I knew, too, that someone could be injured or killed while I was in charge. I routinely pictured and prepared for worst-case scenarios. But, not having been through a professional tragedy, I didn't really *know* what it would be like. I had no idea that the ramifications would be so widespread or the pain would run so deep. Not only do the injured and their families suffer, but so do the program's employees. And so do those who love them.

Although I realized there were lessons to be learned from our experiences, it was still difficult to write this chapter. I wondered: How could I possibly ask the readers to empathize with a distraught employee, knowing that that person's pain could not compare to the victim's or the family's? Something Kate said helped. She reminded me that there are many victims in a tragedy like this. It's like dropping a stone in water. The central players feel the greatest impact. They endure the greatest pain and disruption. But the ripples go out in all directions.

"The pain that the Dzialos feel never leaves me," Kate admits. "Seeing the impact, the devastation that the accident has had on Adam and his family has been terribly difficult. But just because my pain might be different doesn't make it less real."

Kate is right: Although a trip leader's or a manager's suffering might not come close to a family's, they are still in the path of the ripple. The experience might be less intense, but it is not a competition. The employees are traumatized, too.

After exchanging stories with other outdoor leaders who are part of the club, it became clear that we would all like to somehow bottle our learning and share it with others. Not only might it be cathartic, people suggested, but perhaps we can help others—trip leaders, managers, and even future participants—develop a deeper understanding of the realities associated with outdoor activities. Maybe we can articulate what it is like to lose a student when you are the one who is supposed to keep everybody "safe." Maybe we can help our peers prepare to more ably survive a storm or minimize the chaos that is inevitable in an emergency. And maybe we can let readers know what helped us recover so that they might, in turn, be able to someday support a colleague in need.

This chapter is a merger of stories from outdoor leaders who have experienced professional tragedies. In an effort to learn how a serious incident affects a program and its employees, I conducted face-to-face, telephone, and e-mail interviews with 20 or so trip leaders, program managers, and administrators. Some of the interactions lasted hours; others lasted only minutes. Some of the interviewees talked openly of accidents that had occurred years ago; others were more reserved since their cases are still in litigation. In some instances, the participants voiced a desire to recount what they had been through, but the pain was simply too fresh. Although they freely discussed the facts, they stopped short when they were asked to describe their feelings. And though some of the people asked that their names not be included, all of the interviewees were willing to share their insights so that they might be used to strengthen the industry as a whole.

HEALING THROUGH UNDERSTANDING

Webster's Twentieth Century Dictionary defines trauma as an emotional shock with a lasting effect (Allen 2005). The Critical Incident Stress Foundation says a significant trauma will affect everyone who is associated with it, regardless of his or her background, coping mechanisms, or available support groups. Although responses vary by individual, research compiled over the last 50 years has identified a number of common temporary manifestations that can arise after a traumatic event:

- Recurring thoughts or nightmares
- Trouble sleeping or changes in eating habits
- Feeling "on edge" or being easily startled
- Feeling depressed, sad, or lacking enthusiasm for life
- Difficulty concentrating on daily activities or work
- Feeling emotionally numb or withdrawn

When a student or a client is injured or killed, trip leaders and managers are quite often traumatized—sometimes even devastated—by the experience. But why is it that two persons who experience the same event can react so differently? And what is it about the incident, or the handling of the incident, that has the greatest impact on an employee's ability to cope or heal?

Admittedly, personality traits, support systems, and even "stress pileup" make a difference. But after completing the interviews for this chapter, I have come to believe that the strength of an outdoor professional's response is also greatly influenced by the following four factors:

1. **The employee's relationship to the person who was injured or killed.** Trip leaders who are most directly responsible for the welfare of participants appear to be more affected than assistant instructors or guides and non-field personnel. Anecdotal evidence also suggests that a trip leader who has developed a strong bond with a student or a client (which can and often does occur during an extended trip) seems to have a more difficult time recovering from the incident than does a day-trip leader.

2. **The employee's judgment of how the injured person or family is treated following the incident.** The outdoor leaders interviewed for this book expressed a strong desire to "do the right thing" following their incidents. To them, this typically meant providing support to those who were hurt, investigating what went wrong, and learning from the experience. If employees believe that their employers are not doing enough toward these ends, they tend to suffer something of a second crisis.

3. **How the employee is treated after the accident.** Traumatized employees generally will experience emotions and behaviors typical of a trauma "survivor." While survivor responses cannot be controlled, research has shown that recovery can be enhanced or stifled, depending on how the survivor is treated after the event. When survivors feel supported, are allowed to discuss their feelings, and are given the opportunity to take part in the post-incident decision-making process, they tend to feel less afflicted in the long run. When they are isolated, taken out of the post-accident process, and judged responsible or blamed for the event, their trauma is deepened, and their pain becomes more lasting and more severe.

4. **Cumulative stress that is provoked by multiple incidents.** Only two of the people I interviewed had experienced more than one serious incident, but both reported that the cumulative effects were significantly greater than what they had experienced after their initial ordeals.

The following will help explain these findings to a greater degree. I attempt to describe what "survivor responses" look like, specifically as they apply to the interviewees. Clinical information regarding survival psychology is included as well so that readers can better understand what their colleagues might think, do, and experience following a serious incident or death.

Shared Beliefs and Their Effects. According to several mental health organizations, most members of society have a number of shared core beliefs. The majority of people believe, for instance, that the world is a pretty good place and that their friends and neighbors are decent people. These types of beliefs are especially strong in individuals who are young, healthy, and have lived relatively agreeable lives. Trauma changes all that.

Researcher and social psychologist Roy Baumeister examines the ways in which a victim's core beliefs are affected by trauma (Allen 2005). He suggests that the primary psychological impact of a crisis comes not from the event itself but rather from the challenge to a survivor's core beliefs. For example, after a citizen has his home broken into, he might lose trust in his neighbors. If a woman is the victim of a violent crime, she might stop believing that the world is a good place and stop trusting in the goodness of people in general. If core beliefs are shaken, a person is forced to reevaluate his or her concept of life and society. If core beliefs are shattered, it can change the way a survivor views his or her world.

If core beliefs are shattered, it can change the way a survivor views his or her world.

Outdoor professionals have a few shared beliefs of their own. In addition to those described above, they also believe the following:

- As long as I am well trained and use my best judgment, chances are good that a serious accident will never happen.

- Because I am a good person who tries my best, because I like my students/clients and they like me, and because I work for a good employer that supports me, even if an accident happens, things will probably turn out okay.

Any serious outdoor incident can challenge these beliefs. But when that incident is followed by public criticism, media scrutiny, lack of support within the institution, and/or a lawsuit, the survivors can come to feel that their core beliefs have been violated. The outdoor professional might struggle with trust, for instance. Often, it is no longer assumed that "things will be okay." Instead, the guide/educator might begin to believe that:

- The world is not such a good place.
- Things do not always turn out okay.
- I am not sure I trust people. If I let down my guard, I could be harmed.

On a slightly different though related topic, research suggests that people who go through well-crafted outdoor or adventure experiences improve their moral reasoning skills (Garvey and Spencer 2005). *Moral reasoning* is the ability to determine a morally right course of action in a difficult situation. "Morally right" in this sense does not refer to any particular theology; instead, it is based on the understanding that some actions are more appropriate than others if the end goal is to support a common good. Limited empirical data has found that people who have been exposed to intentional programming for problem solving, reflection, and integration—qualities integral in many outdoor programs—will grow morally in a wide variety of contexts.

Outdoor leaders seem to have a shared belief that people (i.e., their employers) will "do the right thing" following a serious incident. To the interviewees, the right thing had more to do with compassion and communication than with protecting an organization legally or financially. The outdoor professionals I spoke with all expected that any injured student or client would be given the care he or she needed. They believed that appropriate support would be offered to the families, other participants, and program employees alike. If a victim was fatally injured, the employees expected to be able to grieve with and offer condolences to the participant's family. In short, they had reached a conclusion that the morally right thing to do would be to show compassion to all involved.

There are those who will find this expectation naive; yet, it was a common thread in my interviews. Consequently, these shared beliefs likely should be considered to at least some degree during the post-incident decision-making process.

According to Dan Garvey, President of Prescott College and a moral-reasoning researcher, "After an incident, a program's decision-makers must carefully weigh the advice they receive from multiple sources. Although a well-intentioned lawyer may give advice for reducing the program's [liability] exposure, that same advice might seriously undermine the expectations of some of the program's employees. That is, the action might not appear to meet the standard of doing 'the right thing.'"

A legal recommendation, Garvey adds, often includes the lowest level of human support required. Staff, on the other hand, might expect something quite different from their employers. Unfortunately, those workers who truly believe that things will be okay following a worst-case scenario can suffer even more trauma when post-incident actions go badly. And if, as a result of the process, their core beliefs are shattered, it can literally change the way they view the world.

The Need to Talk. In 2000, three years after the Ptarmigan Peak accident (see Chapter Four), the University of Alaska Anchorage (UAA) published a book titled *Lessons Learned: A Guide to Accident Prevention and Crisis Response*. In Chapter Six of that text, ethicist Jasper Hunt wrote, "A death or an injury suffered on an outing is often treated as a dirty little secret that we dare not talk about. ... The advice [to remain silent] usually comes from legal counsel concerned about potential lawsuits. But that advice, sound though it may be from a legal standpoint, can interfere with both the healing and learning processes."

Looking back on my own experience, and after sharing stories with a number of other outdoor professionals nationwide, I couldn't agree more. Silence doesn't work. Not only is it okay to talk about our incidents, but if we are to survive them personally and to improve as an industry, we *must* talk about them.

Most of the survivors I interviewed identified "talking" as the most important element in the healing process. According to the interviewees, there appear to be four different *types* of talking that helped: simply telling the story, usually in detail; talking to a friend or a loved one without fearing judgment; talking to someone who has experienced a similar event; and/or talking to a mental health professional. It was the third of these, talking to others who can relate, that seemed to be the most beneficial.

> Trauma survivors often need to talk about an incident over and over again.

According to trauma psychologists, the goal of talking is to render the traumatic experience thinkable and speakable. That happens best in an environment of trust. Jon Allen, psychologist and author of *Coping with Trauma: Hope Through Understanding* (2005), believes that being able to talk in a secure relationship—i.e., being able to explore difficult emotions or memories with someone who cares or can relate—goes to the heart of healing. Perhaps that is why survivors feel such a strong need to discuss events with their peers as well as their loved ones.

Jacob Lindy, M.D., offers a slightly different theory on why talking matters (Allen 2005). He says that shortly after being traumatized, survivors begin to develop a kind of emotional barrier to protect them from further harm. Lindy calls this the "trauma membrane." Although this barrier can prevent further pain, it also can lead to extreme feelings of isolation. Talking—to loved ones, to trained listeners, and/or to someone who has experienced a similar event—can help penetrate the membrane and can ease the feelings of isolation.

Readers should realize that "talking about" an event doesn't simply mean telling the story once. Trauma survivors often need to talk about an incident over and over again. Consider the following case in point: Shortly after a recent avalanche in which a man was killed, the surviving partner told his story to a park ranger. He talked in detail about the accident, describing every action he took to try to find his friend in the debris. (The victim was not wearing a beacon, fell into a crevasse, and was never found.) In less than an hour, the survivor repeated the story, almost verbatim, to a colleague. As soon as two new peers walked into the room, he started over, explaining, yet again, the quality of the snow, the slope angle, and the rescue efforts. According to John Leach, author of *Survival Psychology* (1994), this behavior is both understandable and normal. In his text, Leach describes other survivors who also appear "compulsive" in their need to tell their stories over and over again, with identical detail and emphasis.

Talking to and learning from others who shared the experience is the purpose of a Critical Incident Stress Debriefing (CISD). These structured sessions, first described in Chapter Four, employ both crisis intervention and educational processing. They structure the traumatic experience in a way that binds the different perspectives of the group members together. In theory, the gathering will generate feelings of hope and control, allow for peer support, and provide an opportunity for catharsis. When participants are asked afterward what they found most helpful about the debriefings, they typically mention talking about the incident, realizing they are not alone, hearing others talk, being part of a group that had a similar experience, and hearing how others handled their stress.

When applied properly, a debriefing can be a useful tool for stress mitigation. But negative experiences have been known to occur, particularly when there is poor leadership or poor facilitation. CISDs are not therapy, and facilitators typically are not trained therapists. When a facilitator does not fully understand the group process, lacks the authority to steer it, or does not understand what the participants have been through, a session may not be particularly beneficial. Consequently, if an organization decides to offer a CISD following an incident, it should be careful to use only qualified leaders.

Overall, the most helpful kind of talking seems to occur when survivors can tell their stories to people who have experienced similar traumas. Says Blaine Smith, the lead guide on the Mount McKinley climb described in Chapter Two, "It's been frustrating to try to explain the storm and the bivouac to someone who has no concept of what it might have been like. There is no empathy. I knew I might have made a big mistake by going to the summit. We didn't know if we were going to live or die, and I felt ashamed that the whole thing had happened. But I don't think most people can relate to that. In fact, if they're not guides, they look at me as if I'm from another planet just because I climb mountains for a living."

Blaine adds, "I tried to talk to my colleagues, but it seemed like many of them were judging me. I guess they felt that they had their acts together. It was almost as though they thought it could never happen to them. Ultimately, I found it most satisfying to talk to guides who had been through an emergency, close call, or accident. They could relate, not only to an extreme environment, but to what can really happen out there."

Kate agrees. "I liked talking with folks who had been through their own trauma. It was critical being able to talk to Laurie (a colleague from GCC's Outdoor Leadership Program) because Laurie got it. She understood. In fact, if somebody in a time of need reads this book, consider this an invitation to contact me."

Kirk Shimeall is another member of the club, a manager of a youth program in which a teenage student died. He found it helpful to talk to his wife, family, and coworkers afterward, but he sought professional mental health advice as well. "The enormity of the events weighed me down tremendously. I definitely was not my upbeat self. It was feedback from family and peers about how I had changed that convinced me to seek professional care. It helped to describe what I was feeling in a safe and nonthreatening environment. The therapist never passed judgment and was able to give me some very useful advice."

It should be clear by now that survivors need to talk, and program managers are often faced with tough decisions in this regard. What should the survivors be allowed to say? And to whom should they be allowed to say it? A wise program manager will recognize the employee's need and find a way to allow him or her to discuss the matter in a safe environment. A CISD might be a good start, but other venues can work as well. If a program insists on public silence, it should at least arrange for the survivors to be able to talk with trusted friends or professionals behind closed doors.

What should the survivors be allowed to say?

Program managers and lawyers who try to mandate total silence should beware: Several of the interviewees noted that even though they had been told not to talk about an incident, the need was so strong that they talked about it anyway. Two even admitted to finding a victim's or family's home phone number and calling the people directly, against their lawyers' advice. While attorneys might want administrators to limit a survivor's conversations for fear of litigation, they should realize that most survivors will be negatively affected by this approach, and many will fight it.

One of the hardest parts of Kate's ordeal, she says, was the college's code of silence. "Because I am an educator by nature, I wanted to talk about things, to put things in perspective, and to say what we learned. Although I wasn't given an explicit order to keep quiet, I was cautioned again and again to be very careful about what I said. The legal office made it clear that I should hold my tongue. But it's very, very hard to live that way. The lawyers say 'no comment.' But when that advice runs counter to standards of decency and causes so much extra pain in people's lives, it is 180 degrees in the wrong direction."

Physical Ailments. Because the specific responses to trauma can vary so widely, it is hard to know what to expect. And though talking is important, it does not, by itself, heal all wounds.

Exposure to acute stress generates physiological changes throughout the brain and body. Although these responses can help a person cope in the short term, if the stress is too great or exposure is too long, they also can lead to physical ailments as well as a reduced immune system function. Trauma survivors, in fact, frequently report an increase in aches, pains, and illnesses. When the symptoms become intrusive and long term, they can lead to a diagnosis of Post Traumatic Stress Disorder (PTSD).

Predictably, several of this chapter's interviewees found themselves experiencing a range of ailments. In some cases, the symptoms were minor or temporary in nature. Other times, the symptoms became debilitating.

Liz's experience is a good illustration of how the ailments can affect a survivor's life. Liz had received exemplary support from her organization, and she was allowed—if not encouraged—to talk about the experience. Yet roughly 11 months after Katy's death, Liz's body started to malfunction. "I had a sequence of unexplained injuries that lasted four years," she says. "It felt like tendonitis or chronic joint pain, but there was no obvious cause."

She lost the use of her joints and was not able to swim, cycle, backpack, climb, or even walk more than very short distances. At one point, she could not play guitar or knit. She went to the Mayo Clinic and saw dozens of alternative health practitioners, but none could give her a definitive diagnosis. Some doctors suggested that it was just in her head. One woman said it "might be emotional." "What was I supposed to do with that?" Liz asks. "I wanted an answer. I wanted to know what was causing it. I wanted to know what would make the pain go away. I tried acupuncture, I changed my diet, I tried everything I could think of."

She only recently stumbled onto an explanation that makes sense to her. In Belleruth Naparstek's book, *Invisible Heroes: Survivors of Trauma and How They Heal* (2004), Liz learned that mysterious and chronic physical ailments are a common side effect of PTSD. While she initially was reluctant to accept that there was such a direct cause and effect, she admits now that it is the only explanation that fits. "I had four years of being physically incapable of athletics, and I've had a very long road of emotional processing. I do feel better these days, but it's still very personal for me."

In an equally disturbing case, a 23-year-old healthy trip leader who was associated with an incident was diagnosed with cancer two years after her ordeal. Although no direct correlation has been made in that case either, those who are familiar with the facts say they would not be surprised if there is some sort of connection.

Hypervigilance. Following any trauma, there can be feelings of heightened concern that a similar incident might happen again and the pain will be repeated. At one end of the spectrum, this concern can culminate in paranoia—a true disorder characterized by baseless or excessive distrust in others. Less severe manifestations include hyperarousal (which relates to fear), hyper-responsiveness (which means being easily startled), or simply overreacting (the tendency to make mountains out of molehills).

It is not surprising that outdoor professionals tend to experience their own anxieties following a trauma. Some of the people interviewed for this book suffered from insomnia. Others were irritable and/or prone to angry outbursts. Several had a difficult time concentrating, at least for a while. All of them acknowledged experiencing hypervigilance, a condition of being overly concerned or careful. According to *Coping with*

Trauma, hypervigilance occurs when a survivor maintains a level of anxiety about threats that can be imagined but not seen (Allen 2005). When a person's sense of control and confidence has been interrupted, even temporarily, he or she cannot be sure that danger is not around the next corner. A common theme for the outdoor survivors was that they were simply afraid for people's safety.

"Even years after the incident," says Kirk, "each time the on-call phone would ring, my heart would begin to pound, and my chest would tighten up. I was always expecting another worst-case scenario. I would feel a subtle yet persistent dread, a nagging darkness descending over me every day as I drove to work."

"I remember those early months," says Kate. "I was more conservative, sometimes overly cautious. My kids couldn't go anywhere without a helmet on. Maybe it's a type of paranoia, but the feelings made sense to me."

Very few people who were affected deeply by their tragedies still work in the field.

Blaine's hypervigilance has waned in the seven years since his traumatic experience, but it is still with him. "I'm still jumpy," he says. "I haven't lost my love for the mountains, but I realize what can happen, and I'm more observant of the little things going on around me. I was probably always a bit on edge, even before the accident. But I used to enjoy getting to know my clients and laughing with them during meals or in the evenings. That doesn't happen as much anymore. Now when I'm in charge of others, I can never truly relax."

This persistent anxiety and concern over safety can be so strong and uncomfortable that many trip leaders actually lose the love they once had for the profession. Very few people who were affected deeply by their tragedies still work in the field. Of the 10 frontline instructors or guides interviewed for this chapter, eight stopped leading trips after their incidents. Of the five program managers and administrators interviewed, only two still take others into the wilderness. (The remaining five interviewees were only indirectly involved in their program's accidents. All of them still work in the profession.)

Guilt versus Shame. Guilt and shame are emotions that occur when an individual fails to conform to certain social rules or to uphold the moral order. Although they overlap, guilt typically is associated with a voluntary action that hurts someone else, whereas shame is a pervasive sense of defectiveness that tends to surface from an involuntary shortcoming. In short: Guilt is feeling bad about what you have done; shame is feeling bad about who you are.

Shame is the opposite of pride. Pride is associated with feelings of success and accomplishment. Shame corresponds to failure and inadequacy. Pride has you wanting to be seen and admired. Shame has you wanting to hide.

Shame is a common facet of trauma. Trauma wounds a person's sense of competence and mastery. This is true whether one is the victim of a crime or simply watches but has no control over a tragedy. It is especially true if one feels humiliated for one's participation in a shameful act.

Before his own traumatic experience, Kirk associated accidents with bad organizations. "I had this notion that only poorly run programs experienced death. When we had a fatality, it occurred to me that maybe we were one of those organizations. I felt deeply ashamed. I used to be quite proud of my company. After the incident, I found myself dreading the 'what do you do,' or 'where do you work' question that everyone seems to ask in any new social contact or situation."

According to Blaine, "I'm ashamed that the accident happened, that I allowed us to be caught in a storm. I'm ashamed that the lives of my clients were severely altered. I know I did the best I could, and I'm proud that they came down alive. But I'm embarrassed that it happened at all."

Liz adds, "I knew I was part of something really horrible, and I was afraid it was somehow my fault. Even after I decided that I didn't think it was 'my fault,' I was afraid that some information would surface that would make me change my mind, and that it would turn out to be my fault after all."

Kate believes that her sense of shame may not run as deep as the others, but she can still relate. "Because I'm a couple ripples out, I don't necessarily feel the same type of shame that a trip leader might feel. But I am still ashamed of our response after the accident, in particular the fact that we had so little regard for human feelings."

Interestingly, fewer of those interviewed expressed feelings of guilt. Those who did tended to apportion it according to the role they played in the tragedy. Program managers did not tend to feel guilt over the incidents, although some (like Kate) felt guilty for the suffering that occurred due to a poorly handled response. Lead instructors, on the other hand, sometimes felt guilty about their roles in the incidents, but they rarely felt guilty about their employers' long-term actions. Feelings of guilt typically are associated with *intentional* wrongdoing, which may be why so few experienced this emotion. None of the interviewees considered their actions negligent or malevolent; whatever mistakes were made were certainly not purposeful. And all who acknowledged feeling guilty at some point also seemed able to forgive themselves over time.

Learning from Surprises. It is common practice for outdoor professionals to try to imagine a variety of crisis scenarios and plan appropriate responses. Even so, everyone I interviewed was caught off guard in some way or another during their experiences.

Blaine is a good example. A veteran guide who had already climbed Mount McKinley 12 times before his incident, he had mentally scripted a "what if" scenario to prepare for every eventuality he could imagine. But, he says, "For some reason, I had sort of imagined that bivouacking would be like a really uncomfortable camping trip. I knew it would be challenging, but it didn't really click that, for us to bivvy, things would have to be so bad that we couldn't stand or communicate. I had never imagined that our equipment would be blown out of our hands. I also wasn't prepared for how much work there was to be done once we got back to high camp. I didn't realize how much effort it would take to get the evacuation going."

The aftermath of an accident has its own surprises. Blaine, for instance, also had not anticipated how exhaustive the post-incident ordeal would be for everyone. "The surgeries ... the therapies ... they were endless. I certainly knew what frostbite was (before the incident). I had learned how to avoid it and how to treat it in the field. But I hadn't really thought about how long the recovery would take. I was surprised at how much the accident permeated people's lives."

One program manager was surprised by the overwhelming presence of the media. He would have liked to interact more with the victims and their families in the days following the accident, but he continually was interrupted by reporters wanting an interview. Another respondent was surprised by how difficult it was to try to maintain his composure when making the initial phone call to the next of kin. "I was only able to do it by having someone sit right next to me when I spoke to the family. He [the colleague] would stop me whenever I started to slip into the emotions of the moment by putting his hand on my shoulder."

Several interviewees were surprised by the behavior of their colleagues.

Still another program manager talked about how surprisingly difficult it was to meet everyone's needs after a multi-casualty incident. Looking back, she would have liked to have been able to dedicate one full-time person to each of the injured persons (and/or their families). But, she says, "For a small business like ours, it is often one or two people who are running the show. Addressing the needs of the victims and survivors, working with the insurance company, and keeping the business going all at the same time is almost impossible."

A final anonymous respondent was dismayed by the reluctance of his employer's insurance carrier to allow an external investigation. Once the insurer finally did agree to one, it was only under the condition that the findings would remain confidential and would not be discoverable by the parents' lawyers.

Several interviewees were surprised by the behavior of their colleagues. For example, they knew that their students or clients might become upset during a crisis, but they had always imagined that their coworkers would remain calm. Unfortunately, that didn't always happen. In one instance, an instructor began acting hysterical. In another, an assistant stopped eating and drinking for two days. One guide was simply too exhausted to help with the rescue efforts. And in a fourth case, the dynamics between an instructor and a coworker were so disturbed that it affected their ability to function properly as leaders and teammates.

One explanation for these behaviors comes from survivor research. Author Leach notes that, although behaviors are not necessarily predictable, there are trends that are consistent across studies (1994). The most common first thought of all victims or survivors, for instance, is, "I can't believe this is happening." Most people, about 75 percent, initially will appear stunned and bewildered, and their reasoning and thinking processes will be temporarily affected. These people often will want to be told or shown what to do. About 10 to 20 percent of people will stay calm enough in an emergency that their awareness remains intact and their ability to make sound decisions remains unimpaired. The final 10 to 15 percent will show a high degree of inappropriate behaviors. They tend to respond in a manner that is not only ineffective but may be counterproductive and can make the situation worse.

Leach lists a number of individual reactions as well. He notes that survivors are constantly surprised by post-incident fatigue, as Blaine was, because its onset is insidious and its effects rapid. He also identifies anger, guilt, and psychological breakdowns as possibilities. Readers might be surprised to learn that panic is quite *uncommon* during or immediately after a crisis. If and when it does occur, it is almost always accompanied by a feeling of being trapped—by physical barriers or by lack of resources.

Inevitably, Leach explains, most people respond by falling into reflexive, well-learned behaviors or resorting to habits that require little or no thought (1994). For example, during a crisis, most people will speak in their native tongues. People who like organization and order might stop to clean or tidy an area, as Liz did, even while things around them are in disarray. And people who are used to a certain routine tend to follow that same routine—even in an emergency.

This information is useful in training people to respond appropriately in a crisis situation. The first step is to educate employees so that they know what to expect, so that people are not surprised by the behaviors of those around them. Next, if a person practices effective and desirable behaviors to the point that those behaviors become routine, chances are far greater that he or she will do the right thing during an emergency. Not only are trained people more apt to perform effectively, but their training and response can then be used to guide the masses. Panic is contagious, but so is calmness and control. Group composure can be established and maintained by leaders who have learned to offer support and information as needed.

Blaine is one of many survivors who hopes to help others learn from his surprises. "I try to get guides to more accurately picture their most likely worst-case scenarios," he says. "They tend to assume there will be a fairly straightforward fall or injury. They don't often imagine the bad weather, chaos, or intensity that accompanies it. I tell them, 'You're going to have to run containment on your people. You have to expect that your instructions will not be heard, understood, or followed. You'll need to identify your assets (including clients or students) quickly and use them in order to keep things under control.' If trip leaders have a better idea of how things can fall apart, maybe it will help them keep things together."

Who Hurts the Worst? Who are the people most affected by a student or client injury or fatality? After the victims and their family members, those interviewed agreed that the trip leaders likely shoulder the biggest burden.

"While it's impossible to measure," Liz says, "I think I took the biggest hit. After all, I was in charge."

In one program, all three field staff who had been working a course walked away from their jobs shortly after a student fatality, clearly traumatized by what had happened. Of the trip leaders from Kirk's organization, "Almost all of them are still in the helping professions (social work, group homes, etc.), but none are leading trips at this time that I know of. I think it is just too difficult for them, the possibility of it [a death] happening again on their watch. I don't think they are willing to put themselves in that position." Another manager was happy that one of her guides returned a year after a client died on a trip. But, she says, "If anything happens again, I would be very concerned about his well-being."

In many organizations the trip leaders are cut loose and left to their own soon after the accident.

Unfortunately, in many organizations the trip leaders are cut loose and left to their own soon after the accident. This happened at GCC, for example, as well as at UAA. Almost immediately after each of these incidents, the instructors—who had been employed on a temporary, contractual basis—were dismissed. Kate feels particularly bad for Patrick, one of the instructors in charge in the Deerfield River incident. "The contact with him was over immediately," she says. "I still wonder if he ever received the support he needed."

Although those most directly involved are logically the most seriously affected, other employees (as noted) can be traumatized as well. Neither Kate nor I were trip leaders, for example, yet we both experienced what we consider life-changing events. In our cases, much of the stress came as the result of our interactions with our institutions, and our feelings that we were unable to make a difference in post-incident actions.

The National Institute for Occupational Safety and Health affirms that employees can be significantly and detrimentally affected by a perceived lack of control in their work environments (2005). This is exacerbated if the workers expect to have a say in what's going on around them. Kate and I strongly disagreed with how our institutions responded and felt continually frustrated to be left out of the decision-making process. Consequently, not only were we stressed, but we faced an ongoing dilemma: If we remained with our organizations, we were, in a way, accepting a course we did not believe in. If we left, we assumed a "wrong" course of action was inevitable. Our only hope was to stay and try to make some sort of difference.

Kirk, another program manager who was clearly traumatized, had something of an opposite experience. He did not feel shut off from the decision-making process; instead, he felt as if he were shouldering the organization's grief. "I think I say that because I had to deal with the incident the most intimately over the longest period of time. Others were able to set it aside or at least not have it in their face every day. But every day at work, I faced the 'Sentinel Events' folder on my computer, the ongoing attempts to get information from the coroner, the internal review that couldn't be completed due to a lack of information, the root-cause analyses, the external review that was resisted by the insurance company … the list was endless."

Many service providers become so overwhelmed by the widespread ramifications of a serious incident or fatality that they go out of business. Of the eight providers associated with this chapter, three closed their doors permanently. Although each of these outfitters struggled with lawsuits and finances, their stop-work orders came almost immediately. Mainly, it seems, they succumbed to the pressures brought on by the media, angry family or community members, and the threat of expensive litigation. The interviewees associated with the defunct outfitters noted that though their initial intentions were to learn from the tragedies and move forward, their organizations were unable to survive the stresses of the post-incident process.

Virtually all of the service providers who remained in business were able to learn something from the incidents. Many of the guides and instructors reported feeling a tighter bond with their coworkers in the long run. One interviewee said that the internal and external investigations encouraged her organization to examine specific field practices and staff training procedures which, in turn, helped improve the provider's risk management system.

The Road (and Roadblocks) to Recovery. Once a tragic event has occurred, a normal response is to want things to return to the way they were or, at least, to find a way to "make things better." The "right" path that will lead us to "better," however, is rarely obvious, and the reality is, there often are roadblocks to recovery.

Even though employees need to talk about what happened, lawyers often are concerned that they will say too much. As a result, survivors almost always have their conversations controlled to some extent. Many of the affected professionals do not have adequate built-in support systems. Either they live alone, or they have few close friends, or they are ostracized by their colleagues or the community. In such cases, the healing process can stagnate or be prolonged. Non-affected employees and peers sometimes don't know what to say to survivors. Unfortunately, the silent treatment often is interpreted as judgment—confirmation that the professionals did something bad or shameful—which makes them feel even worse.

How trip leaders or program managers are viewed by others—such as the injured or their communities—also can make a significant difference in their recoveries. This is exemplified by how people respond to natural versus technological disasters. A community tends to pull together following an unexpected natural disaster (such as an earthquake or tsunami). When nature shows its fury and people suffer, victims tend to accept the event as fate or as the will of God, and people usually help and support each other. Technical (or human-made) disasters, on the other hand, are more socially divisive, and attention and energy often are diverted away from helping and directed toward finding fault. In these cases, individuals and organizations may be blamed for their actions regardless of motives. Outdoor accidents often are placed in the latter category.

When we attribute an accident to human acts or omissions rather than to impersonal forces of nature, we are more apt to see those who were hurt as victims and those who did the hurting as perpetrators. Further, psychologist Baumeister has shown that when a victim/perpetrator relationship is assumed, victims (and society members) tend to overestimate the malevolence of the perpetrator. So, depending on how an outdoor incident is interpreted (i.e., as an act of God or caused by negligence) and depending on how a service provider responds to that accident, the employees—who are already feeling shameful—also may be cast as villains. Sadly, the interviewees who had been "villainized" had the most difficulty healing.

Liz had perhaps the best institutional backing of any person interviewed for this chapter. "The support I received from NOLS was fantastic," she says. "The first interaction I had was with two program supervisors who came in by helicopter to help us hike out. They were very clear that even though they were there to assist, I was still in charge, and I could keep as much autonomy as I chose. They provided lots of positive encouragement, kept people busy, and tried to keep us in the routine of our course—at the same time they thought about group closure in the face of Katy's death. I couldn't have asked for anything more. The group came together heroically. We finished the course with a standard barbecue, complete with laughter and hamburgers, and we had a lovely memorial service." Liz is particularly thankful that NOLS's administrators respectfully asked for and included her opinions in risk management decisions after the accident.

Others were not always so fortunate. While Kirk received excellent support from his organization, he also was subjected to "ignorant comments" from other professionals. "It was at least six months after our last fatality, but I was still affected by secondary PTSD. I was sitting on a panel of wilderness risk managers when a colleague made an offhand remark about how some programs 'kill kids.' The intimation was clear: Responsible programs do not experience fatalities. I had a distinctly visceral and angry reaction, but I bit my tongue so as not to seem unprofessional. After all, people had come to learn about accreditation, not to watch programs bicker about fatalities. I think the comment bothered me so much because this person is a professional in the field, and the comment disregarded those who have suffered through this."

"The intimation was clear: Responsible programs do not experience fatalities."

Another key to recovery lies in one's ability to find meaning in the experience. For many of those interviewed, this meant discovering lessons to be learned and coming up with ways to improve their programs or the industry.

"Becoming an active part of the NOLS system," says Liz "was integral in my healing. In my six years of supervising instructors, I have been able to keep the lessons of Katy's death alive." She has done this by sharing her story; helping other instructors become more effective in teaching students about objective hazards; working on their decision-making; and maintaining an active and open dialogue about risk management practices. She says the experience has made her more able to treat trip leaders in a way in which they feel respected, trusted, and pushed to grow.

Laurie Gullion, Kate's colleague at GCC, says, "I speak openly with students and outdoor colleagues about Adam's accident because I think the discussion helps people improve how they can manage kids' programs or train new instructors."

Kate says, "I want to make a difference. I want people who plan, administer, and conduct trips to develop a better understanding of risk. I'm willing to use my experience to help them get there."

By the time the interviews were said and done, a few communal points on the road to healing became clear. Survivors report that talking helps—a lot. Exercise, too, is beneficial. Relaxation and meditation reduce anxieties. Friends and family matter, and survivors appreciate it when people call, write, or e-mail, just to say they care.

When a trauma was more recent, the survivors didn't know what to say when I asked what has helped. Nothing has helped. It was hard for them to imagine that anything good would ever come out of the tragedy. For these individuals, it seemed, time likely would be the greatest healer of all.

INSIGHTS FROM SURVIVORS

The last pages will give readers a sense of how these incidents have changed the survivors. Interviewees also were asked to share learning points that might be useful to others.

The accident on Ptarmigan Peak in Alaska changed my life. Although I continued to work as a program administrator for the university, I did not lead outdoor trips again for six years. The joy of taking others into the outdoors was gone. I became hypervigilant and cynical. I no longer trusted that everything would be okay. In fact, I was scared that even if we (at UAA) created a fantastic new program, something bad would still happen. I felt changed as a human being.

I had to think long and hard about staying in the profession. I had to decide if the benefits outweighed the risks. I questioned my effectiveness as a professional and wondered if I was too paranoid to do a good job. This process took years.

But once I made up my mind that the benefits of outdoor education do indeed outweigh the risks, as great as those risks may be, I was able to commit to my work again in earnest. In the years since, I have become dedicated to helping others develop a greater appreciation for what can happen. I try to help them learn to do everything possible to mitigate risk without eliminating the integrity of the wilderness or the activity.

I wondered if the other survivors had experienced such fundamental changes.

Says one anonymous trip leader, “I miss being really happy. I feel like someone put an anchor around my neck, and I’ve never been able to shake it off. Don’t get me wrong; I love life and play hard. But the innocence (for lack of any other term) is gone. I am more reserved than I used to be. I am less carefree in my day-to-day life. I’m afraid to ask people to go on a trip with me. I'm afraid they will make the connection between who I am and the accident.

"At the same time, I don't think you could find safer people than those who have been through a major incident. I feel like 'we' as a group (accident survivors) have a keener insight and gut feeling that just can't be explained to people who have never had that experience. It's something that no amount of training can prepare you for."

"I don't think you could find safer people than those who have been through a major incident."

"The process of dealing with this fatality," says Liz, "has been repeatedly, to the core, completely and utterly exhausting. On the other hand, I cannot emphasize enough the impact of the goodwill that so many people have extended to me. And interestingly enough, I gained a tremendous amount of confidence from the experience. It was the first time in my life I really needed to work at such a high level from my gut instinct. Successfully responding to the accident and taking care of the remaining 14 students really led me to trust myself. I think the overall experience also played an integral role in my staying at NOLS. It provided a foundation to really believe in and trust what NOLS does on its courses."

Kate says, "Sometimes I have this flash. I look at my son, who is Adam's age, and realize that Adam will never look like that, never be able to do some of the things my son can do. It's very hard to accept that Adam will never have the future he should have had. It makes me realize how fragile life really is. Because of that, I think, I truly appreciate my health, my family's health, and each day that goes by."

Kirk also was deeply affected by a tragedy. And as Kate does, he uses an analogy to describe his experience. But Kirk does not refer to ripples; he compares his trauma to waves. "The entire experience has been like being out at sea. The sadness, grief, and pain of these events come in waves, with peaks and troughs. Initially, the waves are steep, powerful, and close together, so much so that they are overwhelming and you wonder if you can withstand the onslaught. Over time, however, the waves diminish both in size and in frequency until calmness and steadiness prevail.

Kirk adds the ocean itself provided perspective for him. "For me, a powerful healing took place while I was surfing the frigid waters of the Pacific Northwest. As I watched the waves roll in, never changing, I felt at peace for the first time in months. I had an epiphany that my pain was just one little blip in the sea of existence, and I took comfort in knowing that no matter what happened in my life, the waves would continue to come, unceasingly.

"Going through this experience, feeling the depth of it, and surviving it, has strengthened me in effable yet profound ways. I have adopted more of a Buddhist perspective on life and its impermanence. I have also come to firmly believe that whether things are good or bad, 'this too, shall pass.'"

If you had to do it over again and could use what you have learned, what would you do differently?

Kate says, "Without question, I would work more closely with the victims and their families on a human and compassionate level. I'd find out what they need. I'd try to work in a partnership.

"If a program is part of a larger organization, before brochures are put out and programming happens, I would want to make sure I had a conversation with the decision-makers. We'd discuss the benefits, but we'd also discuss the risks [of outdoor and adventure education]. And we'd talk about what will happen in the event of an accident. I'd make sure that my employers know what the industry expects, no matter what the lawyers suggest."

Last, and certainly not least, Kate adds, "If I could tap people on the head, I would want trip leaders to remember that even if the risk is minimal, it's still there, and it can be devastating."

Laurie seconds Kate's thoughts regarding preparation. "It's important for outdoor professionals to educate administrators about their programs, not only by sharing what's written but also by including the higher-ups in different outdoor experiences. It's our responsibility [as outdoor educators] to do a better job of communicating our worth as well as the risks associated with our programs. If those above us better understand how and why we intentionally use risk and challenge, then they will be better able to communicate the value of these programs to the public."

Liz says, "I'd have clearer boundaries. I would be much more effective supervising field staff. I would be more confident. I would not attempt to be everything to everybody. I would be clear about my professional opinion and would feel less threatened by someone disagreeing with it. I would also realize that I wasn't operating alone out there, that I was working to the best of my ability within a given system."

I can relate to what all three had to say. If I could do it over again, I would try to create a better safety net so that, if and when an instructor made a mistake, the consequences would not be so catastrophic. I would push harder for my employer to be more compassionate after an incident. And I would try to educate the institution ahead of time so that it would have a better understanding of what effects a tragedy can have on the participants, their families, the employees, and the organization.

Do you have any final thoughts, or is there anything else you would like to share with the readers?

Kirk's final thoughts come from a passage he found particularly meaningful. It is by Pema Chodron in a book on Buddhism called *When Things Fall Apart: Heart Advice for Difficult Times* (1997). The passage reads: "Only to the extent that we expose ourselves over and over to annihilation can that which is indestructible be found in us."

Kirk says, "In a sense, for a time, I did feel annihilated by the whole experience. I was torn apart by forces larger than myself. Over time, and with lots of help and support, I was able to move out of that barren place. Ultimately, going through it all has left me a stronger person. Do I want to go through it again? Of course not, but like it or not, it has helped shape me into who I am today."

Kate offers, "I do not move through the world in the same way as I did prior to the accident. Early on, my fears crippled me. I think it was that first meeting with the Dzialos that really got to me, that helped me understand the true and potentially tragic consequences that outdoor and adventure education bring. For a while, I questioned the value of risk. But I still believe in adventure education. It can spark confidence in people. It can help people develop a respect for the natural world, even the human world, in a way that is far more powerful than any other type of education I have been involved in. The world has risks we cannot control, but life is still worth living.

"I think maybe Chuck [from Chapter Two] said it best. He said that even after all he had been through, he wasn't going to avoid taking chances. Sometimes things happen. And as awful as those things might be, we can't be afraid of life.

"The world has risks we cannot control. But life is still worth living, and it involves risks still worth taking. We simply need to make the best of whatever comes our way."

Managing the Risks of a Lawsuit

By Charles "Reb" Gregg © 2005

This chapter examines risk management from a legal perspective, with an emphasis on the relationship between an outfitter and its clients. The author describes a variety of pre-trip preparations, in-the-field actions, and post-incident responses that affect the relationship and can either increase or decrease a service provider's exposure to the risk of a lawsuit. Citing examples from the case studies in Chapter One and Chapter Two, the author shows how well-thought-out actions can guide an organization and survivors through even the worst kind of incident to a reasonable, if not uniformly positive, outcome.

The legal lessons to be learned from the Mount McKinley and Deerfield River incidents are stark and predictable. When adventures go bad—and particularly when an accident, injury, or other serious disappointment occurs—the primary factor that determines whether or not a lawsuit is filed and, if so, how it progresses, may not be the accident itself. Instead, it may be the relationship between service provider and participant.

The Mount McKinley and Deerfield River incidents involved serious injuries with quite different outcomes. Together, they provide valuable lessons for understanding the legal implications of the behaviors of outdoor program managers and employees.

This chapter examines three phases of the provider-participant relationship, with an emphasis on the legal implications of actions and events. The relationship is first shaped by early marketing efforts, information exchanges, and pre-trip preparations. In the field, it is influenced by the conduct of the activity, particularly with regard to enlargement of risk. In the event of an injury-causing incident, the relationship depends heavily on the service provider's response, including the type of support it offers, its determination to discover the cause of the accident, and its willingness to share information afterward. Relationships that produce positive outcomes tend to be built on effective two-way communication, a clear understanding of the risks and rewards of the activity, appropriate groundwork, professional standards, and clearly expressed concern for the well-being of all parties. The absence of any of these factors greatly increases the risk of lawsuits and the chance for an outcome that satisfies no one.

A caveat: The opinions expressed in this chapter are based on the events and reports of the Mount McKinley and Deerfield River cases as they are described in this book. Other, even contradictory, facts may exist.

PRE-TRIP PREPARATIONS

Preparing for an outdoor activity involves important work, including identifying the activity's risks, developing a plan or strategy to manage those risks, attracting and informing suitable customers, and establishing a relationship with each participant. The initial contacts between an outfitter and its clients, in fact, provide an early opportunity for the parties to establish relationships that may have to sustain them through difficult times that follow. In the event of a later serious incident or accident, all previous actions can come into play in determining whether or not claims may arise and how aggressively the parties choose to deal with them.

Relationships begin with introductions, as prospective clients become aware of service providers—through reputation, word of mouth, or marketing materials. They develop further through subsequent exchanges of information, including telephone conversations, face-to-face meetings, and whatever additional materials later pass between the parties. This phase usually involves an evaluation of a participant's medical history and any previous recreational experiences that may add to or detract from his or her suitability for the activity. Ideally, all these preparations result in the customer signing some form of a *participant agreement* that includes an acknowledgment that he or she understands, and is prepared for, what lies ahead.

Marketing. An outfitter's history and reputation can be powerful promotional tools. Many participants choose a particular provider largely because they have heard good things about it. Although outfitters cannot control what others say about their programs, those that consistently offer good experiences are likely to favorably impress potential clients. And satisfied clients tell their friends, thereby reaching new candidates for future participation.

Other customers are introduced or drawn to an experience through some form of solicitation that is produced directly by the service provider. With varying degrees of intensity and candor, marketing materials and the exchanges that follow will entice, inform, and finally produce mutual promises, matching the potential participant's desire for an experience with the outfitter's willingness and ability to provide it.

Many lawsuits have been filed by parties who claim the experience was misrepresented in early marketing.

Marketing is an early and effective opportunity to provide information and to develop trust between a service provider and participant. Marketing and promotional materials are designed to excite and tempt, but they also must be accurate and reasonably complete in their description of the experience. Americans have developed a fairly good nose for the "puffing" that typically occurs in marketing, and some exaggeration will be forgiven, even in the description of moderate- to high-risk activities. But it is important not to mislead potential clients about the nature of the activities, the severity of risks, the qualifications for participation, the competency of staff, or any unique issues regarding medical care and remoteness (including access to care and reliability of communication devices). Many lawsuits have been filed by parties who claim the experience was misrepresented in early marketing: They note, for example, that the weather was not as represented in the photographs, the ski slopes were not treeless, the horses were not docile, the instructors were not "the best in the industry," or the activity was not, as the brochure claimed, "safe."

Information Exchange. When the recipient of the marketing effort responds with an application or inquiry, additional follow-up materials are often furnished. These might include information specific to a particular trip or site, physical qualifications and conditioning requirements, gear requirements, issues of weather and terrain, and hazards or risks of the adventure. These materials should be factual, precise, and free of the sort of hyperbole that sometimes accompanies earlier marketing pieces.

The careful service provider also collects relevant information from and about the participants (such as medical conditions, levels of experience, and emergency contacts) and requires some sort of *participant agreement* in which a participant acknowledges and accepts the risks of the activities and forgives the outfitter, in advance, for injuries he or she may suffer. Some organizations also will initiate personal phone calls or other contacts to get to know their clients better and to explore issues previously not addressed, in order to deal with them before the activity begins.

Assumption of Risks. The goal of an information exchange is to educate both the participant and service provider so that each may understand and assume certain risks. The service provider must determine that the customer understands the activity; is competent to participate; and will be prepared emotionally, physically, and with adequate gear to reasonably manage certain risks. Likewise, participants must understand what they will be doing, appreciate the physical and other demands and risks associated with doing it, and acknowledge their own roles in determining their competency to participate and manage those risks.

These understandings are important from both ethical and safety perspectives. As a matter of fairness, participants deserve to be reasonably well informed about what they will encounter. Early information may stimulate questions and clarify the activity and each party's expectations for it. Participants who clearly understand what they are to encounter will be better prepared for events or circumstances that might otherwise be distracting and confusing. Further, an enhanced understanding will greatly improve their ability to manage risks and cope with events in the field. Of course, adequate information may also lead some potential clients to decide that they should not participate at all. But it has been said that if the information regarding an outdoor adventure experience doesn't scare at least some of its readers, it isn't properly written.

The legal implications of the information exchange are based on the concept of a participant's *assumption of risks*. Generally, a service provider has a duty to reasonably manage the risks of an activity. It might not, however, have a duty to protect a participant from risks of which the participant is—or ought to be—aware, or those which, it can be shown, the participant has expressly or impliedly assumed.

Inherent Risks (Primary Assumption of Risks). *Inherent risks* are risks that are so integral to an activity that the community of participants is considered to understand them, whether an individual client does or does not. Inherent risks might include falling from a horse, being thrown from a raft, sudden storms in certain environments, and perhaps certain characteristics of a river bottom. These risks "come with the territory," and in most states, an outfitter has no duty to protect a participant from them. Clients are deemed to understand and accept (assume) them when they participate in the activity—even if they have no direct and personal awareness of them. This is often referred to as *primary assumption of risks*.

Although an outfitter might not have a duty to protect its clients from an activity's inherent risks, it does have a duty not to enlarge the inherent risks—for example, failing to supply a helmet or a personal flotation device in certain circumstances, or spooking a horse by some unreasonable conduct. Such an enlargement can produce a claim of "negligence," which will be discussed in more detail below.

It is better to be generous in the description of risks, including those that are inherent.

One might conclude that since knowledge of inherent risks is generally presumed, there is no need to disclose or discuss them. But failing to do so is both legally risky and ethically unfair. It is better to be generous in the description of risks, including those that are inherent. By doing so, a service provider can argue that 1) an injury was caused by an inherent risk; and 2) the participant understood and expressly assumed the risk, inherent or not. More importantly, disclosure creates trust, confidence, and opportunities for dialogue before the event. The service provider that is frank about potential hazards is more likely to be trusted and respected (and selected) by a potential client than the one that paints an unrealistically carefree picture of the adventure.

Secondary Assumption of Risks. If a judge finds that a loss was not caused by an inherent risk but, rather, by some enlargement of that risk, the judge may compare the carelessness of the person who enlarged the risk with the carelessness of the student or client who chose to participate. The judge may either eliminate or reduce the liability of the person accused of wrongdoing, on the basis of the contribution by the participant (i.e., comparative fault). This is the doctrine of *secondary assumption of risks.*

Expressed Assumption of Risks. The laws of most states protect a service provider from claims arising from injuries caused by risks that are expressly assumed by the participant. An *expressed assumption of risks* is a clearly stated understanding of certain described risks that includes an expression of intent to participate in the activity in spite of those risks. Obviously, a written assumption is more reliable than an oral assumption as evidence in a court of law. Oral agreements have a tendency to be remembered differently by different parties over time. However, in the absence of a written record, the existence of an assumption may be decided by a judge or jury. If it is found to exist, the expressed assumption may eliminate a service provider's duty to protect the participant from those risks.

REVIEW OF THE CASE STUDIES AND PRE-TRIP PREPARATIONS

The Deerfield River exercise and the Mount McKinley climb posed very different hazards and included very different inherent risks. Which risks were greater? The answer is not clear. One might expect the river exercise to be a walk in the park compared to climbing one of the world's most formidable mountains. Yet each activity produced a critical life-threatening event. There is no doubt that the planning, exchange of information, and development of relationships that occurred during the pre-trip phase for these two adventures affected both the outcomes and the attitudes of the victims and their families.

The McKinley story demonstrates responsible attention to informing the client, Chuck, of the activity and its associated risks. It also includes a clearly expressed assumption of those risks on the part of the client. The guiding service (Alaska Denali Guiding, or ADG) took care to ensure that Chuck knew what he was getting into. ADG required that a doctor verify Chuck's physical condition. Its staff recommended a personal fitness program for him to follow as he trained. They also offered reading materials and follow-up phone calls over a period of weeks and months, checking in with Chuck and the other clients frequently to monitor their preparations and answer any questions they might have.

Chuck also did his part well. He carefully researched his trip and selected the guiding service from a number of options, based upon the organization's proven leadership and reputation for managing risks well.

Chuck was a fairly experienced camper, and he gained an even greater understanding of what he would face through conversations with the guiding service and through its Web site, brochures, and reading list. He followed the recommended training program and read the recommended materials. He was able to anticipate what he would experience on the way up the mountain, including the nausea and fatigue of high altitudes, and he believed he was well prepared both physically and mentally for the task. He knew there were certain risks associated with climbing at 20,000 feet, and he accepted those risks as part of the experience.

These steps were effective in preparing Chuck for the hazards and dangers he would face on the mountain, and the pre-trip interactions helped him develop personal relationships with the ADG staff. Those preparations and relationships significantly influenced Chuck's attitude toward the event that produced his injuries and toward the guiding service that he maintains "saved his life."

The Deerfield River case is more problematic. The adventure program run by Greenfield Community College (GCC) promised "five days of fun and excitement" in its marketing materials but included little specific information about hazards or risks. Adam's family appears to have accepted these materials at face value, asking (as far as we know) no further questions and making no particular preparations for the activity.

The Deerfield participants received an equipment list and itinerary, were required to pass a swimming test, and signed a *release of liability* form that identified "foot entrapment and drowning" on its list of risks. But earlier materials had described the day's adventure as a hike, and the revised itinerary listed it only as "river activities." The student-to-staff ratio changed from 6:1 (as promised in the marketing brochure) to 7:1 (as the week's activities unfolded) to 12:1 in the moments before the accident. While each of these circumstances may have seemed reasonable at the time and in isolation, they become more serious when considered together and in the wake of the tragedy.

The activity change was particularly significant from a legal standpoint.

The activity change was particularly significant from a legal standpoint. When GCC changed the activity without modifying its marketing materials or giving the family new information, it rendered these materials misleading, or at least incomplete. The announced activity and the actual activity had different inherent risks, and the switch created a different kind of exposure. Since the river-rescue exercise was neither described nor explained beforehand, the boy's family had no way of knowing what to expect, and no real opportunity to keep Adam from participating. One does not usually expect to swim in moving water. A parent who understood a child to be hiking (or even swimming or canoeing) might have very different expectations than one who expects his or her child to be engaged in a river-rescue exercise, particularly with regard to the risk of foot entrapment.

One cannot know if Adam and his family might have withdrawn from the outing had they known the true nature of the activity. According to the instructors, Adam could have chosen not to participate that day in the field, and some of the boys did in fact opt out. But is a 12-year-old who does not fully understand the risks competent to make such a decision? Does a child that age really comprehend his own mortality? Is he likely to withdraw or express fear or concern in front of his peers? Such issues add to the program's burden of supervision and delivery of reliable information.

The information exchange is no place for subtlety, and the outfitter's challenge is to understand the participant's expectations and level of comprehension and to deliver information accordingly. Even if the early materials did not fully explain the activities, their inherent risks, and possible outcomes, pre-activity talks could have—should have—been used for that purpose. Further, they should have been delivered in an environment that allowed an unwilling participant to withdraw.

In hindsight, it can be argued that Adam and his family were not adequately prepared, physically or emotionally, for the water-rescue activity and its associated risks. The parents reported being surprised (even shocked) to learn—after the injury—of the day's activity, the change in the staff-to-student ratio, and the fact that only one staff member was present at the time of the incident. Clearly, these surprises contributed to the family's concerns about the quality and trustworthiness of the program. When they concluded, fairly or not, many months later, that the Red Cross swimming standards and state licensing requirements applied and had not been followed, their sense of betrayal was deepened even further. Even if it could be shown that these issues did not directly contribute to the accident, they could cause a judge or jury to question the competency of the program managers and staff and could influence decisions regarding fault and damages. In any case, they clearly enlarged the Dzialo family's suspicions and distrust of GCC.

All pre-activity issues, such as the ones described here, can influence a participant's decision to demand compensation for a loss as well as the negotiations and litigation that follow. Participants who feel misled, cheated, or treated as adversaries are understandably more inclined to anger and retribution than those who believe an incident occurred in spite of the service provider's reasonable attempts to manage the risks and prepare the participants for them.

In settlement negotiations or at trial, the legal implications of pre-incident acts and omissions are serious and will be very much in play. Issues of fairness and competency drop dramatically to the bottom line when considering what a service provider might be required to pay—in court or otherwise. A competent plaintiff's attorney will be certain that the jury is aware of those issues.

IN-THE-FIELD ACTIONS

An accident investigation typically begins with a reconstruction of the events that took place in the field. Were there any warnings of impending danger? Should/could the service provider have seen what was coming and somehow avoided it? Did the outfitter in any way enlarge the risks of the activity?

To answer these questions, accident investigators focus on two key elements that contributed to the incident: objective and subjective hazards (discussed more thoroughly in Chapter Seven). Objective hazards include environmental conditions (such as weather, terrain, altitude, and other circumstances of place) and gear issues (such as the appropriateness of personal equipment, safety gear, and any rescue equipment that becomes necessary). Subjective hazards have to do with people: the credentials, training, and experience of the staff; the screening and supervision of participants; participant preparedness and performance; and the ability of both service provider and client to respond appropriately in an emergency. Importantly, subjective hazards also include field decisions, group morale, and other attitudes of the staff and participants.

A primary duty of a service provider is to be reasonably assured that participants are competent to perform the activity in which they are enrolled. Competency is the product of adequate screening, instruction, demonstration, and training. Depending on the complexity of the task and, I would argue, the potential for and severity of an injury or other loss, direct and continuous supervision may be required.

A primary duty of a service provider is to be reasonably assured that participants are competent.

The potential for a severe injury is a measure of *exposure*. The greater the exposure is, the more urgent the need for adequate instruction, demonstration, and supervision. I was told of a ledge on a popular Western climb that includes an intimidating gap nearly five feet across. The ledge leads up to a summit, some 5,000 feet above a valley floor. A mistake in negotiating that gap means almost certain death. By comparison, however, a mistake in negotiating a similar sized gap across a shallow stream on the valley floor might produce only a wet boot. Exposure to harm is the difference, and that exposure mandates precautions in the former situation that would not be necessary in the latter.

Negligence. Both a defense and prosecuting lawyer's accident analysis consider many of the same issues as an accident investigator's, but from a legal perspective. The lawyers will want to determine if the accident was the result of an inherent risk (a sometimes effective first line of defense), if the risk was either impliedly or expressly assumed by the injured party (another effective defense), and if the service provider's actions conformed to standards in the industry or left it open to a potential claim of negligence.

Legally speaking, *negligence* is a wrong committed by one person against another. This "wrong" has four elements: duty, breach of duty, injury, and causation.

1. Duty: The legal obligation to act as a reasonable professional would have acted in the same or similar circumstances. The duty may be altered or modified, as discussed below.

2. Breach of That Duty: A person charged with having acted negligently must have failed in his or her duty not to cause harm to the person making the claim.

3. Injury: There must be harm (in the form of property damage or loss, emotional trauma, other injury, or death) suffered by the person making the claim.

4. Causation: There must be a causal connection between the breach and the injury; that is, as articulated in the laws of many states, the injury would not have occurred "but for" the breach.

A claim of negligence may be effectively defended by showing the absence of any one of these elements. The most effective defenses eliminate or modify the "duty" element.

As was explained earlier, in most states a service provider has no legal duty to protect a participant from an activity's inherent risks. However, if the service provider *enlarges* the inherent risks, it exposes itself to a claim that it has acted negligently. For example, mountain storms are an inherent risk of mountain travel. Ignoring the signs of an incoming storm may be an enlargement of that inherent risk. Drowning is an inherent risk of swimming. Failure to inform or instruct regarding foot entrapment may enlarge that risk.

Duty may also be eliminated by an effective waiver or release. Generally speaking, a participant acknowledges and assumes, impliedly if not otherwise, the inherent risks of the activity in which he or she engages. A participant may expressly assume the risks of an activity (most reliably in writing) and thereby relieve the service provider of an obligation to protect him or her from those risks.

A participant also might decide to participate in an activity in which he knows he will confront risks that exceed those inherent in the activity. The court may then compare the carelessness of the participant's decision to participate with the carelessness of the service provider in creating the unnecessarily (and not inherently) risky situation. The comparison may eliminate or reduce an award of damages to an injured participant.

REVIEW OF THE CASE STUDIES AND IN-THE-FIELD ACTIONS

At first glance, the exposure—that is, the potential for a bad outcome—in the Mount McKinley and Deerfield River examples appears unequal. The risk of injury from a mountain climb in Alaska might seem greater than that posed by a river swim on a summer afternoon in Massachusetts. But on McKinley, the risks were better managed, at least partly because they were better understood by the service providers and participants. The wild card in the Deerfield River exercise was the risk of foot entrapment. Given the activity, plus the volume and height of the water, the participants were exposed to risks with potentially catastrophic outcomes. Unfortunately, it seems these risks were not adequately understood by either party.

In the McKinley case, the most obvious environmental factor was recognition of the incoming weather. An accident investigator might well wonder: Could or should the team leaders have anticipated the approaching storm? Did they ignore important warnings? In this case, the answer seems to be "no." We are told that the guides were aware of the weather and assessed it—and, presumably, the physical condition and performance of their climbers as well—several times during the ascent. They made a calculated and, it appears, professionally defensible, decision to keep climbing.

The guides also appear to have dealt properly with the "warning," such as it was, of worsening conditions. They called for an immediate descent once the wind reached dangerous velocities and the prospect of a serious storm became evident. Their emergency gear was adequate to the task, the guides themselves were qualified, and their reaction to the emergency (including the decision to burrow in, rather than continue the descent) was reasonable. (Note that another climber caught on the summit that day did file suit against his outfitter, claiming deficiencies in gear, staff judgment, and preparation.) The ADG climbers appear to have been well screened and suitably prepared to confront the substantial risks of the climb, and Chuck, at least, appears to have understood them.

Based on this description of events, the McKinley incident does not appear to have been produced by anyone's negligence or oversight. It resulted from an act of nature, a risk that was inherent to the activity and that had been knowingly assumed by the client. It is unlikely that the suddenness and severity of the weather change could have been anticipated and avoided. Once the storm was upon them, the guides acted reasonably to minimize further injury to their participants. In essence, the incident appears to have been properly managed before, during, and after the crisis on the mountain.

The Deerfield River incident can also be attributed to an act of nature, but in this case it is not clear that instruction, supervision, or rescue preparations were adequate, or that either the program or the clients sufficiently understood the hazards and risks of the river activity.

The day of the trip began well. The instructors prepared the boys for the activity ahead of time. They fitted them with appropriate life vests. They gave instructions that conform to common practice. They divided the teens into two manageable groups, and they allowed boys who wished to opt out to do so.

Matters began to break down, however, as the activity got under way. As the full water release arrived, the river rose and the current strengthened. One instructor left the site, and the other continued the exercise without him. As a result, Adam entered the water for his second swim without direct supervision or the benefit of an instructor to remind him of the proper procedures, including the correct floating position and the danger of foot entrapment. The remaining staff person, now responsible for 12 students, remained 200 feet downriver from where Adam entered the water.

Inadequate rescue and recovery often are among the claims made by an injured person.

It could be reasonably argued that the departure of the upstream instructor was a critical event—that the accident might not have happened if a staff person had been directly supervising Adam's preparation for his swim, reminding him to keep his feet up as he began his float. The instructors apparently warned the swimmers to keep their feet up in their initial training, but it is not known how well they explained the reasons for it. In interviews after the accident, none of the other boys appeared to understand the term "foot entrapment" or what had happened to their friend. We will never know if clearer instructions or a longer training period at lower and slower water levels might have better prepared Adam to swim the rapids. In any case, Adam did not assume the correct swimming pose, or lost it in an attempt to stand up, and the result was his serious injury.

Inadequate rescue and recovery often are among the claims made by an injured person or his or her family. When Adam went under the water, the remaining instructor immediately ran to the site and tried to conduct a rescue, but the current kept her from reaching Adam. In fact, several people attempted swimming and wading rescues in the first few minutes, and all attempts were thwarted by the force of the current. It eventually took a concerted effort by several men who happened to be on the scene, using a combination of boats and ropes, to pull Adam from the river.

Did the GCC instructors carry appropriate gear to quickly extract a student from foot entrapment? No. Was there an emergency plan to address that contingency? Apparently not. Foot entrapment was listed on the release document as a risk of water activities, so it might be reasonable to expect that GCC would have a plan for recovery from it. Yet no such plan is evident. In fact, it seems clear that even if both instructors had been present, they would not have been able to rescue Adam without a great deal of help.

The rescue attempts in this case, though heroic, were ultimately inadequate to save Adam from severe injury. The reduced roles played by both instructors at the scene, the lack of suitable rescue gear, and the absence of a strategy for extraction from foot entrapment might be argued as evidence of the program's lack of preparedness for such an emergency.

On the other hand, GCC might assert that foot entrapment is an inherent risk of the activity in which Adam was engaged, and that by virtue of having signed the release form, Adam and/or his parents recognized and explicitly assumed this risk. But as previously noted, when Adam's parents signed the release document, they had no reason to believe that Adam was going to participate in a river-rescue training session, let alone one in swift water.

Since Adam could have chosen not to be a floater, it might be argued that he impliedly, perhaps even negligently, assumed the risks with his own decision to participate. But the family would almost certainly counter with the argument that Adam could not have understood the mysteries of the river bottom without adequate instruction and training. A 12-year-old might be aware that fast moving, moderately deep water poses certain dangers, but it is unlikely that foot entrapment is an issue of which the community generally is aware. The investigator's (Charles Walbridge's) notation that none of the other boys seemed to understand the term is an indication that the hazard had not been adequately described to them by the staff. Could Adam reasonably assume risks of which he was not aware?

The accident investigation found no gear issues that might reflect negligence. Adam was wearing "sneakers" as recommended by the college program, and the investigator concluded that these were appropriate. The family was particularly concerned about the fit of the life jacket, which separated from Adam when rescuers tried to pull him from the entrapment. Although Adam reportedly was small for the jacket he was issued, the staff considered it to be an acceptable fit, and the accident investigator concurred. The fit of the jacket did not appear to affect Adam's ability to stay on top of the water. The investigator concluded that no jacket could have done that, given the force of the current.

The investigation authorized by GCC nonetheless raised predictable questions about the objective and subjective factors that might have contributed to the accident and its outcome. The credentials, training, and experience of the people leading the activity were all called into question, as was the part-time status of the program manager. The site was examined for suitability.

The major contributing environmental hazards were the depth, volume, and velocity of the river—factors that were affected by the timing of the water release. The trip leaders were aware of the release time, and we might assume that they had experiences with the water at different levels. Although investigator Walbridge did not find the site inappropriate, a different fact finder might conclude that the deeper, faster moving water was not properly anticipated and dealt with, and omissions in this regard might have been found to be negligence. Additionally, preliminary training in water safety is best conducted in slow, low water, with students graduating to deeper and faster flows. It does not appear that this occurred.

While noting the possible deficiencies of instruction and supervision, the investigation found no clear case of negligence on the part of GCC. References in the report to "bad luck" and "poor swimming technique" upset the family and made its members feel that Adam himself was being blamed. The investigator's conclusion that "all outdoor activities contain an element of uncontrolled risk" remains, to me, unclear. Recall that an organization has a duty to reasonably manage the risks of an event, but has no liability for an accident produced by an inherent risk. Did the investigator mean that Adam's accident was the result of inherent risks that the college had no duty to control? The family clearly disagreed.

The fact that this was not a scheduled activity, combined with evidence of the inadequacy of instruction and supervision, make it difficult to argue that either Adam or his parents were adequately prepared to assume the risks.

Further, as previously discussed, when a service provider enlarges an activity's inherent risks, and when that enlargement causes an injury, the service provider may be found liable for negligence. The Deerfield River accident presents several points at which it might be argued that the inherent risks of the water-rescue exercise were enlarged, and that the parties responsible for that enlargement—the program and its staff—might have been called upon to defend a claim of negligence.

Whatever sustainable claims the family might have had arising from deficiencies in the conduct of the activity would be influenced by other failings that, whether or not they contributed directly to the accident, frustrated and angered the family and caused it to question the basic quality of the program. This latter category of deficiencies includes changing the activity without notifying the families, increasing the number of participants, and, importantly, as discussed below, inattention to the family and to Adam immediately after the accident.

POST-INCIDENT RESPONSES

A service provider's post-incident conduct may have a greater influence on a participant's decision to sue than the accident itself. Post-incident issues include stabilizing and protecting the participants; transferring injured persons to definitive care; managing relations with injured persons, their families, and the media; investigating the accident; and modifying policies and practices as appropriate. Failures in any of these areas can create or deepen the divide between participant and outfitter, and ultimately can lead to angry, protracted, and expensive litigation.

A service provider's post-incident conduct may have a greater influence on a participant's decision to sue than the accident itself.

As noted in Chapter Four, prudent organizations address key post-incident questions in their emergency action plans (EAPs). Before they take to the field, they will have formulated a serious-incident protocol that considers the following issues: whether or not and how to conduct an investigation; whether or not and how to release internal documents and reports to injured participants or their families; and under what circumstances the organization might settle a matter even if it feels it did nothing wrong.

Obviously, all post-incident responses have legal and financial implications. The lawyer's perspective is likely to be conservative when it comes to allowing an organization's representatives to speak to the media or to "the other side" (i.e., the family). Lawyers may wish to adopt the "hunker down" approach as a matter of policy, fearing that something will be said or done (perhaps expressing sorrow at the family's loss or releasing a potentially unfavorable investigative report) that may affect the defense of the case. Similarly, the insurance company will expect to make the ultimate decisions regarding payment and settlement, since usually it is the insurance company's dollars that are most at risk.

These matters can and should be negotiated as part of EAP discussions and contracts between the organization, lawyer, and insurance provider. The roles each will play in accident response can and should be worked out in advance. This is the best opportunity to thoughtfully develop strategies that take into account the organization's culture and values, its professional reputation, and its commitments to its own staff. Hunkering down may be legally defensible, but how does it affect the organization's relationships with the participant, the participant's family, the media, and the community in which it will continue to operate? As noted elsewhere in this text, the more completely these matters are decided in advance, the more comfortable an organization (and its insurance carrier) will be with its choices, and the better those choices will be executed during a crisis. The hope and expectation are that all players will act instinctively and without question, confident in the strategy they have adopted.

REVIEW OF THE CASE STUDIES AND POST-INCIDENT RESPONSES

The crisis response demonstrated in the Mount McKinley case study was impressive. The guiding service helped facilitate a successful rescue off the mountain, effectively managed the care and support given to Chuck and his family, and maintained an active and positive relationship with Chuck even after he returned home. The ADG staff called Chuck's wife while events on the mountain were still unfolding. The staff informed her about what they knew as soon as they knew it. They met the rescue helicopter at the hospital in Anchorage. They provided a reassuring presence to Chuck and his family from the time of the accident to well after Chuck's recovery from it.

The attention the organization paid to Chuck and his family and the apparently genuine expressions of concern and compassion from staff members contributed to Chuck's attitude, not only toward the incident, but also toward the role of ADG and its guides in that incident. The entire relationship between Chuck and ADG seems to be one of openness, respect, and collaboration to achieve mutually understood goals. The fact that Chuck did not sue ADG may be, in part, attributable to the inherency of the risks encountered and his understanding and assumption of those risks. But it was probably also influenced by the guiding service's professional post-incident management and by the care shown to Chuck and his wife.

Again, the Deerfield River incident is a very different story with a very different outcome. The GCC program representatives were notably absent from the earliest contacts with the family in the hours immediately after the incident. It was the hospital, not a Greenfield employee, that reached the parents and told them about Adam's accident and condition. Although the college president did call and leave a message that evening, no college representative visited the hospital until the following day. And those persons, when they did arrive, came across as guarded in their dealings with the family (according to the boy's father). At that time, according to Mr. Dzialo, the president of GCC said that the college would answer all questions later, when they were ready.

Adam's father believed that the college representatives had all received legal advice to minimize contacts and conversation with the family. When he phoned the program director, he was told she was not supposed to talk with him. The college later took an official position of "no comment" and, in effect, ended its dealings with the family, in spite of earlier assurances of cooperation.

Mr. Dzialo reports that he very much wanted a "partnership" with the president of the college—one that would include conducting an accident investigation, sharing of information, and developing a plan to reduce the chances of such an accident happening again. Yet when the college hired an expert to conduct the accident investigation, the family learned of the appointment from a newspaper report. From this, we can assume that the family was not consulted about the nature of the accident review or the selection of the expert who would conduct it.

The benefits of involving the family in an investigation are clear.

Of course, there is nothing illegal about GCC's refusal to allow the family to participate in the investigation. An organization may, by law, protect an investigation's results from its adversaries. However, it must weigh the relative advantages of excluding the family and withholding the report findings against a more inclusive approach that tends to get the parties to a better ultimate outcome. The benefits of involving the family in an investigation are clear. By doing so, the report becomes, in part, the family's report and becomes very difficult to challenge. If the report reveals wrongdoing, so be it. Inevitably that conclusion, reached by others with arguably equal credentials, will become a part of the case in any event.

Months after the Deerfield River accident, Adam's family learned that the GCC program was operating without a camp license that would have required a Red Cross swimming certification of all participants. The college did not disclose this information to Mr. Dzialo; he discovered it on his own. With that discovery, Adam's father became even more convinced that the college was hiding information from him. GCC defended its actions, explaining that Adam had been required to pass a swim test and that the licensing requirement did not apply because the adventure program did not fall into the "summer camp" category. But in matters of this sort, it is the perception, rather than the reality, that controls the emotions and subsequent conduct of the families involved. In addition to feeling lied to, Adam's father said that he found no display of humanity or kindness in the actions of the college. Whether this is a proper characterization of the attitude of individual employees is beside the point. Perception, not reality, is what drove the actors in this sad drama.

In the end, the Dzialo family found it necessary to file a lawsuit. The timing of the filing, according to Adam's father, was dictated by the impending expiration of the statute of limitations (that period of time, provided by state law, in which a suit must be filed). The filing halted the college's plans to hold a previously planned fund-raising event for Adam and caused the institution to withdraw an invitation to Mr. Dzialo to participate in the presentation of a safety workshop. Obviously, by this time the relationships had become hopelessly adverse.

We will never know if the outcome of the GCC/Dzialo story might have been different if the program's post-accident conduct had reflected the compassion, understanding, and cooperation that Adam's father found lacking. But it is hard to imagine how the relationship between the parties could have been any worse.

By the time this matter was scheduled for trial, it was,

most lawyers would agree, a potentially "bad" case for the college. There was evidence of mistakes by GCC in preparations for the activity, in the conduct of the activity and rescue, and in its response after the accident. The mechanism of injury was not easily explainable. Adam and his family were certain to attract the sympathies of the community and a jury picked from that community. GCC came across as uncooperative after the incident, or at least the school did not reflect the care and compassion a parent would hope for and expect. GCC's lawyers must have recognized the challenges of defending the program under these circumstances. To make matters even more difficult, as noted in Chapter One, the potential for a significant—arguably even adequate—monetary recovery was limited by state law.

Presumably, both sets of lawyers were competent, understood the strengths and weaknesses of their respective cases, and were aware of the limited potential for monetary recovery. Perhaps the college attorneys even regretted that more money was not available to satisfy the family or to at least bring about a dismissal of the lawsuit. Regardless, after acrimonious and expensive trial proceedings and negotiations, GCC found a way to craft a settlement that worked somewhat around these limitations. It would be interesting to know why GCC did not try to seek that accommodation earlier, either on its own or in collaboration with the family.

It could be argued that a "bad" case requires stronger efforts than a "good" case to reach some form of accommodation and resolution that allows the respective parties to get on with their individual and institutional lives. Typically, both sides share a desire to understand what occurred, to reduce the chances of it happening again, to provide adequate compensation where appropriate, and to return to some sense of normalcy. In a bad case, the aggressive pursuit of these issues is absolutely necessary.

Particularly in a case where the facts and applicable law are "bad," other considerations might ultimately outweigh the potential for financial loss. These include the reputation of the person or organization accused of wrongdoing, staff morale, the setting of precedent in the event of future incidents, and the importance of a resolution consistent with the culture of the institution. Generally, the more serious the controversy, the more significant these other issues become.

CONCLUSION

The principal legal lessons to be learned from the Mount McKinley and Deerfield River incidents relate to the ways a service provider's actions can affect future litigation. Pre-trip preparations, in-the-field actions, and crisis response all have powerful effects on the nature of the outfitter-participant relationship. Together, they influence the likelihood, the tone, and the outcome of subsequent legal actions.

As expressed by Phil Dzialo, survivors and their loved ones need, more than anything, to find some meaning in what has happened to them. Meaning begins with information. If information is withheld, the survivors and family members are denied the most important component of the healing process, and anger and frustration almost certainly build. This animosity can often be avoided by establishing a partnership as presented in the Mount McKinley case, in which Chuck and ADG came together to try to achieve mutual goals.

Survivors and their loved ones need, more than anything, to find some meaning in what has happened to them.

The outfitter-participant collaboration begins in the earliest planning stages. It continues into the field and throughout the activity. The relationship of cooperation and trust reaches perhaps its greatest potential in the aftermath of a tragic accident. When the two operate as adversaries, they sow seeds of distrust, anger, and resentment that can continue to haunt them long after the legal "settlements" have been reached. But when service providers and their customers come together as partners at all three stages, they create a foundation that can help them withstand even the most painful of tragedies. An organization best prepares itself for a worst-case scenario by regarding its participants as members of the team—in planning, in risk management, and in finding and sharing the lessons to be learned when an adventure goes bad.

Understanding "How Accidents Happen" in Outdoor Pursuits

By Drew Leemon © 2005

This chapter explores the current state of thinking on how accidents occur in outdoor pursuits. Thoughts and theories on incident causation and decision-making are included. The author also addresses the importance of analyzing and investigating incidents, and uses examples of real events to demonstrate the practical applications of these ideas. The information presented here is intended to help outdoor professionals and managers prevent serious injuries and fatalities, but it can benefit anyone who has an active interest in outdoor activities.

(Updated from Lessons Learned: A Guide to Accident Prevention and Crisis Response [Ajango 2000]. *Drew Leemon and Deb Ajango would like to thank Scott Erickson for his contribution to the original work.)*

At first glance, it seems easy enough to say how an outdoor accident happened. A mountaineer dies after falling down a mountain, a river kayaker drowns in a whitewater rapid, a backpacker breaks his leg descending a steep snow-covered slope. But this level of description is really only a statement of the end result. It tells us *what* happened without really explaining *how* or *why* it happened.

While a fall from a height might be the reason a person died, and a slip might be to blame for his tumble, those facts do not really say much about the story behind the tragedy. What led to the slip? And why did an experienced outdoorsperson fall from the same slope he has successfully negotiated dozens of times before?

The information presented here will answer some of these questions. By studying the thoughts, actions, and decisions of people, and by recognizing the contributing factors that tend to be associated with outdoor mishaps, we can start to better understand how accidents happen in the first place. This chapter also will identify ways in which accident analysis can be used to improve judgment and hopefully reduce the number of future incidents. It is hoped that by the end of the chapter, readers will better understand how and why that "worst-case scenario" ever came to be.

Is It Really an Accident? When we first hear about an accident, we might think that the event was unpredictable. But if we are able to examine and categorize the variables that led to the injury or fatality, we often find that the outcome, though unplanned, was not such a surprise after all. Some people might consider getting struck by a falling tree on a calm clear day while hiking down a trail a true accident. However, trees do fall, and being struck by a falling tree can be viewed as an inherent risk of hiking through forests. In fact, if one walks through an old forest shortly after a windstorm, one should not be surprised to be hit by a falling bough.

The point here is not to suggest that people should "know better." Nor is it to suggest that most accidents are the result of foolish errors. Instead, the point is that the connotations associated with "accident" might lead one to believe that there is little we can do to avoid what is in actuality a potentially preventable outcome.

The word "accident" is commonly used to refer to events that cause injury or harm. A dictionary definition of the word, however, is "unforeseen and unplanned event." In reality, many, if not most, of the so-called accidents that occur in the outdoors are not random. They are in fact foreseeable and can be avoided through the use of control strategies or practices. These controls might include such things as training for leaders, education for students or participants, and activity planning. In other words, an outcome *often* can be modified if one is able to effectively assess hazards, anticipate problems, and identify and use accepted or appropriate practices to address the risks. When viewed in this way, it is possible that events that result in property damage, injury, or perhaps even death are not really accidents at all.

The word “incident” is gaining more acceptance as a term that can be used to describe an unwanted ending. *Webster's* dictionary, for instance, considers an incident an occurrence “that is a separate unit” from the original or intended experience. Given this definition, it seems that “incident” might be a more appropriate word for referring to an unintended outcome that results from a force of nature, an error in judgment, or the inherent risks of an activity.

This type of shift in terminology is beginning to appear in a variety of publications in the safety and risk management realm. The *British Medical Journal* in 2001 made an editorial decision to no longer use the word “accident.” The National Safety Council no longer calls its annual report “Accident Facts.” It is now titled “Injury Facts,” with a category of injuries called unintentional. We also are seeing a change in terms such as automobile *crash* or *collision*, as well as human or system *errors,* to describe these “separate” events or unintended outcomes.

We in the outdoor industry might consider joining this trend and modifying how we think and talk about our unwanted outcomes. Not only would it be worthwhile to admit that many incidents are foreseeable, but it also would be beneficial to recognize and modify or avoid the factors that often contribute to those undesired end results.

Recognizing the Foreseeability of Incidents. Almost every situation in the outdoors contains the potential for an undesired outcome. For instance, when we combine a novice climber who is using unfamiliar equipment with an instructor who has to provide supervision from the end of a 50-meter climbing rope, the chance of something going wrong can be fairly high. While one might not *expect* an injury in this type of situation, the potential for injury should not come as a surprise.

Consider this example as another case in point: A student on a backcountry climbing course took off her climbing harness after she had crossed some third-class (moderately easy) terrain. When she put her harness back on to finish the fifth-class (technical) portion of the climb, she failed to attach the leg loops to the waist belt. A little later, while on a top belay, she fell. She hung for approximately 30 minutes before an instructor could descend to assist her. When the instructor reached her, he noticed the improperly attached harness. Once she was lowered to the ground, he corrected the problem. The student later complained of soreness to her lower front rib cage, but fortunately she was not seriously injured. This seemingly small error could have resulted in damage to her internal organs, asphyxiation, or worse … death.

While the outcome in this scenario certainly was not intended, it was foreseeable.

While the outcome in this scenario certainly was not intended, it was foreseeable. It is not uncommon for climbing students to make mistakes with their equipment—such as not fastening their harnesses correctly, not tying into the climbing rope correctly, or incorrectly clipping into or out of an anchor. A nearby leader might anticipate this and can usually spot these errors and correct them. But when the leader is 150 feet away, the effectiveness of his supervision is reduced significantly. Consequently, the responsibility to prevent or to identify and correct these types of mistakes often falls to the student.

Another example of a foreseeable and undesired outcome occurred on the Clearwater River in Alaska. It was day 71 of a 75-day-long expedition. A group of four students and one instructor decided to wade across the river. They held hands and crossed as a chain. As part of the group reached the swiftest part of the current, one student fell down. Two other students and the instructor also fell into the water, but all three were able to get to the water's edge in no time. The student out front, closest to the shore, scrambled out of the river as well.

The fourth student, the one to first fall, was not so lucky. She could not unfasten her backpack's sternum strap, which she had forgotten to unclip when she unfastened her waist belt before the crossing. As she struggled to get her pack off, she was carried off by the current. She floated sideways facing the opposite bank. She traveled roughly 100 yards, with her head above water, before the instructor and another student were able to help her from the river. Once ashore, the students and instructor warmed themselves by changing clothes and hiking the remaining two miles to camp. Fortunately, other than getting wet and cold, no one was seriously hurt.

Like nearly all incidents, this example illustrates how several elements combine within a sequence of events to produce an unwanted end result. Had the student unbuckled her sternum strap, had the group used a different technique to cross, or had it attempted to cross at a different spot, this incident might never have occurred. And although the outcome was not expected, given the interaction of circumstances, it should not have come as a surprise.

More Than Meets the Eye: The Complexity of Incident Causation. A common model used to help increase our understanding of how incidents happen examines the interplay of two types of contributing factors. The *Dynamics of Accidents Theory* was developed in 1983 by Alan Hale, one of the first people to apply this type of theory to outdoor adventure programming. Hale's theory organizes elements into two broad categories: 1) objective factors, which are the ones we usually cannot control, such as the environment; and 2) subjective factors, which are things we may be able to control, such as our decision-making and actions. These two categories exist separately and at times interact to create what Hale referred to as the *accident potential*.

As illustrated in Figure 7.1, as the interaction between the objective and subjective factors grows, so will the accident potential.

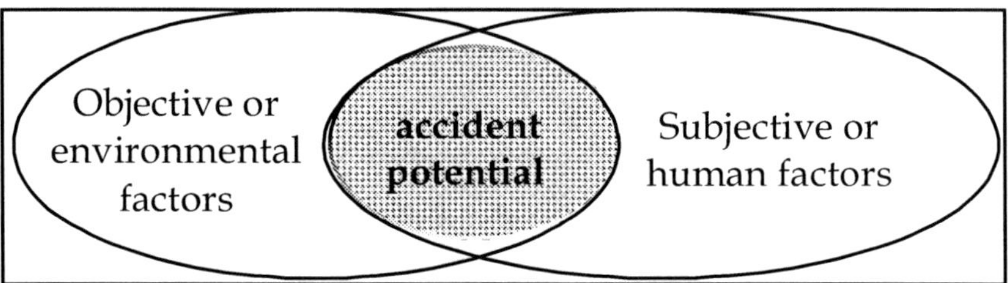

Figure 7.1 *The greatest potential for incidents occurs when objective and subjective factors overlap or interact (adapted from Hale's 1983 work).*

Figure 7.2 shows what the objective and subjective factors associated with the Clearwater River close call might look like. The river was the objective factor, but it certainly did not *cause* what happened. Superficially, one might say that a stumble or fall led to the close call. But the subjective factors, the choices as well as the mistakes that people made, had the greatest effect on the outcome. On closer examination, the following can all be considered contributing factors:

- The group was "heading for the barn." The expedition was almost over, people were thinking of home, and team members were complacent about the seriousness of the crossing.

- The group underestimated the hazard, thinking that the Clearwater River was easy and that the "real" challenge on this route was the McKinley River.

- The fact that the water was clear and the river bottom visible (thus making it "easy" to cross) diminished the hazard in their minds.

- The group had not carefully scouted the crossing site and had not determined if there was another better spot to cross. (The simple act of scouting can heighten one's awareness of, and get group members to focus on, the hazard.)

- Instructor supervision was inadequate. The instructor was conflicted between letting the students make their own decisions and intervening. The instructor was concerned about not being condescending to the students and wanted this to be a learning experience.

This example clearly illustrates what most investigators already know: The true nature of any incident is almost always far more complex than it first appears. In fact, incidents generally involve a combination of environmental conditions as well as human decisions and actions. While a fall might be considered a primary cause of one's injury, on closer look it becomes apparent that a multitude of factors contributed to the outcome. In the end, it is the myriad and overlapping contributing factors that ultimately led to the close call, injury, or death.

The mere presence of subjective and objective factors, one should remember, does not guarantee that an incident will happen. Even in the most extreme situations—such as guiding non-mountaineers on Mount Everest—trips can end with fine results. But when the contributing factors begin to add up and overlap, the potential for an incident increases significantly. In theory, if one takes the same basic set of circumstances and conducts identical scenarios, a change in just one element could lead to a completely different outcome.

Objective Factors	**Subjective Factors**
The depth and current of the river	The actual and perceived physical ability of each group member
The time of day	The group's knowledge of river crossing methods
The type of riverbed (mud, sand, rocks, etc.)	The experience level of the group in crossing rivers of this size and type
Effects on river level: snowmelt/rainfall	The condition of the group: Are people rested, fed, and hydrated? Are they tired, hungry, and cold?
Geography of the watershed	
Presence or absence of bridges either man-made or natural	What are the options? Are there alternatives to crossing the river? Are there alternatives to crossing at this particular spot?
Presence or absence of downstream hazards such as rapids, waterfalls, or sweepers	Is there a basic awareness of the hazard?
Entry and exit points	Communication within the group: Was there a "buddy check" to assess if hip belts were unfastened?
Weather: temperature, precipitation, or wind	Are there impediments to decision-making, such as eagerness to get to camp?

Figure 7.2 *This analysis of the Clearwater River incident breaks down relevant hazards into subjective and objective factors.*

To continue, let's examine the thoughts, actions, and decisions of a second group that finds itself in a similar river-crossing scenario. This time, let's look at how a high school backpacking class with eight students and two leaders might handle the situation.

On the seventh day of a 10-day trip, the backpackers encounter a 30-foot-wide river. The current is four miles per hour, and there is no bridge. Their scheduled pickup is in three days, at a road head 15 miles beyond the river. From an initial unsuccessful attempt to cross, the group learns that the river is at least three feet deep.

It is 2:00 p.m. The group already has hiked seven miles that day. It has been raining for the past three days, but now the rain has ended and the weather seems to be clearing. The leaders knew that they would have to cross this river but did not anticipate it being so deep. The students have had classes on crossing rivers and some practice doing so.

Some students are tired, but others are eager for the challenge. The water will be at least waist deep on the two shortest members of the group. There is a bridge 12 miles downstream. The headwaters of the river are 15 miles upstream, and a significant tributary joins the river two miles upstream.

This situation sets the scene for a potential incident. The degree to which the river presents a danger to the group is related to many variables, including the decisions the leaders or group might make. A simple look at the river, with a goal of crossing it, is not enough to assure success. Instead, if the group expands its perspective and evaluates how to—or even if it should—cross the water, it might discover new, and perhaps better, options. That is, by thinking in terms of objective and subjective hazards, the group potentially can minimize the likelihood for an incident.

In this scenario, the leaders think the group can successfully cross at the present location, but they want to give the tired students time to rest. After discussing the situation with the participants, they decide to camp where they are, watch the water level, and see if it goes down overnight. They will reevaluate and possibly attempt to cross the river in the morning. If the river proves to be too much for the group at that time, then they will hike up to the tributary and attempt to cross what should be two smaller rivers.

If we compare this scenario with the first river-crossing scene, we might ask: What contributed to the differences in decision-making? And why is it that the two scenarios, similar in appearances, ended so differently?

As this example illustrates, by looking beyond the immediate obstacles or hazards, and by carefully evaluating the big picture, one can often discover a better option that allows the risks to be minimized. The leaders in this story understood the objective factors presented by the recent weather; the size, depth, and current of the river; and the topography that showed where the river might be smaller and possibly easier to wade. They also understood their students; some were smaller and possibly weaker than others, and some were tired from hiking in the rain all day. Aware of the accident potential these overlapping factors created, the leaders were able to make a good decision based on all of the facts and their own experience.

The Art and Theory of Decision-Making. As demonstrated through these two scenarios, our ability to make good decisions is often based on our ability to identify and assess all of the aspects of a situation and see the big picture rather than just the immediate challenge facing us. Further, the ability to accurately assess a situation is closely tied to how we perceive the hazards around us.

Typically, people fear the unknown more than they do the known. People also tend to fear gruesome death (e.g., being eaten by a crocodile) more than they fear death from the mundane (e.g., heart disease), even if the latter is the leading cause of death in the United States. People often worry more about dangers that in reality are not that threatening (such as nuclear threats to their community) while overlooking the common ones (such as car crashes). They also are more afraid of hazards that are new (like a terrorist attack), and they become more complacent once a threat, such as smoking cigarettes, becomes familiar.

In other words, one's perception of a risk can influence, rightly or wrongly, one's ability to assess that risk. When people overestimate or underestimate a threat, due to lack of knowledge and/or overfamiliarity, they increase the likelihood of making an error in judgment.

A key in incident prevention involves helping people improve their risk assessment skills.

So a potential key in incident prevention involves helping people improve their risk assessment skills. One's ability to accurately assess risk, and thus make better decisions, can be improved with practice and experience. The skill of risk assessment and decision-making is achieved through education, training, and feedback. And being open to feedback about the decisions one has made is the most important factor in sharpening this skill.

Good leaders contemplate their decisions after all is said and done. Just because a decision led to a positive outcome does not mean it was a good decision. In other words, "luck" can be misinterpreted as good judgment. If the group in Alaska (Clearwater River) made it across the river without incident, for example, it would have received reinforcement that its technique—right or wrong—was appropriate.

In order to better understand how people make decisions, let's look at a few theories on the topic. The ability to reflect on the outcomes of experiences and be open to receiving feedback from decisions fits into what noted psychologist Al Seibert refers to as the "survivor style." Seibert describes the survivor style as "interacting with everyday life in ways that increase the probability of survival when survival is necessary."

People who exhibit the "survivor style" of thinking have three basic characteristics: 1) They can "quickly absorb information about what is happening." 2) They "expect that something can be done to influence events in a way that leads to a good outcome." 3) And they are "willing to consider using any possible action or reaction." They can "rapidly read reality" and adapt to changing situations in their daily lives. When faced with a challenging situation, a survivor subconsciously will use what Seibert calls "open-brainedness" to assess risks and decide how to respond.

In his research, Seibert has studied the personalities and attributes of people who have survived amazingly difficult and trying experiences, such as prisoners of war and people who have been adrift at sea in a life raft. These survivors each exhibited similar traits that helped them get through their respective situations. These traits included curiosity, playfulness, a sense of humor, empathy, and a belief that they were responsible for good outcomes in their lives. A person with this open-brainedness is not limited by preexisting patterns or assumptions. Rather, Seibert found, the person can adapt and be flexible in his or her response or reaction and choose a course of action that best fits the situation.

Survivors often are thrown into abnormal situations without warning. In some cases they are completely out of their element. Wilderness leaders, on the other hand, have (or should have) an expectation that things can go wrong. Further, by remaining open-minded and not assuming that events will progress a certain way, wilderness leaders, like survivors, have the ability to choose a course of action according to each unique situation. Seibert suggests that perhaps the best decision-making method is the one in which a person has "the ability to not impose preexisting patterns on new information, but rather allows new information to reshape [his or her] mental models."

Ian McCammon, an accomplished outdoorsman who has studied the way people make decisions, has applied his research to outdoor settings. He describes four primary decision-making methods that are generally used by wilderness leaders: analysis, heuristics, expertise, and random choice.

The first, *analysis*, involves a logical step-by-step process that is used to sort through all the variables, as well as the "pros and cons" of each, to reach a decision. This is an exhaustive process. If done correctly, it can lead to a good decision. However, it takes time to rationally process all the information, and *all* the information needs to be available at the start of the process. It is useful for group decision-making, especially if the rationale for a decision needs to be explained or justified.

Heuristics are simple rules that each person develops from his or her own experiences. These rules, or learning points, might be obvious (e.g., when it rains, you should put on a raincoat so you don't get wet). But you arrive at this decision quickly, without weighing the pros and cons and without seeking alternatives. Instead, your decision is based on experience: You know that you will be warmer if you stay dry, and you will not have to spend time drying out your clothes.

Heuristic problem-solving also can be complex, however, and it can be applied to specific activities. Domain heuristics, for example, can be taught or learned (e.g., for better balance when downhill skiing, keep your hands in front of your body). Typically it involves knowledge that can help people avoid negative results (such as falling down while skiing at high speed). Heuristics are used frequently in everyday life because they operate at the threshold of our conscious thought. They also lend themselves well to wilderness settings for making decisions when the leader needs to be free to handle other demands.

For example, on a multiple-pitch rock climb, a leader might use the acronym "SERENE" when building a belay anchor. SERENE provides "cues" for constructing and evaluating an anchor. It stands for Solid, Simple, Equalized, Redundant, and Non-Extending. The cue can help a climber assess his anchor while he also is deciding where to stack the ropes, monitoring rock fall hazards, watching the weather, reorganizing gear, checking on the student climber below, and starting a belay.

The third decision-making method is *expertise*. At this level, decisions are made because a person has developed the ability to recognize familiar patterns. This recognition allows the expert to make quick and effective choices. Decisions at the expertise level do not require conscious thought and are often regarded as intuition. A simple example of expertise at play is a whitewater kayaker who is able to make many quick decisions in succession as she descends a rapid. By recognizing the patterns of the waves, rocks, riverbank, and velocity of the water, she can make fine adjustments in body position and paddle strokes for a smooth run through the rapid. Experts always make it look easy—that's because they do not have to think; they can just react.

Random choice may seem like a complete abdication of responsibility for a decision, but it really is a legitimate method to use in some situations. If you do not have the experience or expertise or if all the information is not available to make an informed decision, random choice can be effective. If the consequence of the decision is low, simply taking a guess can be better than long and endless discussion. By taking action you will gain more information and experience.

Each of the four decision-making styles has pitfalls or "traps" where they can fail. For example, analytical decision-making is often time consuming and complex. Also, it is difficult to compare and evaluate all of the variables if/when they are unknown, which is often the case in wilderness settings. Random choice is simply your best guess, so the probability of being wrong is high.

Heuristics and expertise fail when we rely on them in spite of contrary information. In fact, McCammon has identified six heuristic traps: familiarity (because the situation is familiar, we think we are safe), acceptance (we want to be accepted by others whom we respect), consistency (we are determined to be consistent with an earlier decision), expert halo (expecting knowledge of someone in one situation when that person's expertise is in a different situation or skill), scarcity (a goal is more valuable if others are competing for it), and social proof (because others have done it, it must be okay).

The expert can make a mistake if/when she tries to use her expertise where it doesn't quite fit.

The expert can make a mistake if/when she tries to inappropriately use her expertise where it doesn't quite fit. This is called the overconfident expert trap. An example would be if our expert whitewater kayaker assumes that she can use her river paddling expertise to perform a sea kayak surf landing, even if she has never sea kayaked before. Although the situations are somewhat similar, her experience is not applicable enough to apply to the new situation. A variation of this is the expert halo trap. This is when others expect knowledge and expertise of someone in one situation because that person has expertise in a different situation or skill.

Understanding how people make decisions is useful for wilderness leaders since the decisions they make are such an important element in how incidents occur. Understanding the traps of these decision making methods is equally important.

Digging Deeper: Investigating Incidents. A post-incident investigation is a means to unravel the particular sequence of events that led up to an incident. By identifying the sequence, one can reveal possible turning points all along the way, including small changes that might have led to a completely different outcome. Understanding the full complexity of the event also can help reveal countermeasures that might have prevented it or that might have mitigated its consequences. It is reasonable to conclude, therefore, that incident investigations provide a road map for learning how risk management can be improved.

To explore this concept further, let's start with the basics. When we seek to apply the knowledge gained through incident analysis, we tend to look at 1) cause and 2) correlation. Cause, or cause and effect, is the more easily understood of the two. If we kick a loose rock on a mountain, it will fall or roll down the slope. Our kick *caused* it to fall.

If we cause a rock to fall but no one is below us, nothing bad happens. The rock just rolls or bounces, hitting other rocks until the angle of the slope decreases to the point where the rock stops. But what if a hiking partner is 10 feet below? There is now the possibility that the rock will hit her and cause injury.

Correlation seeks to find the more subtle connections between events and requires that we review contributing factors. Rockfall can cause an injury, but not all hikers who are exposed to rockfall get injured. Instead, there are many variables within our control that can reduce or influence the probability of an injury or the correlation between actions and results. If a hiker below the rockfall is astute enough to realize that she is exposed to the hazard, if she is aware that a rock is heading her way, and if she is agile enough to move out of the way of the falling rock while carrying a heavy backpack, then she will not get hit or injured. In fact, each of these factors will affect the probability of her getting hit or injured.

Dan Meyer and Jed Williamson developed a matrix (2003) that allows investigators to analyze the interplay of (i.e., correlation between) objective and subjective factors. Figure 7.2 lists contributing factors that can affect an outcome. But by looking at how the factors interact, Meyer and Williamson suggested that we can improve our understanding of how incidents happen.

The Meyer/Williamson matrix is organized into three main categories (see Figure 7.3). As in the Hale matrix, there is a single category for objective factors; however, the subjective factors in the Meyer/Williamson matrix are separated into two categories—behavioral (acts) and cognitive (thoughts and judgments). Under each of the three categories are more specific, yet still fairly broad, subcategories.

Potentially Unsafe Conditions are the objective or environmental factors that contribute to incidents. Often the factors listed under this category are used to describe what happened, such as "the victim was hit by a falling rock" or "he died of exposure to the weather." While environmental conditions are significant and are often referred to as the cause of an incident, it is important to realize that environmental factors are only hazardous when we put ourselves in a potentially harmful situation in relation to them.

Potentially Unsafe Acts are subjective hazards that represent actions we take. When considered individually, these acts may seem inconsequential. But in a potentially unsafe environment, the combination of seemingly insignificant acts (such as crossing a river while wearing a buckled sternum strap) may in fact contribute significantly to the end result.

Potential Errors in Judgment are subjective hazards that represent the decisions we make that lead to the acts we take. A single prominent judgment error or a combination of minor miscalculations ultimately can lead to an incident.

Our judgment, or the way in which we make decisions, is influenced by our experiences and decision-making traps. Simon Priest, an outdoor educator and researcher, defines judgment as "drawing on past experiences to substitute for current uncertainties." An error in judgment can occur if we draw from incorrect past experiences or if we lack relevant experiences altogether. An error also may occur if we do not

Potentially Unsafe Conditions Due to:	Potentially Unsafe Acts Due to:	Potential Errors in Judgment Due to:
• Falling objects (rocks, etc.) • Inadequate area security • Weather • Equipment/ clothing • Physical/psycho-logical profile • Swift/cold water • Animals/plants	• Inadequate protection • Inadequate instruction • Unauthorized/ improper procedure • Inadequate supervision • Unsafe speed (fast/slow) • Inadequate food/ drink/medications • Poor position	• Desire to please others • Trying to adhere to a schedule • Misperception • New or unexpected situation • Fatigue • Distraction • Miscommunica-tion of participants and/or staff • Disregarding instincts

Figure 7.3 *This chart identifies the principal factors that lead to incidents in outdoor pursuits (Meyer and Williamson 2003).*

fully anticipate all of the uncertainties. Other factors that influence judgment include the emotional state of group members, how well the group communicates, and how the group perceives its abilities.

Unfortunately, potential errors in judgment are often difficult to perceive or predict in ourselves (or our group members). Well-trained and experienced leaders, however, are cognizant of all three of the Meyer/Williamson categories and can consciously think about if or how the subcategories might be influencing their decisions.

The Meyer/Williamson matrix is useful in organizing an incident analysis. By listing all of the factors that contributed to the end result, the investigator can better understand how that undesired result truly came to be. To see how this works, let's apply the matrix to the real world.

Case Study No. 1: Avalanche

At 9:30 a.m. on the fifth day of a 10-day backcountry ski trip in Wyoming, a group of 11 students and two leaders set out to ski three miles to the base of Patterson Peak. They would break trail to what was to become their next campsite, and once there, they would mound snow for snow shelters. They planned to move into this camp the next day.

Willy, one of the leaders, was at the front of the group. Dave, the other leader, was at the back of the line, about 15 to 20 minutes behind. During the morning, as they crossed some flat areas, Dave felt a collapse of the snowpack. He did not think it was indicative of any instability in the snowpack, however, and did not mention it to Willy.

About mid-morning, the group broke out onto a 20-degree NNE-facing open slope. The skiers could see that it extended uphill about 100 feet to a tree band. The slope angle then gradually increased. There were small and large trees located midway up the slope. Above the band of trees, and not immediately obvious to the leaders or anyone else in the group, the slope steepened for about 400 feet as it rose to a cliff band. Willy decided that neither the slope nor the snowpack was a danger. He made a gradual descending traverse across the slope to the valley bottom and the future camp location. The rest of the group followed, arriving about noon.

Willy and Dave discussed whether to return by the route they had come in on or break a different trail back to camp. Willy liked the path they had just traveled. Dave wanted to avoid crossing the same route because he felt it would be difficult for students who would be carrying full packs and pulling sleds (the next day). Plus, there was a slope on that route that Dave thought posed some avalanche danger. These concerns, together with the collapsing snow he felt earlier, made him want to establish an easier route back. The two instructors had a terse conversation about which route to take but failed to reach a decision. For the next hour and a half, they busied themselves making snow shelters.

At about 1:40 p.m., a student, Steve, came to Willy and Dave complaining of pain in his feet. Willy inspected Steve's feet and decided that the group needed to head back to camp. Again, Willy and Dave discussed their route options. Willy felt that using the already broken trail would be more efficient and would allow them to get Steve back to camp more quickly. Dave acquiesced.

Willy started out leading the group back on the existing trail. Dave again brought up the rear. Willy reemphasized to the group what to do in the event of an avalanche: ski downhill, struggle to stay close to the surface, and create an air pocket. Though Willy did, by now, recognize the slope as a possible avalanche hazard, he didn't think it was threatening, and so he didn't establish spotters or have the students ski across one at a time.

When Willy got across, he turned to watch the students. Suddenly he heard a sound (like a crack) from up slope, and looking up, he saw the avalanche. He yelled at the students in the slide path—five of them—to "ski down!" Steve was already out of the way. Denise easily skied out of its path. Frank and Molly skied downhill and to the side, but were caught by the avalanche.

Roger looked at the avalanche and then at Willy. He then waved his arms and yelled. He did not attempt to ski down out of the slide path, even though he was a capable skier. The avalanche caught Roger and carried him downslope. He was on the surface for 20 to 25 feet before he was buried.

When the snow stopped moving, Frank was buried to his chest and Molly was buried to her waist. Willy saw that Frank and Molly were not in imminent danger, and he focused his attention on Roger.

About five or six minutes after the slide ended, Willy located Roger by using an avalanche transceiver. Willy quickly uncovered Roger's face. Roger was buried about three to four feet under the surface. He was completely encased in snow and was not breathing. There was no pulse. Rescue breathing was begun immediately, and chest compressions were started as soon as his chest could be uncovered. The CPR efforts were continued for two hours. Unfortunately, they were unsuccessful.

Late that night, the instructors were able to contact the managers of their organization and inform them of the incident. Roger's body was flown out by helicopter the next morning. The students and instructors skied out that next day as well.

The avalanche path ran NNE. The starting zone was at the base of a limestone cliff. The width of the avalanche was roughly 350 feet; it ran downslope approximately 420 feet. The crown face varied in thickness from one foot to four feet, suggesting that wind had redistributed snow in the starting zone. The bed surface slope angle ranged from 33 to 40 degrees, with an alpha angle of 26 degrees. Roger was the 21st person to cross the slope that day.

An autopsy cited the primary cause of death as suffocation.

INCIDENT ANALYSIS: AVALANCHE, THREE STUDENTS CAUGHT, ONE FATALITY

The Meyer/Williamson matrix is useful for analyzing incidents and offering distinct points of inquiry. An analysis of the above case study, if organized into the Meyer/Williamson matrix, would be as follows:

Potentially unsafe conditions due to 1) falling objects (in this case snow, in the form of an avalanche), 2) inadequate area security (not paying attention to the snowpack history or stability indicators), and 3) physical/psychological profile

The slope was not secured because it was not considered a hazard. The leaders did not recognize how the cliff band above them could affect the stability of the snowpack. They could have avoided the slope entirely and chosen a different route.

Potentially unsafe acts due to 1) improper procedure and 2) poor position

Dave and Willy did not accurately evaluate the stability of the snowpack or fully evaluate the hazard presented by the slope. Instead, they relied on their evaluation of the snow from the snow pits they had dug in another location the day before. Transferring data from a pit dug on one slope on one day to a new slope on a new day is an inadequate method for evaluating a particular slope.

The instructors also ignored important signals. On the previous day, they had noticed two naturally occurring avalanches that had run on northeast-facing slopes. Also, Dave did not fully realize the importance of the "whomping" (the snowpack collapsing) he felt earlier in the day.

It is often difficult to predict with any certainty how someone will behave, no matter how well we think they've been taught.

Position was certainly a contributing factor in this incident as Roger, Molly, and Frank were close together and all three were caught. The leader allowed the students to group up and get into an improper position. Willy took the time to reemphasize the actions to take if there was an avalanche, yet did not instruct the students to cross one at a time.

Roger's actions, once the slide began, also could be considered inappropriate. Though Roger was a capable skier, he reportedly seemed to "freeze in place" when the avalanche began to slide. It is often difficult to predict with any certainty how someone will behave, no matter how well we think they've been taught.

Potential errors in judgment due to 1) misperception, 2) desire to please others, 3) disregarding instinct, 4) distraction, and 5) miscommunication

Since the condition of the slope was not accurately assessed, Willy and Dave misperceived the danger. They also failed to recognize some obvious signs. It was estimated in the post-incident investigation that the slope probably slid every 10 years. There were groups of small trees in the slide path that abutted mature trees. The mature trees had branches broken off on the uphill sides. Further, neither instructor noticed how the slope steepened (to 40 degrees) above them as it rose to the cliff band.

Willy's desire to please the students (by not having them break a new trail back to camp) and to take the easiest route (once Steve's foot condition was discovered) clearly affected his judgment. The condition of Steve's foot became a distraction, contributing to the miscommunication that already existed between Willy and Dave.

Dave's and Willy's communication was poor, and there was tension between them. Their differing evaluations of snow conditions and route choice earlier in the day were not adequately discussed. As a result, Dave's concern about snow-pack stability and another possible avalanche slope were not effectively articulated to Willy. Though Dave, too, failed to recognize the avalanche potential of the slope, it appears he may have disregarded his own instincts about the snowpack.

The Meyer/Williamson analysis matrix will now be applied to the Deerfield River and Mount McKinley incidents, described in Chapters One and Two.

Case Study No. 2: Deerfield River

Potentially unsafe conditions due to 1) Swift/cold water; mainly swift because we do not know the temperature of the water, and it was not cited as a contributing factor. 2) Inadequate area security; by the time Adam entered the river, the "bubble" of water from the dam release had arrived. 3) Equipment; the PFD was the wrong size and was pulled off Adam during the rescue. Although it is doubtful that a properly sized PFD would have kept Adam's head above water in these conditions, it may have helped the rescuers get his head above water earlier.

Potentially unsafe acts due to 1) Inadequate instruction and inadequate supervision; by having one leader for 12 participants, standard group size ratios were exceeded for this type of activity. There was no one to coach/supervise participants as they entered the water. 2) Poor position; since the single leader was positioned downstream, she was not in a position to assist a participant if he encountered difficulty upstream.

Potential errors in judgment due to 1) Desire to please others; continuing with the activity after one leader left rather than calling off the activity or waiting until the other leader returned. 2) Misperception; the leader(s) apparently did not take into account the time of day and when the "bubble" of water would arrive. It seems that the window of opportunity between when the dam release occurred and the bubble arrived at the activity site had closed. Adam's foot entrapment coincided with the arrival of the bubble. It may not have mattered if there were two leaders present once he was caught.

Case Study No. 3: Mount McKinley

Potentially unsafe conditions due to 1) Weather; the severe storm with high winds and snowfall. 2) Altitude; the extreme altitude contributed to the climbers' dehydration and might have contributed to the climbers' cognitive abilities.

Potentially unsafe acts due to 1) Poor position; the group was caught in the storm while on a very exposed part of the mountain. This is due more to chance than to any actual action.

Potential errors in judgment due to 1) Misperception; the building weather conditions were misperceived, but mountain weather is capricious and can change rapidly. The weather is an inherent risk of climbing Mount McKinley. Everyone in the party understood this risk, and they were prepared to handle the weather by having proper equipment and well-trained, strong, and experienced leaders who showed wise judgment in stopping and digging in rather than trying to continue their descent. The leaders in this case are excellent examples of people who possess "survivor style."

Applying analytical tools to real incidents can help us increase our understanding of how an incident occurred. The application of the Meyer/Williamson matrix to these case studies shows the correlation of the contributing factors that led to the incidents. It further demonstrates how a post-incident analysis usually reveals a step-by-step sequence that led to an unfortunate result.

The Role of Human Error in Risk Management Systems. Risk management in the outdoor industry tends to be uniquely complex. We rely on systems that are technical, as in ropes and anchors; cognitive, as in assessment and decision-making; and behavioral, or being able to perform without error. As a result, the potential for minor errors to cascade into significant incidents is great.

The human factor and the role of human error are often the most difficult aspects to accurately document in any sequence of events, but they are typically prominent in the end result. Further, given that the human element comprises the largest portion of an incident equation, it is the most important to understand.

James Reason is a professor of psychology at the University of Manchester in Manchester, England, who has studied human error and its effect on outcomes. Reason acknowledges that incidents, in part, result due to the failures of individuals (i.e., from errors in judgment and/or procedural violations) (1991). But he also believes that incidents result from failures within organizations.

If we look at the Clearwater River incident described earlier, we can better understand Reason's concept. The expedition was part of a wilderness education program designed to teach leadership. This was its organizational arena. The group objectives for the day were twofold: 1) to cross the river to get to camp, and 2) to provide practical leadership experience. The environmental hazard was the river. There were a variety of human errors, including one student's failure to unfasten her sternum strap, the whole group's complacency regarding the hazard, and the leader's decision not to intervene.

An organization should reflect on how it might have contributed to an incident.

From an organizational perspective, the actions of the leader (to remain silent and allow the students to make their own decisions) fell within the parameters established by his employer. Instead of simply evaluating the leader's supervision of the river crossing, it might be more enlightening or appropriate to assess the educational objectives and methods for teaching leadership established by the organization.

Admittedly, a leader can benefit from reflecting on his behaviors and decisions. But an organization also should reflect on how it might have contributed to an incident. Following an analysis of the Clearwater River incident, perhaps the key questions are: Should a leader allow students to learn from their own mistakes? Or should he or she intervene when the wrong decision is being made? This is a paradox faced by many outdoor educators and programs.

Similarly, let's consider the Deerfield River incident. After hearing that a young, inexperienced boy nearly drowned when only one instructor was present, one might conclude that the instructors made an error in judgment by allowing a relatively unskilled group to continue without adequate instruction or supervision. If that was the case, the organization would simply need to fire the instructors to ensure that a similar incident never occurred again. But to truly learn from the experience, it is important to consider how the organization contributed to the end result.

The Greenfield Community College instructors' supervisor and program as a whole knew about and approved the activity. They sanctioned the instructor training regimen. Further, the program, not the instructors, came up with the prerequisites for participants (i.e., age and background). So was it reasonable for the college to think that nothing would ever go wrong? Or should the school have done more to anticipate a worst-case scenario and thus modify the activity or rescue plans? Reason believes, in fact, that both individual error as well as organizational influence should be addressed if one wishes to improve overall risk management within any system (1991).

Reason's theory is premised on the fact that human beings make mistakes. This fact is the foundation upon which all analysis of human error (and the factors that induce human error) rests. Perfect human performance in all situations is simply impossible. What works brilliantly in one set of circumstances may be quite imperfect in another.

Interestingly, when addressing mistakes from an organizational approach, errors are seen as consequences rather than causes. That is, Reason focuses on the conditions in which people work. He also focuses on building defenses that can help avert errors and mitigate their effects. Ultimately, Reason believes, when an incident occurs, it is more important to understand how the defenses failed than to identify who made the mistake.

In his research, Reason has found that errors are not random but fall into patterns that repeat themselves regardless of the people involved (1991). By understanding this concept, astute managers can seek out and change aspects of the system that provoke or allow the mistakes to be made. When an incident occurs, consideration must not only be given to the specific human failure. It also should include an assessment of why that error occurred. Managers who seek to use a risk management "system" approach strive for a comprehensive plan that targets not only the people in the organization, but the task, the workplace, and the organization as a whole.

Some researchers differentiate between task errors (actions) and decision errors (judgment). Others maintain that there is no real difference—they are both examples of people errors. But if we can study and learn to understand how and why people make mistakes, we will stop blaming people for making decision errors. This does not mean that we should accept poor outcomes. In fact, the opposite is true. The discovery of an error should be the beginning of the inquiry rather than the end. The real work is to find out the complete range of factors that resulted in the undesirable outcome.

Organizational Cultures and Their Influence on Risk Management. All organizations develop their own culture, which is reflective of the personalities of the people working in or involved with the organization. The culture can greatly affect the productivity of the organization, both positively and negatively. When an organization is involved with high-risk activities, the culture can greatly affect how risk is managed and incidents are prevented.

Scott Sagan, a professor of political science at Stanford University, studied highly complex systems such as those used in air traffic control. He developed a theory to describe how these systems work. Sagan called this the *High Reliability Theory* and proposed that safety can indeed be achieved through the implementation of appropriate organizational design and management techniques (1995).

Within this theory, Sagan identified four components that can be found in effective and reliable organizations:

1. Leadership Safety Objectives
2. The Need for Redundancy
3. Decentralization, Culture, and Continuity
4. Organizational Learning

Leadership Safety Objectives means that an organization's management and leadership have established safety priorities and emphasize these priorities regularly. By admitting that people make mistakes and by acknowledging that systems can fail, high reliability organizations also accept *The Need for Redundancy*. As a result, they build backups or safety nets into their operations. In an outdoor adventure context, this redundancy might include such things as using multiple instructors per group; making sure each instructor has a common minimum level of training; and creating a safety net (i.e., using backup anchors for climbing, wearing PFDs while paddling, etc.) to guard against human error.

Decentralization, Culture, and Continuity, in an industrial context, means that anyone on the assembly line can stop production when there is a safety concern. In the outdoor context, it means that any on-site leader can exercise his or her judgment and make decisions appropriate to the situation at hand. High-reliability organizations also have a pervasive "culture of safety" that permeates all levels. Each employee embraces the organization's safety priorities and applies them to his or her area. High-reliability organizations also rely on continuity and consistency in their staff trainings.

The fourth component, *Organizational Learning*, simply means that an organization can learn from its experiences and mistakes. This aspect of the theory is quite relevant to this chapter. It suggests that the analysis of incidents can greatly enhance organizational learning.

An organization can learn from its experiences and mistakes.

While Sagan (1995) has identified the ways in which reliable organizations can prevent or limit incidents or their severity, Charles Perrow, in his *Normal Accident Theory*, poses that complex systems inevitably will fail (1984).

Perrow, a sociology professor from Yale University, has studied high-risk and highly complex systems, such as nuclear reactors and petrochemical plants. He believes that, because of the high degree of complexity in these systems, accidents are normal, and though rare, they are going to occur. It is also Perrow's contention that risk factors can be linked in multiple and unpredictable ways. These links create interactive complexity that can defy organizational management. The failure of one part may coincide with the failure of a different (and possibly unexpected) part.

Perrow (1984) suggests that the components of an organization's risk management system can be "tightly coupled" (that is, the linked parts are closely related) or "loosely coupled" (the parts are not directly connected). When tightly coupled components fail, it may be difficult to stop the ensuing and cascading outcome. In fact, when tightly coupled safety components fail, the result often is catastrophic. On the other hand, when loosely coupled components fail, there is more time for intervention, either from another part of the system, or more often from a human, to stop the chain reaction.

On a basic level, Perrow's theory purports that these system characteristics produce normal, inevitable incidents. Additionally, in complex systems, the way in which the characteristics interact is often incomprehensible. As such, the end result may indeed be a true accident.

Applying *Normal Accident Theory* to outdoor incidents can be valuable to the outdoor professional. When we look at the avalanche case study, we see that Steve's sore feet, the "whomping" that Dave heard and felt in the snowpack, and the fact that the two leaders did not recognize the slope as an avalanche slope all were loosely coupled components. Sore feet do not cause avalanches, and while whomping is a sign of snowpack instability, skiers can make decisions to avoid terrain where unstable snow can slide downhill.

The tightly coupled components of this incident were the failure of the two leaders to communicate effectively, the decision to backtrack rather than make a new trail, and the failure to follow standard procedures for crossing avalanche slopes. It is interesting that two of these components were considered, at least by one leader, as appropriate safety measures. Backtracking was going to be a faster way to take care of Steve's sore feet. Willy offered some direction for the possibility of being caught in an avalanche, but he did not follow the practice fully, and he did not have people cross the slope one at a time. Once these tightly coupled variables began to fail, there was little anyone could do to intervene and contain the incident.

Whether one favors Sagan's (1995) or Perrow's (1984) theory, or prefers the Meyer/Williamson matrix, the analysis of incidents can greatly enhance organizational learning. As the data is analyzed, it often reveals patterns, which in turn suggest improvements an organization can make in its programs and practices. By studying its own mistakes (and the mistakes of others), an organization with a strong desire to learn can adjust its routines and activities, thus achieving greater effectiveness and a higher degree of reliability.

Collecting Injury and Incident Data. Within the outdoor industry, there is an ongoing debate about whether or not injury or incident data should be collected. While some people believe the information is useful, others think the practice can expose an organization to legal liability.

According to Reason, "Effective risk management *depends* on establishing a reporting culture" (1991). Without a detailed analysis of mishaps, incidents, near misses, and these 'free lessons,' he goes on to say, "we have no way of uncovering recurrent error traps, or of knowing where the 'edge' is." Reason is so adamant about the practice of collecting incident data that he adds, "The complete absence of such a reporting culture … will lead to disaster."

"The complete absence of [an incident] reporting culture … will lead to disaster."

In fact, injury and incident data can indeed be used to create a statistical database for analysis. It can be used to identify trends and predict future problem areas. The accounts of actual incidents presented here, in fact, illustrate the usefulness of this information exchange.

The incident data presented by the American and Canadian alpine clubs in their annual summary in *Accidents in North American Mountaineering* can be used to identify the primary and contributing causes of climbing incidents. From the collection of reports through the years, one can learn that 59 percent of the incidents occurred on ascent, while 36 percent happened on descent. Five percent were unknown.

Figure 7.4 provides an overview of some other interesting facts. The first list identifies the leading causes of injury, from most frequent to least frequent. The second list identifies contributing causes. The two lists are independent of each other.

PRIMARY CAUSES	CONTRIBUTING CAUSES
Fall or slip on rock	Climbing unroped
Slip on snow or ice	Exceeding abilities
Falling rock or object	Inadequate equipment
Exceeding abilities	Weather
Avalanche	No/inadequate protection

Figure 7.4 *Leading primary and contributing causes of climbing incidents, from* Accidents in North American Mountaineering *(1951 to 1997). The items are listed according to frequency of occurrence.*

Unfortunately, it is often difficult to find incident data specific to certain niche professions, such as outdoor education or outdoor adventure. This typically is due to the fact that there is no single or central reporting agency, nor is there a mandate for programs to report the data.

In an effort to change this situation, the Wilderness Risk Managers Committee (WRMC) initiated a voluntary incident reporting project in 1991. Contributions have been meager, however, apparently due to a hesitancy of programs to make this data public (even though donors would remain confidential), a lack of incentive to report, and the extra workload reporting might add to an organization. In 1999, the Association for Experiential Education (AEE), which offers accreditation services for outdoor and adventure programs, began requiring accredited outfitters to submit data to help support the project. While this latter step has helped boost contributions, the number of programs responding is still low.

Working together, the WRMC and AEE have now published two reports (1998 and 2002) that document the results of the project. A brief summary of the findings is included in Figure 7.5.

AEE/WRMC Injury Profile	1989 to 1997	1998 to 2000
Athletic (sprain/strain)	248	73
Soft tissue: wound/bruise/sting	138	69
Fracture	54	8
Head w/o loss of consciousness	19	8
Dislocations	16	6

Figure 7.5 *The five leading injury types that occurred to participants (from the AEE/WRMC incident reporting project). During the period 1989 to 1997, a total of 534 participant injuries were reported. During the period 1998 to 2000, 20 programs submitted data, and a total of 180 participant injuries were reported.*

Although a list of causes is not included in Figure 7.5, the AEE/WRMC project noted that the leading (primary) cause of reported injuries was falls or slips.

Another organization, the National Outdoor Leadership School (NOLS), has maintained a database of incidents since 1984. Figure 7.6 and Figure 7.7 provide an overview of the data (types of injuries, contributing factors, and activity at time of injury) recorded by NOLS over a four-year period.

It is interesting to note that in each of the sets of data provided here—from *Accidents in North American Mountaineering*, AEE/WRMC, and NOLS—slips and falls were the leading cause of incidents. Further, slips and falls are also near the top of the list for the most common cause of incidents in Outward Bound USA programs (Patton 1992).

Readers might be interested to learn that musculo-skeletal injuries (including strains, sprains, and fractures) are the leading type of injury, followed by soft tissue injury, in all of the above studies. These are also the top two injury types documented in another outdoor profession, the United States fisheries (Ajango, Cullenburg, and Dzugan 2004).

Injury Type	No.	Percent	Contributing Factor	No.	Percent
Athletic	301	49.9	Fall/slip	171	28.2
Soft tissue	186	30.8	Overuse	161	26.7
Head w/ no LOC	23	3.8	Previous history	40	6.6
Fracture	22	3.6	Animal/insect/plant	35	5.8
Dislocation	20	3.3	Stove fire/spilled hot water	24	4.0

Figure 7.6 *Injury profile for the National Outdoor Leadership School (NOLS). This chart identifies the five leading types of injuries and contributing factors of injuries on NOLS courses during the four-year period from September 1, 1998, to August 31, 2002. Athletic and soft tissue injuries combined account for over 80 percent of all injuries during this period. Athletic injuries, which account for 50 percent of all injuries, most commonly include sprains and strains of knees (35 percent), ankles (30 percent), and backs (13 percent).*

Activity at Time of Injury	No.	Percent of All Injuries
Hike with pack	278	46.1
In camp	103	17.1
Hike with no pack	33	5.5
Mountaineering	29	4.8
River—all types	25	4.1

Figure 7.7 *Profile of the five leading activities that resulted in injuries for the National Outdoor Leadership School.*

By gathering data such as this, organizations no longer need to rely on anecdotal accounts and myths. Instead, risk managers can focus on known and documented problem areas. Organizations, as well as outdoor leaders, can develop a better understanding of which types of incidents and injuries are most common, and in turn, they can modify trainings, education, or policies accordingly.

The Importance of Tracking Close Calls. Incidents that result in serious injury or death often receive the greatest amount of attention, both within an organization and from the media. Another very important type of incident that should be monitored, however, is the close call (sometimes referred to as a near miss). The story of the Clearwater River crossing at the beginning of this chapter is an example of a close-call incident.

While close calls and minor incidents are certainly not as concerning as fatalities, they should not be taken lightly.

A close call is a dangerous situation in which safety was compromised but no injury resulted. It is a situation in which those involved expressed relief when the event ended without harm. It is not a situation that involved a routine slip, trip, or fall, where there was little chance for serious injury.

Near-miss incidents often are predictors of future incidents. Cathy Haddock, an outdoor educator from New Zealand, researched studies of industrial incidents and found that "for each serious injury or fatality, there were 10 minor injuries, 30 cases of property damage, and 600 incidents with no visible injury or damage" (1999). In other words, while close calls and minor incidents are certainly not as concerning as fatalities, they should not be taken lightly. In fact, if an organization is able to recognize where, when, and why the close calls and minor incidents are occurring, and it makes appropriate modifications, it might be able to prevent the fatality down the road.

Post-Incident Challenges. Following a serious incident, there is often an urge—sometimes driven by public pressure—to "do something" immediately. Unfortunately, rarely are knee-jerk responses and quick implementation of significant changes good moves.

An incident, particularly one with serious injuries or fatalities, tends to create a high-stress situation. The pressure to act hastily is all too often based on preliminary speculation and incomplete information. Unfortunately, quick action can lead to overreaction, with demands for more rules, regulations, and restrictions that ultimately may be unnecessary or overly redundant.

Additionally, sometimes legal action is brought against an organization following a serious incident. While the organization has an obligation to protect its financial stability, as other authors have noted throughout this book, it also must consider the needs of the injured parties (and their families), and it should think about how it wants to be perceived by the affected parties as well as the public. Because this issue is addressed elsewhere in this book, it will not be addressed further here.

> We should always focus on saving lives rather than saving jobs.

Exactly what an organization decides to share or do post-incident is not the essential issue. What is most important is to remember that when politics interferes with organizational learning, we lose out on valuable lessons. The fear of admitting possible mistakes and exposing a program to possible legal action inhibits outdoor leaders and our profession from improving. It is only through careful examination and the open sharing of information that we can learn from our experiences and advance the potential that future incidents can be prevented.

We should always focus on saving lives rather than saving jobs.

Is Anyone to Blame? An undeniable aspect of human nature seems to be in our desire to identify responsible parties whenever a serious injury or fatality occurs. By focusing on the actions of individuals or organizations, we are able to place blame on their failures. But, throughout this chapter, we have seen that incidents are rarely the result of a single event or cause—such as instructor incompetence or disregard for another's welfare. Instead, the people involved in the incidents—generally good people who truly care for their students and clients—simply do not see the entire picture as it unfolds. Their decisions are based on the continually changing and often subjective information they have at the time. It is only in hindsight that their decisions appear to be so obviously flawed.

Although incident analysis can prove beneficial, it can become counterproductive if the goal is merely to find fault. According to Reason, identifying the "cause" of an incident serves no purpose unless some preventative action is taken (1991). The ultimate outcome following any investigation should not be to assign blame, but to reduce the potential for future incidents. We need to be less concerned with who made a mistake and more concerned with how the controls—which are intended to prevent an incident—failed.

So the question remains: Is it truly possible to learn a lesson when someone is hurt or killed? The answer depends on whom you ask. What is certain is that, given the subjective and ever-changing nature of our work, achieving perfection is impossible. Risks from hazards can be moderated or hazards can be avoided altogether, but at what cost? Eliminating the risk completely means eliminating the benefits that come from participating in outdoor and adventure education.

While we might never reach our learning potential, we can acknowledge that incidents will always exist. And we can do our best to reduce their numbers and severity. The lessons we can garner from the study of incident data and from investigations, while not a substitute for actual experience, can be very useful to outdoor leaders and managers, and the subsequent discussions are important and necessary if outdoor leaders and organizations are to improve.

The Loss of Leadership in the Outdoor Industry

By Blaine Smith © 2005

Chapter Eight is authored by a guide/educator who has more than 20 years' experience leading trips. Blaine Smith, the lead guide in Chapter Two, Chuck's Story, identifies how the outdoor industry has changed over the past two decades. He also offers insight into how this transformation has created significant challenges for field staff and program managers. While he acknowledges that some of the current trends appear to be working against the industry, he ends the chapter by offering a number of ideas for enhancing the quality and professionalism of today's aspiring leaders.

The bad weather arrived quickly, and it came when we were the most exposed and vulnerable. We had just summitted North America's tallest peak, Mount McKinley. As we reached the top, the sky began to change from blue to gray; by the time we were able to reorganize and start our descent, we could barely stand against the wind.

We were a group of seven, and I was in charge. We were hours away from the safety of our tents. It was minus 30 degrees Fahrenheit, and we couldn't see farther than five or six paces in the blowing snow. It was apparent that we couldn't continue to travel in those conditions; the chance of something going wrong was simply too great. I knew it would be tough to try to "camp" for the night, but I made the call anyway. It was time to dig in.

The snow was rock hard and offered very little opportunity for building a shelter; yet, somehow three of us managed to cobble together a small igloo for the rest of the team. Our survival gear gave us a fighting chance, but the fragility of the situation was apparent to everyone. We were scared, and later I learned that some of the men thought that they might not live through the storm. Despite the odds, the clients retained their composure, looked to me for guidance, and followed instructions. The next day, we were able to descend to our high camp. We were battered, but we had survived.

What does it mean to be a leader, and just how do leaders come to be?

Looking back on that night—what it took to endure that storm—I marvel at the team's dynamics. What, I wonder, had transpired over the previous three weeks to transform us from a group of strangers into a team, able to take such a licking? And what had I done to create such trust in me?

As I reflect on that experience, I also consider my past, my training, and my growth as an outdoor professional. Although I was climbing and guiding 20 years ago, I'm not sure that I could have led a group of beginners through such a storm and survived back then. I can't help but ask: Where and how did I develop my skills and judgment, and at what point did I become a *leader*? On McKinley, we all knew who was in charge, but not because I strutted around announcing my place on the team. Instead, everyone simply had a confident acceptance of my role. The incident has led me to question, not only for myself, but for others as well: What does it mean to be a leader, and just how do leaders come to be?

Without a doubt, the outdoor industry has gone through a transformation of sorts. More and more people—often quite inexperienced people—are venturing into the hills and woods. Competition among companies trying to solicit these potential customers is fierce. To meet the demands, there is a growing need for qualified trip leaders. At the same time, the demands placed on outdoor instructors and young guides are even greater than they used to be.

Before, all that was required to get a foot in the door was a positive attitude and a strong back. Today's newly hired guides and instructors are expected to be skilled in a variety of activities, to have a list of certificates, to attend annual trainings, and to remain calm in a crisis—all for slightly more than minimum wage. There is little room for error, especially in the current legal climate. But mistakes are part of learning, and it seems unreasonable to expect perfection from anyone—particularly from those who are still learning a trade.

I have no doubt that the outdoor industry as a whole is more professional today than it was two decades ago. But while leaders are expected to grow their list of talents, they also are losing the ability to be experts in any given area. As a result, a leader today is a "jack of all trades, master of none." And as such, I have serious concerns about the status and future of the industry. Do today's guides/instructors really have the knowledge, skill, and judgment to keep their groups out of trouble? And if/when trouble strikes, do they have the ability to get their groups home, safe and sound?

A leader today is a "jack of all trades, master of none."

THE EFFECTS OF A CHANGING WORLD

The Changing Client Profile. In the early 1980s, it was a given that before people would even consider climbing Mount McKinley, they would first spend several years ascending peaks of lesser stature and gaining valuable personal experience. If they hadn't quite mastered certain skills, then they would hire a guide. Those early McKinley "clients," consequently, had solid backgrounds and generally knew what to expect. They knew that they would be cold and uncomfortable at times. They knew that they would be expected to carry heavy packs. Their understanding of mountaineering had likely disabused them of any notions of a risk-free adventure, and they knew that there were no guarantees of success or safety.

Most of today's McKinley clients are much different. Despite a blizzard of information that exists on how to prepare for a high-altitude ascent, it isn't uncommon for customers to be surprised by the most basic things. I've heard them say in disbelief, "You mean I have to carry a share of the group gear? But it's so heavy!" They are curious as to why they need to learn glacier travel and crevasse rescue. "I thought that's what guides are for." I even know of one gentleman who couldn't believe he would be sleeping on snow throughout the entire trip.

Of course, not all current clients are so ill-prepared or misinformed, but good organizations must be careful to minimize assumptions—their own as well as those of their customers. They should not, for example, function as if today's participants mirror those of yesteryear. They should learn as much about their participants as possible, and if they find that the client profile has changed, then they should modify their marketing and/or practices accordingly.

The changes in the client profile affect not only the outfitters, but they also affect how trip leaders do their jobs. Not only are today's guides expected to lead their customers through unfamiliar environments and activities, but they are expected to be "teachers" as well. They are expected to help their customers know what they're getting themselves into, and they are expected to help novices recognize hazards that can hurt or kill them. Today's trip leaders must help clients understand what is meant by *remote* wilderness, even though the participants' interpretation of the term might evoke images of northern county parks in their home states. Today's instructors also are expected to be effective communicators and skilled listeners. They must recognize nonverbal cues that indicate a client's fear and confusion, so that when they see either one in a team member, they can patiently explain the directions a second time.

If these changes in client backgrounds and expectations had happened overnight, they inevitably would have been noticed. But shifts occur slowly, one client at a time. And it is only in hindsight that reality becomes so obvious.

The Effects of a Changing Society. Over the past 20 years, Americans seem to have become more averse to taking risks. No one wore bike helmets when I was a kid. Seat belts in cars were available, but wearing them certainly wasn't required. Today's media insists that smoke detectors, avalanche beacons, satellite-based roadside assistance plans, and cell phones in the backcountry should be required, and people who don't use them are foolish. The manufacturers claim that their products can virtually erase the risks that our society has faced for generations.

At the same time, there is something of an explosion in *extreme* sports, and athletes who are willing to take extreme risks are held in high esteem. Young adults admire these role models and seek out activities that provide similar adventure and stimulation. In essence, they go out of their way to find the same risk our society has so efficiently tried to protect them from.

So which reality is closer to the truth? Probably both. According to recent studies, the human brain is not fully developed until age 25, and the area that remains "under construction" in the late teens and early 20s has to do with judgment and decision-making—attributes that can affect one's risk tolerance and tendency to engage in risky behaviors. This group of young adults, not surprisingly, tends to make up a significant portion of the outdoor industry's clientele, as well as its guides and trip leaders. People in their 30s, 40s, and 50s, on the other hand, seem to gravitate toward more tame activities. Their priorities have changed, and they are willing to take fewer chances over time.

Gerald Wilde, in his *Risk Homeostasis Theory* (1997), proposes that people do not wish to eliminate risk from their lives at all. Instead, he suggests that everyone has a certain tolerance for risk (which is described in more detail in Chapter Nine). When an environment or activity seems too stressful, a person will try to find a way to reduce the risk. If the risk seems low, however, the person might actually engage in riskier behaviors simply to keep things at the status quo. In other words, as program managers try to make activities safer through improved equipment and techniques, our young, risk-tolerant clients counter with behaviors that are ever more extreme.

While some people enjoy the perception of risk, the average Joe appears to be less willing than ever to get hurt.

Does this incongruence influence today's customer? I believe so. Increasingly, today's clients expect a big show, but many of them (or their parents) have little tolerance for true danger. That is, while some people enjoy the perception of risk, the average Joe appears to be less willing than ever to get hurt.

Further, the majority of today's visitors seem more interested in "trying out" the outdoors than in reaching competency. They seem to embrace an instant gratification concept supported by a number of media outlets: "I want it now, and I don't want to have to work too hard for it." Consequently, true wilderness is such a foreign environment to this group that they are not capable of caring for themselves when conditions become challenging. Plus, they are surprised when nature cannot be contained.

To truly eliminate injuries in the outdoor industry, we would need to replace current activities with simulated ones. Maybe we should simply have customers sit in a mounted raft, surrounded by large-screen movies showing the shoreline pass by. We could splash a bit of water on them as the boat seems to plunge through the rapids. A ridiculous idea, perhaps, but certainly more plausible—and safer—than when I was a boy.

I admit there is value in providing a safer environment in which to live, but risk in life can never be eliminated, and risk in the outdoors is part of the game. Unfortunately, many of today's clients seem to assume that their guides will keep them *safe*. In the end, when the best-laid plans go awry, there likely will be a need to blame.

The Changing Look of Service Providers. As today's general public seeks stimulation, adventure, and novelty, more businesses than ever offer a wide variety of experiences to meet everyone's needs. And in order for today's outfitters to survive and compete, they sometimes expand their menus of available services. Companies that once offered backpacking-only trips now offer multifaceted packages through which clients can enjoy canyoneering, rappelling, and canoeing, all within the same week. Cruise ship passengers can enjoy onboard sport climbing as well as a dozen onshore excursions. Transportable climbing walls show up at parks and state fairs. Even scouting groups, once known for their traditional merit badge options, now embrace adventure sports. No longer satisfied with the overnight campout, scouts climb, scuba dive, and sail without hesitation.

What does this mean for the outdoor industry as a whole? I believe it reinforces the delusion that one can have it all: the adventure of a lifetime with little effort or risk, at a price that many members of our affluent society can afford. When outdoor organizations choose or feel compelled to increase risk in order to stay in business, however, they are treading on very thin ice. Not only are these providers allowing students and clients to engage in potentially dangerous activities, but they often are employing less-than-stellar leaders to keep these thrill-seeking novices from getting hurt.

The Face of Reality. In the end, the mix looks volatile: Clients and students in search of adventure are looking for sexy-but-safe thrills. They expect a great time and will hold the guide or guiding organization responsible if something goes wrong. Service providers are giving in to their demands in order to stay in business, but managers around the country complain of a shortage of qualified leaders. Consequently, outfitters employ whomever they can get, maybe provide a bit of training, and hope for the best. And while supervisors recognize the precariousness of the situation, most are at a loss when it comes to solutions. They would love to snap their fingers and find a magic fix. Instead, they cross their fingers and say to their employees, "Give 'em a great show, but please don't let them get hurt."

How can anybody possibly make it work? Although it's hard to change the desires and expectations of the clientele, we certainly can work to modify their expectations so that they are more realistic. We can do this by educating potential customers and helping them understand the real risks associated with adventure and outdoor activities. We also can work harder to be fair and honest in our literature and marketing, and to avoid unrealistic promises.

And although we might prefer to simply hire instructors who have extensive personal experience and are wonderfully qualified, the reality is that there are not enough of these dream leaders to go around. The following advice cannot be used in place of the benefits provided by quality field experiences coupled with a solid education, but it might help outdoor managers in their quest to create the competent outdoor leader.

ATTRIBUTES OF A QUALITY LEADER

Given the number of outdoor education classes available these days, much of an aspiring leader's learning comes from structured experiences in which he or she makes pseudo-decisions under the watchful eye of a paid instructor. If/when the weather gets bad or challenges arise, the instructor can coach the students so that they do not have to "learn the hard way." Even the month-long or semester-long courses offer only a few days of "student-led expedition" in which the leaders-to-be actually experience success or failure.

These structured experiences often are so positive that a small number of participants subsequently choose to devote their lives to the profession. With minimal field days under their belts, they are promoted to paid positions through which they can, in turn, introduce others to this wonderful thing called wilderness.

These new guides/instructors are eager to reap the satisfaction that comes with leadership and being top dog, but the same individuals have yet to learn the vital skills required of their positions. It doesn't seem to bother them that only last month, or maybe last year, they were students themselves. They have been able to learn theories and the technical skills associated with the activity, and they are naive enough to believe that they are ready to make important, sometimes life and death, decisions. Unfortunately, unless these leaders-in-training are allowed to practice and test their decision-making skills under real conditions and learn from their experiences, it is doubtful that they will be able to rely on good judgment when it is needed most.

It is *imperative* that employers articulate very clearly what they expect from their employees.

Many people in the outdoor industry have offered inventories of what are considered "core competencies" for wilderness guides. Entire books have been devoted to the topic. While lists like these certainly are helpful, there is something about leadership that cannot be easily categorized or measured. Further, while I believe that it is important for employers to be familiar with the core competencies of leadership, it is *imperative* that they articulate very clearly what they expect from their employees. They must role model the types of behaviors they wish to see, and they must help guide and mentor these aspiring leaders.

The "Right" Attitude. When I first started guiding, I encountered many situations that were new to me. My confidence was sometimes lacking when I was required to think on the fly. I would often mask my insecurities with a bold and emphatic attitude. As I gained experience and became more comfortable in the role of leader, my style became much less controlling and more inclusive. I was more open to the opinions and ideas of others. I began to see my job as not so much "the guy out front," but more as the "builder of the team."

Guides and instructors should learn early on that even though they are in charge, they are not the most important members of the team. Instead, a good leader will assume the attitude of a good coach. All team members should be encouraged to reach their highest potentials. The more it can be engineered so that the younger guides and the students feel responsible for their own progress, so much the better. Not only can this help improve team performance, but when all group members become engaged in safety (rather than following the leader), everyone wins.

The ultimate leader is confident yet humble. His or her confidence should come from experience and a solid knowledge base that grows over time. Humility evolves from the same things. Admittedly, no one likes to be wrong or look foolish. But a good leader is able to admit mistakes as well as acknowledge weaknesses. Fortunately, when one has the right attitude, it isn't that hard. I have found that the more I know, the more comfortable I have become admitting, "I really don't know."

Compassion. It is often easy to recognize passion in an employee. Passion is a zest or love for the job that is contagious. When new employees love to climb, for example, they tend to exude enthusiasm for their work. But passion is not the same as compassion. The bottom line is that teaching and guiding are people businesses. To be successful, potential leaders must care about people.

What does it mean to care about people? It means being concerned for the physical and emotional well-being of others.

It means being able to put oneself in the clients' shoes, to be sensitive to their needs, and to reduce their physical or emotional stress as much as possible. It means remembering what it was like to be a beginner.

Being a good leader requires the ability to make people feel important. Good leaders know the clients' names by the end of their first session. They also try to learn what is important to each team member. What are the names of their spouses and children? What do they do, and where have they been? What are their goals for the trip, and what are their concerns? In order to lead effectively, one must have the trust of one's followers. A big part of this trust is gained when the students feel that the leader has their best interests in mind and knows and cares about them.

Stressful situations can expose the worst in anyone. And the stress of a new outdoor adventure can change an annoying client into an unbearable one. So what should a leader do when a client is acting inappropriately, if not belligerently?

A friend of mine told me of an encounter that provides a good case in point. She was leading a group, including an esteemed doctor, through Pittock Pass in the Ruth Amphitheater of the Alaska Range. The area is glaciated, and large blocks of ice (that had fallen from above) littered the narrow route. Halfway to the pass, the doctor sat down on one of the chunks of ice and refused to budge. Although my friend warned him of the dangers of stopping at that spot, he told her that he was tired and needed a break. My friend then pointed to an ice scarp directly above them that could easily avalanche at any time. According to my friend, the doctor began pouting like a child and whining about how he only wanted to rest there for a minute. My friend had to resort to being a mother. She didn't want to humiliate him in front of others, but she was forced to scold him until he got the message that there were bigger issues to be aware of than his personal discomfort or desires.

When students or clients exhibit inappropriate behaviors, it takes real mental discipline to tolerate and sometimes address their unlikable traits. But a good leader must do whatever it takes to motivate the clients and protect group members. Although some people might be draining, a quality leader does not allow them to bring down the team. Most students can contribute on some level or in some way, and it is up to the leader to bring that out in everyone. Failing that, a good leader makes sure expectations of acceptable behavior are crystal clear and takes steps to assure that participants know that their well-being is the primary objective.

Communication Skills. I once had a discussion with an ocean kayak guide who told me how he had prepared his group to complete a two-mile, open-water crossing. He had the team of relative beginners stand in a circle and asked whether or not they were comfortable with what they were about to do. He made eye contact with each, and he gave participants a brief time to respond. No one expressed any doubts.

Halfway into the crossing, two kayaks capsized. No one was injured, but the students were wet and cold. The instructor seemed to shrug it off, as if saying, "no harm, no foul."

Later, two students complained to the instructor's supervisor that they had been quite scared prior to capsizing. They added that they did not believe they were given the opportunity to voice their fears. The leader was stunned. He felt that he had been blindsided, and he was angry that the students hadn't been more honest with him.

During the debriefing, it was discovered that several of the students had felt stifled and unable to express themselves throughout the trip. Due to the instructor's brash disposition and gung-ho attitude, they claimed that they never felt safe to voice their concerns. The instructor, on the other hand, assumed that each student was confident enough to speak freely in front of the group at any given time.

As everyone knows, communication is far more than what a person says through words. Instead, good communication, integral in leadership, involves effectively sharing as well as receiving messages. Good leaders remember that their "lingo" and field habits have become second nature to them due to their experiences. As a result, good leaders do not make assumptions that their customers understand their language. Instead, they cover all bases, check for understanding, and modify methodologies if/when the message is not getting through.

Good communication includes being a good listener. In order to receive a message, a good listener should be able to assess all communication—verbal or nonverbal—that is occurring. A good listener is able to read body language and understand that crossed arms, silence, or short tempers might indicate fear or distress. It's not that stress is all bad. But clients who are too stressed often focus more on their fears than on directions or warnings. Although many organizations recognize the importance of watching out for stressed clients, few teach how to do so in staff trainings.

A good leader creates an atmosphere in which it is acceptable for students and colleagues to express themselves. As part of a pre-trip briefing, good leaders empower their colleagues and clients to be partners in the quest for group safety. As a trip leader, I do what I can to practice this philosophy. "Ask me any question concerning our activities," I'll say. "If I can't explain why this is a good thing to do, then we probably shouldn't be doing it." I let clients know that there may be times when we need to do a task quickly to limit our exposure to a hazard, but I am always careful to identify those times beforehand so that everyone is prepared. I also let all of the students know that each and every one of them has the power to say "stop" if something doesn't look or feel right or needs further explanation.

To make sure clients are comfortable sharing their fears, I am careful to check in on people outside the "whole group setting." I visit them in their tents or talk to them individually, out of earshot of their teammates.

Other times, instead of asking people face to face about what frightens them, I ask generic questions that apply to everyone. I might ask, "Can anyone tell me what could go wrong with our open-water crossing today?" By couching the question this way, not only can I get them to voice their concerns, but they are validated in front of the group. If someone brings up a potential problem, I follow up by asking, "And what would be the best thing to do if that happened?" In this way, I can get the whole group to participate, share, and learn.

Quality leaders learn to anticipate the "next move."

Finally, I have become confident enough in what I do that I am willing to poke fun at myself. Humor and self-deprecation can make a leader "real" to his or her students, and that's a trait that I certainly admire in others.

Initiative and Foresight. Quality leaders learn to anticipate the "next move." When their teams arrive at the campsite, they have checklists in their heads. They know that the tents need to be set up, kitchen areas need to be established, latrines need to be built, and water needs to be secured before nightfall. They know, too, that though a break would be nice, trying to complete the chores in the dark while tired would add unnecessary risk to the day.

Good leaders learn to modify their plans as an outing progresses. They realize that, due to changing snow, water, or weather conditions, Plan A might no longer work. They continually watch the group for fatigue or errors, and they are willing to move to Plan B, even if it angers the more driven participants.

Perhaps most importantly, good leaders learn to recognize the beginnings of difficult if not dangerous situations before it is too late. Over time, they develop the ability to anticipate "foreseeable" events and student errors (which is addressed again later in the chapter).

Physical and Mental Toughness. A good leader sometimes can be referred to as a "rock," or someone who can withstand even the toughest conditions. A good leader is fit for the activity, not just to the minimums, but to a degree that enables him or her, and hence the group, to have an adequate margin of safety in a bad situation.

Physically, trips and classes should not be overly taxing for those in charge. If leaders are exhausted when they arrive in camp, they are less able to deal with contingencies that could endanger the group.

In the past, some of the younger guides considered it a point of pride to show up for an outing after a poor night's sleep, maybe dehydrated, sometimes hungover. These folks confused having the ability to perform under these conditions with toughness. While I used to think this type of behavior was somewhat humorous, I now consider it foolish.

As I grow older, I no longer have the wide latitude to use or abuse my body and expect an endless reservoir of strength. I am more militant about making myself eat and drink on a regular schedule. I get as much sleep as possible. It is too bad it has taken me so long to change my behaviors. Not only would it have saved some wear and tear on my body, but it would have increased my margin of safety as well.

Finally, what cannot be changed must be endured, and good leaders endure discomfort without complaint. Whining, in leaders especially, is contagious. It also is destructive to group morale. If a particular job needs to get done, it doesn't matter how many mosquitoes are feasting or how cold it is: Good leaders attend to business.

Punctuality and Organization. A guide I worked with a few years ago used to have problems getting his act together, particularly in the morning. He was incredibly disorganized.

His tent site always looked like a garage sale with gear and clothing scattered hither and thither. Consequently, for the first two hours of the day, he was of little help to the clients or to me. Thankfully, after some coaching, he improved to the point where he was worth his pay.

Organization and punctuality are linked, and both are essential qualities in a good leader. Punctuality equates to professional attention to detail, and the quality is reassuring for novices who are headed into a new environment or situation. Being a bit early also will go a long way toward keeping the boss happy, and conversely, guides/instructors will earn little respect from their colleagues or clients if they sleep late while others are up, prepping for the day. Punctuality includes maintaining a schedule in the field, and it's a quality aspiring leaders should emulate.

Leaders need to be organized in their personal lives as well as in a group setting, and one can't happen without the other. Being personally organized sets an example for the clients to follow, and keeping equipment organized is the "safe" thing to do. Imagine trying to find a shovel during a blizzard, searching for a throw bag after a client has been swept downstream, or chasing after loose items blown from a tent that came apart in the wind. Leaders should know where key items are at all times, and they should be diligent in attending to details.

Group or time management is a form of organization. Not only can leaders improve their time management by planning ahead, but clients and students are more comfortable if they know what the future holds. They will perform better if they have a clear goal in mind or know how much time will be devoted toward a task. In order for leaders to provide this information, they first must have a map in their own minds.

Social Etiquette and Good Grooming. When I graduated from high school, I thought that I had left the world of vulgarity and coarse jokes behind. I was wrong. Unfortunately, when people—clients and trip leaders alike—leave their structured social lives behind to enjoy a wilderness experience, they often leave societal norms and etiquette behind as well. The wilderness, it seems, can bring out the "wildness" in almost anyone.

Good trip leaders address issues of social etiquette head on. People from all walks of life seek out wilderness to enjoy themselves, and they hire a guide or an instructor to enhance the experience. Good leaders role model appropriate language and behaviors and make sure that their colleagues and customers do the same. I have never read an evaluation in which clients complained of clean language, but I have heard from clients who were hurt, disappointed, or offended by vulgarity and inappropriate jokes.

Good trip leaders address issues of social etiquette head on.

I have learned that bad first impressions take extensive time to correct. People will assume that the way the leaders present themselves physically is a reflection of how seriously they take their jobs. Good leaders take pride in their professional appearance and maintain high standards even in the field. Not only does this show that we are at home in the environment (reassuring for the clients), but it also sets an example of cleanliness, which is an important quality in maintaining group health in the field.

TECHNICAL COMPETENCY REQUIREMENTS

While the personality characteristics described here are important, without technical competency, an outdoor professional might find the task of leading others not only difficult, but dangerous. The following text is not a detailed checklist of the types of skills and certificates every outdoor leader should have or obtain, but it does provide an overview of the kinds of generic technical competencies that outdoor leaders should possess if they hope to effectively teach or lead adventure activities.

Solid Technical Skills. Obviously, trip leaders need to have solid hard skills applicable to their activities. But what does it mean to have solid technical skills, and just how competent must a leader be? Do rock climbing instructors need to be competent climbing 5.12 routes if they are only expected to teach in 5.7 terrain? Do raft guides need to be able to row all classes of water if they are to take participants down a Class II river? Not at all.

A leader should be able to facilitate an activity on auto-pilot.

To be considered solid, a leader should be able to facilitate an activity on auto-pilot. When the activity—or the basic skills and equipment associated with that activity—is second nature, the leader can focus nearly all of his or her attention on the students'/clients' behaviors and interactions, the environment, and/or the changing weather.

In fact, most leaders actually are quite competent in the technical skills needed to do an activity. Field skills are often easy—and fun—to learn as well as to teach, and progress is easy to see. Consequently, it seems that many organizations devote considerable time to teaching or reviewing the technical skills that are part of the activity.

Without a doubt, it is important for a leader to have solid technical skills. But because of the nature of the industry, good teaching and communication skills are as, if not more, important. Program managers would be wise to remember this. They should spend time helping their employees learn how to teach and how to communicate with the students so that problems can be prevented in the first place.

Emergency Preparedness. A program audited by my wife conducted a top-rope climbing and rappelling class. The instructors had fairly strong climbing, belaying, and rappelling skills, and could teach these with ease. But when asked what they would do if a student froze midway up a climb or was injured on descent, these same instructors struggled. They were not prepared to keep a foreseeable problem from becoming an emergency.

Beginning students make mistakes. Sometimes they do things they've been instructed not to do. In fact, it sometimes seems as if they're out to kill themselves. The only way to respond quickly to an emergency is to have a plan thought out ahead of time.

Emergency preparedness means being able to deal with the unexpected. An instructor might be quite skilled at setting up and running a rappel; however, he or she also should be able to quickly and efficiently respond if/when a student gets clothing or hair caught in the rappel device and/or jams a prussik.

To be prepared for an emergency, a good leader needs to consider all of the "what ifs" that might occur during an activity. In order to help leaders hone this skill, supervisors might consider playing a "what if" game with their employees. Trip leaders could do the same with the students prior to or during an outing. Not only might this leader-student interaction help make sure that the instructor isn't missing anything, but it could help the students learn how to look out for dangers as well.

A good leader does everything possible to avoid situations in which a foreseeable mistake could lead to disaster. For example, imagine asking a group of novices to traverse a steep snow slope above a cliff band without putting in running protection or placing a fixed line for safety. Even if the students learned how to use ice axes, it would be inappropriate to put them in a position in which their own safety would be dependent on their ability to achieve an effective self-arrest. While this scenario might be acceptable for a skilled group of professionals, it is inexcusable for almost any team of beginners—no matter how short the exposure to danger might be.

Good leaders carry appropriate emergency equipment and know how to use it. I am not sure that we would have survived the storm on McKinley if we hadn't been carrying ours. Although few other teams (at the time) carried heavy steel shovels or snow saws to the summit (they claimed that the weight would slow them down), those tools probably saved our lives. Sure, it was inconvenient to carry extra food, a thermos, and sleeping bags, but as it turned out, we needed every extra bit of help we could muster. Even though we were not able to use everything we carried (some of it froze or blew away), a number of the items were invaluable.

Because leaders rarely use or practice emergency rescue and emergency skills in the field, they need to engage in continuing education in town or back at base camp so that they can polish their skills in realistic scenarios on an ongoing basis. Annual rescue trainings and refreshers can increase the chances that trip leaders will perform appropriately if and when an incident occurs.

Medical Training. Twenty years ago, it was acceptable for trip leaders with little to no medical training to take groups into the field. Outfitters that did require training asked that their guides obtain certifications in first aid and CPR. The few Emergency Medical Technicians (EMTs) who worked in the field were highly prized. Specialized training in wilderness medicine was only beginning to come into being.

Wilderness medical training differs from its urban counterpart in five basic ways. First, instruction in urban-based courses encourages the rescuer to "call 911" in any potentially serious situation. The focus is on getting the patient off the scene as soon as possible, and the primary goal is to place the patient in a qualified medical facility within minutes of the injury. Wilderness medicine, on the other hand, presumes that the ambulance (or transport) is hours to days away. This is a very real possibility when an injury occurs in the backcountry and when someone may well have to walk miles to summon help or the patient may have to be laboriously carried out.

Second, urban medicine touches upon a wide variety of emergencies but focuses on accidents or illnesses that tend to occur in town. Wilderness medicine spotlights the types of emergencies most commonly faced in the outdoors. The latter not only addresses athletic and tissue injuries (which are most common), but it also covers treatment of environmental injuries and illnesses from exposure to cold, heat, and high altitude, as well as from toxic plants and animals.

Today, wilderness medicine training is an accepted standard of the outdoor industry.

Third, by necessity, wilderness medicine courses address evacuation decision-making and the basics of rescue and transport in backcountry settings. None of this information or training is part of the traditional urban course.

Fourth, in a backcountry emergency, caregivers must consider *potential* problems that can transpire in the hours or even days it might take to get the patient to help. In urban courses, there is an expectation that the patient will get to a hospital quickly, and even EMTs often lack the ability to anticipate the challenges associated with weather and temperature, delayed transport, and/or the lack of resources.

And fifth, in wilderness medicine, participants are taught to improvise equipment. Because backpackers rarely carry enough medical supplies to effectively deal with serious trauma in a nonurban setting, it is important that they understand the design of standard medical equipment such as splints or backboards—so that they can create workable versions of these items from materials they might find in the field.

Today, wilderness medicine training is an accepted standard of the outdoor industry. While there is no consensus on which certifications are best for various classifications of employees, there seems to be growing agreement that the following are minimums: If and when an organization conducts an activity in an environment in which it would take one hour or more to get a patient to definitive care (i.e., a hospital or medical clinic), at least one on-site employee should be trained in Wilderness First Aid (typically 16 to 20 hours in length). If a program works in a *remote* environment in which a patient might not reach definitive care (or be handed off to appropriate rescue personnel) for four to six hours or more, at least one on-site staff member should have a current Wilderness First Responder certificate (72 to 80 hours or more) or Wilderness Emergency Medical Technician training (which takes 150 hours to complete).

INTANGIBLE NECESSITIES

Learning to Assess and Manage Risk for Others. I received an uncomfortable lesson about managing risks for others early in my career. I was working with a group of beginning students in the Chugach Mountains on a winter weekend. We had to break trail through 24 inches of newly fallen snow to get to camp. Shortly after setting up our tents, the wind began to blow. By the time the sun went down, the wind was howling.

The next morning dawned clear and comfortably warm. The wind was finally still after blowing throughout the night, and the students were a bit tired from having to get up repeatedly to patch their wind walls and dig out their tents. We decided to dedicate the day to avalanche hazard observation rather than climb. The ridges were scoured and barren, which meant we would have easy access to teaching spots above snow-loaded terrain. The avalanche conditions were prime, and I knew that a single step onto a loaded slope could certainly produce a large, long-running slide. Consequently, we proceeded carefully.

The following day, we decided to attempt a summit climb. An additional eight inches of new snow had evenly blanketed the area and obscured the route. The visibility was poor and the lighting was flat. Despite the accumulating hazards, I felt I could avoid danger and weave through the terrain.

As the students and I reached some of the steeper and more exposed slopes, I felt increasingly uncomfortable. Stopping the class on a lower-angled pitch, I climbed ahead to explore the route and assess the hazard. I looked around in the nearly whiteout conditions and, feeling less than confident about the situation, decided to return to the students.

As I approached the group, we all heard a loud crack. The snowpack high above us had collapsed, and an avalanche was rumbling straight toward the class. It stopped before it hit anyone, halted by the low angle of the runout slope where we were standing. I can clearly recall the shock I felt as the snow slid toward the students. I was amazed not so much by the avalanche, but by my inability to accurately assess the risk for the group. They had trusted me with their lives, and I was ashamed to have placed them in such danger.

After almost 20 years, that experience still haunts me. All the components for an accident were in place. I was an instructor new to managing groups in hazardous terrain. I lacked the ability to see and avoid the hazard. The students deferred to my supposedly better judgment. And we were all blindly excited about achieving our summit goal. A more experienced leader could have seen an accident in those circumstances a mile away. I had to learn the hard way.

People with extensive personal field experience have more than likely learned to manage risk for themselves. That is, they are able to assess their own strengths and weaknesses. And because they are quite familiar with their own (and perhaps their close friends') abilities, they can look at a situation and accurately evaluate the likelihood of success or failure.

Good leaders, on the other hand, also can assess and manage risk for others. Good leaders not only are familiar with the objective hazards associated with the environment and the activity, but they also are familiar with the most common human errors that instructors and students tend to make. Good leaders know what injuries typically are associated with the activity, and they know how to assess and manage the potential for those injuries occurring.

Good leaders look through "instructor eyeballs." They might ask themselves, for instance, where the best place would be to observe the exercise and give instruction as necessary. Good leaders imagine possible problems that could occur and think about what they would need to do to prevent or fix them.

Accidents have trails. Unfortunately, the trails often are noticeable only in hindsight. Good instructors look for the accident trails as they are being created; i.e., they learn to identify those seemingly minor events that individually seem harmless but in combination with other hazards can potentially lead to misfortune. Good leaders fix or mitigate those events and get off the trail before it is too late. The trail for my close call included an instructor who thought he was smarter than he really was. Thank goodness no one was hurt.

Learning to Anticipate Beginner Errors. My wife recently worked as a consultant for a college outdoor program. During one of the field outings, she observed a beginner rappel into a canyon. By placing herself directly across the slot from where the student descended, she could see that if he maintained his current route, midway down, he would reach a slight overhang and would no longer be in balance. Although the student attempted to move toward the fall line and away from the overhang, the instructor (who was standing above the student and was unaware of the depression in the rock) encouraged him to stay on his route so that he would remain in sight.

Recognizing what was about to occur, my wife called a colleague over to watch. My wife predicted that as soon as the boy reached the depression, he would lose his footing and pendulum into a nearby rock wall. In order to protect himself from getting hurt, he would raise his hands before hitting the wall and would let go of the rope. She also considered it likely that, since he was large and not wearing a chest harness, he would flip upside down. Seconds later, the scene played out, just as predicted. My wife knew the student would be okay because he was on a second belay line, but for a short time, chaos reigned.

When my wife and the instructor debriefed the situation, he could not identify anything he had done wrong. Instead, he seemed pleased that he had thought to include a backup belay. He was quite surprised when she explained that the close call was actually foreseeable.

Learning to assess and manage risk for others is not an innate ability. In fact, it often takes considerable time and experience to develop. Before a leader can predict and avoid accidents, he or she likely needs to spend time teaching beginners. My wife does not have ESP, but she has spent an awful lot of time in the field, teaching beginning students and learning from their mistakes.

Learning to assess and manage risk for others is not an innate ability.

Good leaders learn which skills students or clients will have trouble with—an ability that also takes time to develop. Good leaders not only are able to predict where mistakes will most likely be made, but they can conduct an exercise so that students learn from their errors without getting hurt.

Good leaders are seldom surprised by a student's actions or errors. Because they have seen so much, have been teaching so long, have heard so many stories, and/or have such a good grasp of what might occur, they are prepared to deal with whatever comes their way.

Learning to Teach and Assess. I remember so well standing next to a fellow student on a glacier in Alaska many years ago. The instructor commanded us to set up a crevasse rescue system. The student turned to me, appalled. She said, "Do *you* remember that stuff? We learned it weeks ago! I didn't think we'd have to *remember* it." It obviously had not registered that we were learning these skills for a reason.

Most students who go through the American educational system are not good at applying information. They are expected to memorize, take tests, and then replace last week's information with "new" material from the current lesson. But application of material is essential for safe wilderness travel.

Guides and trip leaders often are expected to get participants to perform new skills. They also are expected to know when participants are ready for greater challenges, and they need to make sure that they do not expose participants to certain risks before they are ready. In other words, today's leaders need to be *teachers*, even if "teacher" is not part of their job description.

Just because job applicants can *do* a skill does not mean that they can *teach* it, and program managers should not assume that applicants with strong technical backgrounds are skilled in teaching or assessing students. Instead, any leader who is expected to take on these responsibilities should be trained accordingly. If a supervisor does not have the expertise to provide mentorship in this area, he or she might consider enrolling in a train-the-trainer class for educators. Or perhaps he or she could bring in a teacher from a local school district to provide some tips.

Good teachers are familiar with a variety of presentation methodologies and learning styles, and they know how to sequence activities so that fundamental skills are taught and mastered before students move on to more advanced techniques. Further, good teachers are not satisfied with a student's single proper performance. Instead, they understand the importance of repetition and kinesthetic memorization. As soon as a student appears to have mastered a skill, good teachers will ask him or her to demonstrate it and explain it to someone who hasn't reached competency.

Rather than simply answering students' inquiries, good teachers help students find the answers on their own by asking provocative questions. Good teachers also make sure that new skills and knowledge are applicable to real-life situations beyond the textbook. They might even try to set up a scenario in which significant consequences ride on the successful performance of the new skill.

In outdoor education, it is especially important that a teacher is able to accurately assess the students' skill levels, their understanding of the material, and their decision-making abilities. In fact, good teachers find ways to assess students on an individual basis. If/when students are simply herded through an activity, like cattle through a gate, accurate assessment will be nearly impossible. Yet, if student testing is not conducted properly, it is much more likely that participants will be allowed to attempt advanced skills (or make decisions) before they are adequately prepared.

SUPPORTING BEGINNING OR NEW LEADERS

I recently read a book by Atul Gawande called *Complications: A Surgeon's Notes on an Imperfect Science* (2002). Although the author offered some interesting chapters on medical mysteries, what I found most fascinating was his discussion on *learning to lead*, or, in his terms, what it takes to become a lead surgeon. Although outdoor leaders are not asked to make life and death decisions nearly as often as surgeons, I found several similarities between the professions. For example, both industries are required to take *students* and somehow turn them into *quality professionals*, able to make quality decisions, without hurting anyone in the process.

As I read along, it dawned on me that many of the techniques used by the medical profession to enhance the progress of beginning surgeons (laid out in the next section) are similar to the techniques used to tutor leaders in the outdoor industry. I realized, too, that the outdoor industry could likely learn from the medical profession—from its successes as well as its failures.

The Importance of Practice. Many studies of elite performers have tried to identify what, specifically, separates them from their counterparts. The biggest difference, researchers note, is the amount of deliberate practice they have had. In fact, it seems that one's willingness to engage in sustained training and practice, even when one doesn't feel like doing so, is essential. As noted earlier, it is important that leaders are able to put certain tasks on autopilot. And although we tend to want perfection without practice, trip leaders need to practice fundamental skills to the point that correct performance has become a habit.

> One's willingness to engage in sustained training and practice, even when one doesn't feel like doing so, is essential.

Not only is it important for leaders to refresh fundamental skills on an ongoing basis, but they also should be willing to spend significant time learning new skills. If, for example, a program purchases new avalanche beacons, program managers should ensure that trip leaders are given significant hands-on training with the tools. It is not enough that the leaders know *how* to use the equipment; they should be *adept* at using it, and practice will help them get there.

Consider the following case in point: In *Complications*, Gawande referred to a Harvard Business School report that studied learning curves among surgeons (2002). It followed 18 cardiac surgeons and their teams as they learned a new medical (cardiac) technique, and the findings assessed how well the teams did. While each team was given the same amount of time to practice, the researchers found that *how* the surgeons and teams practiced made the greatest impact on their progress.

Although the surgeon on the fastest-learning team actually was quite inexperienced when compared to his slower counterparts, he made sure to pick team members with whom he had worked before. He also made sure to keep them together through the first 15 cases before allowing any new members to join the team. He had the team perform a dry-run practice before conducting an actual surgery, and he scheduled multiple surgeries the first week so that little could be forgotten in between. He also conducted briefings prior to each surgery, and the team discussed how things went afterward. He made sure the results were tracked carefully.

The leader of a second team, on the other hand, chose his team members almost randomly and did not keep them together at length. In the first seven cases, in fact, he selected different members each time. The surgeon conducted no briefings or debriefings, and progress was not tracked.

In the end, the first surgeon's team was able to learn and become proficient in the new technique nearly twice as fast as the latter surgeon and his team.

One should not be surprised by these results. Not only does practice help, but the more deliberate we are in how we train, how we track progress, and how we reflect on results, the better our learning will be over time.

Minimizing Skill Diversity. As noted previously, a key to perfecting performance lies in repetition. That is, when a person performs a narrow set of procedures over and over again, he or she can become a specialist in that area. The medical profession provides plenty of evidence that true specialists make fewer errors than the generically trained practitioners who attempt to perform the same skills. Perhaps the outdoor industry should take note of this fact.

Today's outdoor leaders, on the other hand, are often expected to be skilled in a number of disciplines. Johnny is no longer simply a good skier and snowboarder who has training in backcountry travel; today Johnny is also a whitewater raft guide, an international traveler, a rock climber, and a survival specialist. But can we realistically expect Johnny to be an expert at all of these? If we look at how other industries train their "experts," I am tempted to say no. While Johnny might be pretty good in many areas, chances are, he will be an expert in few to none.

According to Lucian Leape, a Harvard surgeon who has studied errors in medicine, "A defining trait of experts is that they move more and more problem-solving into an automatic mode" (Leape, Berwick, and Bates 2002). With repetition, he adds, a lot of mental functions become automatic and effortless, much like driving a car. Novel situations, however, usually require conscious thought, and unique solutions are slower to develop, more difficult to execute, and more likely to be wrong. Outdoor program managers should beware: The Harvard Business School study found one other interesting tidbit (Gawande 2002). No matter how accomplished an expert was in a given skill area, when introduced to a new skill, his or her competency (as well as pride) suffered before it got better.

This is called an implementation gap. One of the key reasons why people do not want to learn new things is because they will be worse before they will be better. For some people, the thought of ineptitude, of looking foolish in front of peers, is unbearable.

When we ask our outdoor leaders to be everything to everyone—that is, to be dynamic, funny river guides who also can climb 5.12 rock while pointing out the fascinating geology—we are, in fact, minimizing their ability to become experts in any given area. It also is likely that we are putting them in situations that will, sooner or later, require adroit decisions.

Instead of pushing these new leaders too far too fast, it might be more prudent to come up with a realistic schedule whereby they are given the opportunity to train, practice, learn, debrief, and assimilate new skills, one at a time. Only after they can demonstrate consistent competency in an area should they be expected to add a new skill to their repertoire.

Role Modeling versus Mentoring. Much of my leadership training came about by watching others lead. Whether they knew it or not, my instructors were role models. Through their actions, role models can teach a great deal. Because there is a propensity for students to copy whatever the authority presents to them (partly because they desire to be like the leaders and partly because they lack the experience to discriminate between examples), it is important that leaders are always "on." That is, good leaders consistently model the highest caliber behaviors, knowledge, skills, and fitness levels.

Although role modeling certainly has a place in the outdoor industry, far more can be done to facilitate a new leader's skill development, decision-making, and overall progression, and *Complications* provides a great analogy of what it means to mentor (Gawande 2002).

Imagine, for example, surgeons-in-training who are allowed to observe skilled role models over time. By watching an experienced doctor in a variety of circumstances, the surgeons-in-training can potentially learn a great deal about the medical profession, about patient care, and even about making difficult decisions under stress. But if the surgeons-in-training are only allowed to watch from a distance, if they are not allowed to practice, to make mistakes, and to learn from those mistakes, how good can they really become?

> The bottom line is that student surgeons, sooner or later, have to be given the opportunity to practice on real people.

Consequently, surgeons-to-be are, in fact, allowed to practice on people. To start, they simply watch while someone with more experience performs an operation. But as their training progresses, the budding surgeons are given more and more responsibility while an attending surgeon supervises.

Gawande describes in detail how this mentoring system works (2002). The student surgeon, for example, is expected to do the prep work while the attending stands back and watches.

Before the operation begins, the mentor checks to see that nothing has been forgotten. The mentor does not stand over the patient and make all the decisions; instead, the surgeon-to-be is given quite a bit of latitude. The mentor offers occasional advice and is present in the event that something goes wrong. Ultimately, before a surgeon is allowed to "go it alone," he or she will have had plenty of opportunities to become competent.

But the bottom line is that student surgeons, sooner or later, have to be given the opportunity to practice on real people. As disturbing as this thought might be to the fellow who is going in for an operation, it is the only way for doctors to ultimately improve. As long as there is a risk management plan in place, the system should work. And in my opinion, the same holds true in the outdoor industry.

Currently in the outdoor industry, however, very little mentoring takes place. Instead, assistant leaders are expected to learn mainly through role modeling, by watching their experienced colleagues who might or might not explain their actions and thinking processes. Leaders-to-be might also develop their skills through staff trainings or by adventuring on their own, but they are not allowed to practice on real people, in real situations.

Assistant instructors seldom are given the opportunity to plan an activity, go through a briefing, and practice their decision-making under the tutelage of a mentor. In fact, it is as if they are surgeons-in-training who are expected to become experts simply by watching the lead man in action. After putting in a number of days or trips, it is almost a given that they will be promoted to lead positions.

Mentoring is one of my favorite parts of being a leader. It is when I get to reveal the secrets of teaching or guiding as I understand them. It is also when I get to watch a new leader gain confidence and grow. Mentoring is an active process. Ultimately, it is how I can help new instructors or guides develop their own styles and learn how to anticipate problems and/or student errors.

In order for a mentoring system to work, the mentor needs to be confident in the assistant and needs to be willing to stand back and let him or her potentially make a mistake. Before being allowed to lead, an assistant must be given the opportunity to face real challenges and real decisions; he or she cannot become an expert simply by watching others succeed or fail. The mentor must remember that it is not the trip leader's responsibility to do everything; it is just his or her responsibility to see that it gets done. Mentors should accept that there are different ways to accomplish various tasks, and they should not reject something just because it's not the way they would do it.

Mentors should transfer responsibility on a gradually increasing basis. To guide this process, they should take active roles in helping the assistants improve. It is important, for example, that each and every trip or experience be briefed and debriefed, and learning points should be tracked. Mentors should allow assistants to make decisions free from interference. They also should be diligent in having the assistants explain their logic, and assistants should be required to review their thought processes and decisions. Whenever something does not go as planned, or in the event of a close call or incident, the mentors should ask, "What would you do differently?"

From what I have seen, the outdoor industry has a long way to go before it embraces a mentoring program like the one used by doctors. Opportunities certainly exist, however, and perhaps by learning from others, we can take a step in the right direction.

The Importance of Reflection. Sometimes outdoor leaders "get away with things." Just because a group summitted or the trip ended with no injuries, the leaders assume that the positive outcome was the result of good decisions. As Paul Petzoldt, founder of the National Outdoor Leadership School, once said, however, "There are too many people with a lot of experience who don't know what they're doing. Some people say that experience is the best teacher. To heck with that. I know people who've been making the same mistakes for 40 years" (Graham 1997).

The best way to develop good judgment is through plenty of experience *plus* accurate reflection. The more—and more varied—experiences a person has, and the more he or she is able to reflect on and learn from those experiences, the better his or her judgment likely will be or become.

A common way to help new instructors develop judgment is to encourage personal trips and then help them reflect on their experiences. Encourage them to evaluate their decisions and learn from their successes and mistakes. Have each employee reflect upon a trip, from start to end, and then share those reflections with the employer. How did things go on an interpersonal level? Was the food adequate? Were there equipment problems? How accurate were his or her mountain weather skills? It should be treated as a learning experience and not just as another cool trip. The overt goal "to learn" is key.

Managers would be wise to avoid attaching undo importance to a potential employee's connection to past accidents or emergencies, and focus instead on what the employee learned from those accidents or near misses. How did he deal with it? What did she learn? Depending upon how the person processes the event, he or she could emerge with valuable new skills.

On the other hand, managers should probably be suspicious of someone who seems to have a long list of mishaps and mistakes. As my uncle says, "The harder I work, the luckier I get." It is worthwhile to remember that many of life's circumstances often have little to do with luck—good or bad.

The real challenge to staying safe in the outdoors, or anywhere else for that matter, is knowing oneself. Did it really grate on a guide that he received criticism for not getting his last group to the summit? Was the instructor insulted that student evaluations called her aloof? An aware leader will recognize his or her allergy to negative feedback and take steps to mitigate it. Regardless of which technique is used, the importance of reflection should not be underestimated.

Using Case Studies. Much can be learned from others' errors. Incident data, for instance, can be helpful to outdoor professionals. It (the data) helps professionals recognize trends and can provide guidance when it comes to identifying staff training topics. But simple numbers don't tell a story.

The myriad case studies used in this book provide examples of how someone else's misfortune can be used to enhance an instructor's judgment. Close-call accounts and case studies like these can be used to help beginning instructors improve their knowledge of potential student mistakes without having to experience them for themselves. By presenting and reviewing personal accounts in a nonjudgmental manner, trip leaders also can learn the importance of reflecting on all experiences, whether the outcome was desired or disastrous.

But for accident accounts to be used effectively as teaching tools, they need to include more than data. For example, I recently taught an avalanche safety course for the National Park Service (NPS). The NPS keeps track of statistics, but the avalanche data (e.g., the number of people caught and killed) was only marginally useful to its employees and visitors. To enhance learning from the case studies, I encouraged the agency to collect details regarding the parties involved, including their perceptions of the hazard and their decision-making processes.

Our propensity as human beings is to use data, no matter what it indicates, to support our desired or predetermined conclusions. In the world of avalanche educators, this is termed the *human factor*. If we couch case studies purely in terms of statistics, we lose touch with the human factors. To remind people that accidents entail more than an act of God (or an act of a fool), we need to tell the story with people in mind.

Who were the victims or survivors? What were their goals? How were decisions made? Were they good communicators? Were there errors in judgment?

In most avalanche accidents, for instance, the victim and/or the victim's party was able to identify the objective hazards that contributed to the avalanche event. Such signs might include nearby avalanche activity, collapsing layers within the snowpack, recent weather events, and/or steep slope angles. (Drew Leemon notes in Chapter Seven that Willy and Dave recognized several of these hazards prior to their incident.) The breakdown—the human error—is in the inappropriate interpretation of that data. This inappropriate interpretation is a reflection of our shared humanity, our propensity to be influenced by our past experiences, our fear of speaking up when we have concerns, plus many other factors.

If guides can't abide by the rules, they should quit and find different employment.

It is indeed rare that an "accident" doesn't have a trail of thinking errors or predispositions that made it all possible. If we can connect or identify with the people who made mistakes, perhaps we can take steps to mitigate our own weaknesses. The more we can empathize with those who have been involved in accidents, the more we can learn to recognize and avoid the traps and nuances that are often only noticeable in hindsight.

Policies, Procedures, and Written Guidelines. Seasoned trip leaders realize that techniques and/or decisions that might be justifiable on personal trips might be wholly inappropriate in work settings. New employees, on the other hand, often have a more difficult time understanding what is meant by *institutional risk management*. They don't necessarily understand the differences between personally acceptable behaviors versus professional or institutional standards. Through the use of a good staff manual, an organization can make many of these differences crystal clear.

Written policies and procedures are not intended to replace judgment. Instead, well-written guidelines can help identify and communicate an organization's risk tolerance, as Jerry Dzugan describes in the next chapter. Such guidelines also can help new employees—talented in the areas of technical skills but new to leading trips—develop a better understanding of how to sequence their activities, how to assess student progress, and what to do in the event of an emergency.

Some employees resent policies and feel that their managers don't trust their decisions. I've seen guides and instructors, once in the field, ignore directives for a variety of reasons. They might find a "rule" inconvenient, for example. Although they might acknowledge that the policies make sense for some guides (especially the beginning guides), they don't think the rules apply to them—at least not at that time. Not only is this type of attitude selfish, but it can put an entire organization at risk. If guides can't abide by the rules, they should quit and find different employment. Employees need to understand that, in addition to the clients, whole companies (including the livelihoods of the owners and other employees) are riding on their decisions. Employees need to align themselves with their companies' missions and follow their requests. Knowing and supporting what's in the manual is a positive step in this direction.

There is a good chance that outdoor leaders will never be able to demand high salaries. The jobs are seasonal, and clients seem most interested in selecting an outfitter based on cost. Unless or until we can educate the clients and can make a compelling case for choosing quality of service, there will be little incentive for businesses or outdoor leaders to be "the best." Even if there is little financial reward, however, good leaders can take pride in striving for personal excellence.

Program managers need to do more than remember what it was like when they were trip leaders. Times have indeed changed, and managers need to know what it means to be a quality instructor in today's world. By developing concrete plans for prospective leaders, by building upon their strengths, and by working on their needs, managers will be taking a giant step toward helping these employees realize their full potential.

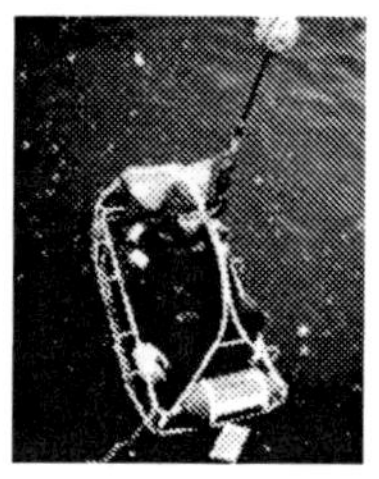

The Role of Perceptions, Genes, and Culture on Risky Behaviors

By Jerry Dzugan © 2005

In this chapter, Jerry Dzugan, marine safety expert and educator, takes a look at the roots of risky behavior and addresses the question: Are potentially unsafe actions the result of ignorance, experience, or genetics? The author explores the concepts of risk perception and risk tolerance, and he speculates about how each can affect not only an individual's behaviors, but also an organization's or industry's safety culture. The second half of the chapter provides ideas on how program managers and industry leaders can modify an organization's view of risk.

Much of this chapter is based on information and evidence obtained through the commercial fishing industry, but it easily can be applied to any risk-based industry.

In the late 1970s in Southeast Alaska, a small fishing vessel sank in a winter's gale. Two young, adventurous people were aboard: a man who was the owner of the vessel and a woman crew member. As the vessel was going down, the owner had to deal with a moral dilemma that would influence the safety culture of commercial fishing in the region for years to come. There was only one immersion (survival) suit available to protect a wearer from the near-freezing waters, and the owner had to decide who would use it. He gave his crew member the protective suit to don, and they both went overboard. Unprotected from the cold, the owner died of hypothermia within an hour. The crew member made it to shore and was rescued a number of days later.

For centuries, mariners have been aware of the hazards of the sea. Fishermen certainly had been aware of the existence of immersion suits prior to this incident. But few mariners purchased them, and at the time of the casualty, there was no law that required that the suits be carried on vessels. Many fishermen, in fact, considered the suits to be "body finders," at best. Others viewed them as objects of ridicule.

But for some reason, when word of this particular incident spread throughout the fishing fleet, vessel owners started voluntarily buying suits for all their crew members. In essence, a change in the region's safety culture began—more than a decade before immersion-suit rules were established. Today, the crewmen who do not carry the suits are the ones who are ridiculed. People who go to sea without them are even considered reckless.

Fishermen generally are an extremely independent and high-risk-tolerant group. Yet without being told to do so, they collectively agreed to change their risky behaviors for the better. While the subsequent changes in behaviors and attitude among this population have been unmistakable, the impetus behind those changes is not as clear. Could it really be that a single, relatively low-profile tragedy influenced an entire industry? And what were the contributing factors that influenced this group's long-held tolerance for risk?

Could it really be that a single, relatively low-profile tragedy influenced an entire industry?

Safety-oriented technology exists everywhere. Helmets for bikers, life jackets for boaters, safety harnesses for roofers, and avalanche beacons for those on snowy mountains are just a few examples of products that are available, are affordable, and have proven to save lives. Nonetheless, the products are not used consistently despite their beneficial qualities.

Then something happens—via a single event or through a gradual shift—that influences the way people think, believe, and act. The tide turns. Bike helmets become the "in" thing. Seat belts become the norm. Fishermen carry survival equipment. A whole country no longer smokes indoors.

This chapter looks at how and why this type of change occurs. I'll start by introducing a concept called risk tolerance; that is, people's willingness to be exposed to (if not seek out) potential dangers. Given that risk is integral to the lives of most outdoor professionals, I'll examine whether risk tolerance is developed or bred in people. I'll also define the term risk perception and describe how it affects people's behaviors. And finally, I'll talk about how a "culture" (the shared values of a group) can influence behavior and identify what it takes to change the safety culture of an organization or an industry.

Long before extreme sports and outdoor education became popular, at-sea adventures were accepted (if not respected) as high-risk activities. In the early days of the Dutch East India Company, most sailors did not return alive; yet, sailors were always found to go out on the next ship. Mariners had an extremely hazardous life no matter where they worked. In 1876 in the Bering Sea, 30 whaling ships were lost in just one winter. Some ports such as Gloucester, Massachusetts, lost hundreds of fishermen in the 1800s. Conditions were so bad in Norwegian ports that the government forcibly moved whole communities because so many of their fishermen were being lost. Nonetheless, people continued to go to sea.

For generations, fishermen, like many others who work and recreate in the outdoors, have seemed to accept that they might be hurt or killed. It was understood that the risks come with the territory. But fishermen seemed to tolerate an inordinate amount of risk, even when compared to the average adventurer. Why do I think so? Because fishermen risk more than just harm to themselves: They are willing to risk the well-being of their families, too. If a fisherman gets hurt, his family does not get fed. A fisherman's success is based on his ability to remain healthy while working in an unpredictable environment that can fluctuate greatly from year to year if not day to day. Fishermen are, perhaps, the ultimate risk managers.

Until recently, commercial fishing was the most hazardous major occupation in the United States. But over the last two decades, this statistic has changed. In the year 2000, for instance, commercial fishing lost its dubious distinction of having the highest occupational fatality rate in the country. And during the last decade, the fishing fatality rate in the United States has fallen 20 percent; in Alaska, it has fallen 61 percent.

By examining how this industry—steeped in a tradition of accepting high risks—has evolved, it is hoped that we, as outdoor professionals, can begin to understand what it takes to change a safety culture. While fishing and fishermen might be used to make certain points, the same influences that affected this profession ultimately can alter the behaviors and/or attitude of any group of people, whether they work in the office or outdoors, on land or at sea.

Risk Tolerance versus Risk Perception: What Is the Difference? In 1914, Antarctic explorer Ernest Shackleton supposedly published the following advertisement for shipmates:

> *Men wanted for hazardous journey. Small wages. Bitter cold. Long months of complete darkness. Constant danger. Safe return doubtful. Honor and recognition in case of success.*

Rumor has it that over 5,000 men applied.

Risk is ubiquitous. We face it every day. And while some people do everything possible to avoid being injured, other people, such as the 5,000 men who responded to Shackleton's ad, seem to thrive when the chance of harm is prevalent. Shackleton made it clear that there would be risk associated with his journey. He did not hide the fact that the men could be hurt, if not killed. So why were so many people willing to accept this challenge? Was it the small potential for "honor" and "success" that Shackleton mentioned? Or did other factors play a greater role? And why do some people seem to be averse to risky situations while others embrace it?

Risk perception is an individual's awareness of the likelihood of loss or injury. Risk perception is affected not only by the characteristics of a situation (i.e., some situations are more dangerous than others), but it also is influenced by a person's assessment of his or her own personal abilities. That is, if a person overestimates or underestimates his capacity to deal with a situation, his or her perception of the risk associated with the situation will be lower than someone else's. As long as a person has good risk assessment skills and is able to realistically determine the probability of harm in a rational way, things likely will be okay. He or she can conduct an effective risk-benefit analysis and make an appropriate decision.

Risk tolerance, on the other hand, has to do with one's threshold. Risk tolerance may be defined as the amount of risk an individual is willing to accept in the pursuit of a desired goal. Some goals may be judged as worthy of higher levels of risk than other goals. This threshold ultimately will help a person determine if or when the benefits outweigh the risks. Consequently, a person's risk tolerance will make a significant difference in that person's decision-making process.

Though the two concepts—risk perception and risk tolerance—differ, they are integrally related. Each affects how and why people engage in risky behaviors. In addition, several theories follow that attempt to explain why people do what they do.

The first proposition, which Gerald Wilde calls *Risk Homeostasis*, states that people in any given activity have a target level of risk that is considered acceptable (1997). Wilde believes that people do not attempt to eliminate risk. Rather, they seek to maintain equilibrium, and they adjust their behaviors so that they are able to perform within the accepted level. People create technologies and even laws to "make people safe." But Wilde postulates that for many, this just won't work.

According to Wilde, when hazards or risks are reduced in one area, people will compensate by changing their behaviors in another area. For example, studies have shown that once safety features were added to cars—such as air bags and antilock brakes—people began driving faster, more carelessly, and closer to the cars in front of them. The people modified their behaviors to bring the risk back up to acceptable levels.

The people modified their behaviors to bring the risk back up to acceptable levels.

This same type of compensatory response can be found in the fishing industry. Larger vessels, overall, are considered "safer" than their smaller counterparts. But operators of larger vessels usually are more willing to work in bad weather; thus, they take greater risks because they are in safer vessels. Further, when people fish or travel close to shore, especially if the weather is calm, they often feel little need to wear life vests or carry immersion suits, even though the water may be breathtakingly cold.

If Risk Homeostasis was the only factor affecting people's decision-making processes, technological or regulatory "improvements" would likely be wholly ineffective in changing behaviors. If it is a fact that some people simply have a high tolerance for risk, one can conclude that they will engage in actions that unnecessarily expose them to dangers regardless of rules or safety features. In fact, if risk tolerance reflects a basic personality trait of an individual, then it would be exceptionally difficult to substantially change that trait by using simple intervention programs.

A second theory that attempts to explain behaviors is called the *Zero Risk Theory* (Hunter 2002). This theory assumes that decisions are based on motivation. It suggests that one's assessment of a situation has to do with the perceived likelihood of a hazardous event. The risk perceived is influenced by the importance attached to the potential consequences—good or bad. According to this theory, as self-confidence increases (largely due to one's experience), perceived risk diminishes to the point of zero. In other words, people who are very experienced at doing risky things feel that there is no real risk at all.

To help readers understand how this might work, consider the following examples. Research has found that the more experience a pilot has, the lower his (or her) risk perception score will be. As the hazards become more familiar and as the pilot becomes more experienced in assessing and managing those hazards, the less he or she worries about them. A 1984 study, in fact, found that a significant number of experienced pilots indicated that they felt virtually no concern when they were asked to assess a risky scenario (Hunter 2002).

Economists observed the Zero Risk Theory at work when they studied the behaviors of people who have been impacted by suicide (bus or outdoor café) bombings. They found that *casual* bus passengers and café visitors reduce the amount of time they spend in these locations when bombings increase. But the *regular* users, largely undeterred, maintain their habits. To the latter group, the cafés and buses are comfortable and are used as part of their daily routines.

People who abide by the Zero Risk Theory believe that the key to changing inappropriately risky behaviors is education. They believe if people can improve their risk recognition and assessment skills, and if they are able to see that the dangers apply to them, then they will be equipped to avoid the risks around them.

A third theory that might help explain human behavior is the *Threat Avoidance Model* (Hunter 2002). This theory suggests that people will learn to anticipate hazardous events and situations and will then simply avoid them. Because the potentially hazardous situations are never encountered, the individual rarely feels threatened.

To put this third theory in context, consider the following: Novice kayakers sometimes avoid large open-water passages due to the potential of rough or hazardous sea conditions. Although this response might make sense at one level, it can lead to problems in the long run. Because these paddlers always stay close to land, and because they may have never experienced the rougher conditions, they might be unable to deal with a situation if/when it does arise. Not only would these people never feel the need to train to advance their kayaking skills, but they likely would be unable to accurately assess risk due to their limited experience. Consequently, a rogue wave/wake or a sudden change in water conditions could be quite dangerous, especially since it was not anticipated.

On land, this theory might imply that hikers who have poor orienteering skills will stick to established trails to avoid getting lost. Unfortunately, because they have not learned to look around and recognize environmental features, they likely would be unprepared if they ever had to deal with an unexpected off-trail experience. To them, the probability of ever having to deal with such a situation is virtually non-existent; it doesn't even register as a perceived risk.

The truth is, life is full of risks, especially if we venture into the outdoors. So while the Threat Avoidance Model might apply to the average citizen, it cannot fully explain why some people actually seek out risk. And to the adventurer, seeking out the unknown is what it's all about.

The *Type T Theory* examines what drives the adventurer (Temple University 2003). In the 1970s, psychologist Frank Farley came up with the idea that some people actually seek out risk due to an inheritable trait. These people, Farley suggested, thrive in intense environments. The men who applied to work on Shackleton's vessel likely would have fallen into this group.

Farley, who coined the trait as "Type T" (as in thrill seeking), has spent decades figuring out what makes risk-taking and thrill-seeking personalities tick. "Extreme behavior, and extreme sports, are fascinating," he says. "Climbing Mount Everest is one of the riskiest things a person can do. The mountain is strewn with bodies. One hundred seventy-five people have died attempting it." But, he adds, people line up and pay lots of money every year for the opportunity to join the ranks. Why do people do it? It is an interesting question, and Farley is working to come up with some answers. Not only is the researcher examining psychological differences between men and women who have ascended the mountain, but he has explored the implications of Type T personalities beyond sports to include business, work, relationships, and education.

In evolutionary terms, the risk-takers (who survive) may be the ones who advance a species.

In evolutionary terms, the risk-takers (who survive) may be the ones who advance a species. In commercial fishing, these are the people who fish the hardest, the most hours, and in the worst weather. By bringing in the greatest haul, they get the greatest reward. In turn, they are able to afford bigger boats, which allow for even bigger catches. And they are able to support the biggest families, who then pass on those T cells.

Farley's theory can indeed be used to help explain why certain people tend to take more risks (Temple University 2003). But if risk-taking behaviors are genetically "hard wired," one might surmise that it would be difficult, if not impossible, to change them. Yet even Farley acknowledges that, with guidance, people can learn to take risks in more socially acceptable ways. The fact that Type T fishermen have altered their perception of risk and have modified their behaviors suggests that there is more to the story than genetics.

The Effect of Culture on Risky Behaviors. In the context of this chapter, *culture* is defined as the sum of all knowledge, skills, attitudes, and behaviors that are passed down from one generation to the next. This definition is important since it suggests that major changes in any culture will need to be passed on through (or embraced by) family members, coworkers, and society at large.

Cultural differences often are rooted in how people within a group collectively view the world. For example, countries built from immigration (e.g., Australia, New Zealand, and the United States) tend to have more of an individualistic culture than a collective one. In an individualistic culture, the efforts, or at least successes, of an individual tend to be more valued than those of a group. As such, individual risk taking is encouraged—it can be used to differentiate the best from the rest.

Culture also can affect how people view the role of "fate" in their lives, and fatalistic beliefs can influence risky behaviors within a group. Fatalism has to do with an acceptance that some things are out of a person's control (they are a matter of fate). Fatalism is especially strong among people who have to confront the forces of nature for a living.

Fatalism is one of the reasons why mariners have had a long and strong history of superstition. Even today, leaving port on a Friday or bringing a black bag aboard is avoided by some of the most technologically advanced mariners. Historically, fishermen would not allow safety to even be discussed on the vessel; to discuss the topic was to tempt fate. The belief that "stuff happens" is so strong among certain fishing cultures that, until recently, leaded boots were available in several American ports (so that a fisherman who went overboard could avoid suffering and sink quickly).

Cultures that are heavily fate-based can be especially challenging to change, even through education and training. At a maritime survival school in the United Kingdom, for example, a group of mariners once refused to practice CPR skills. Their logic: "If it is willed that one must die, why bother?"

In other words, collective values garnered from one's family or community can and do influence an individual's view of risk. While we might be able to modify an individual's behavior through rewards, punishment, or education, to change an entire culture, we would have to change the way an entire population thinks and reasons. It is no small task, and shifts in attitude and behavior usually happen incrementally. Changes in safety, in fact, often are more of an evolutionary, rather than revolutionary, process.

Psychologists believe that an "organizational culture" can be established if and when people in a group see themselves as having unique qualities. When members or an organization or industry, for instance, are able to share myths, rituals, legends, and even a specialized language (as mariners, paddlers, and climbers do), they develop a sense of identity that separates them from other groups. And, ultimately, that organizational culture will develop certain beliefs about risky behaviors and safety.

Investigators noticed that an employee's risky behaviors typically were a reflection of the organization's behaviors as a whole.

Research on the safety culture of an organization or an industry has been fairly recent, but the findings are quite relevant to this chapter. Following some well-publicized accidents (the Challenger Shuttle explosion and the Chernobyl disaster, for instance), investigators noticed that an employee's risky behaviors typically were a reflection of the organization's behaviors as a whole (Wiegmann et al. 2002). Ultimately, they realized, an entire industry's views on safety can be influenced—for better or worse—by the behaviors of a few.

So what does it all mean? Are potentially unsafe actions the result of ignorance, experience, or genetics? The bottom line is that no one theory can be used to explain why people do what they do. I am certain that some people are more prone to risky behaviors than others. But while the born risk-takers may be the ones to start a new country or a new business, there is no doubt that encouragement, support, and approval (or disapproval) from others influence behaviors within a society. Consequently, if an organization's or industry's leaders hope to modify their employees' dangerous ways, they will need to incorporate a variety of techniques in order to address individuals as well as the masses.

THE KEYS TO MODIFYING RISKY BEHAVIORS

Although few readers will advocate for a truly "safe" society, we can probably all agree that some behaviors and attitudes are more injurious than helpful. And while theorists likely will never agree on exactly what motivates people's behaviors, nearly all behavior scientists acknowledge that behaviors—including risky ones—can be modified. So if we hope to create safer industries, the question becomes: How do we do it?

According to experts who are charged with changing an organization's or an industry's safety culture, the following elements are required for success: The industry's leaders must share the same core values in safety. These same leaders must understand that the operative word in safety is not accident, but error. They also must understand and accept that the most concerning errors exist in the systems, not in the people. Employees and field workers must be confident in their leaders. And, finally, the field workers must perceive that by changing their ways, they are doing the right things for the right reasons (Weigmann et al. 2002).

So how is this accomplished? The answer lies in education, training, improved technology, and regulations. The rest of this chapter will look at how each of these steps might be used to positively modify safety culture across outdoor industries.

Education. Education has long been a leading tool in the quest to modify behavior. In fact, if one believes that improved risk perception will lead to less risky behaviors, education could be the means to the end. That is, if we can help people accurately assess the risks, the rest (safer behaviors) should follow, right? Unfortunately, behavior modification isn't quite that simple. While education is a key to improved safety, unless safety information is presented carefully, it likely will fall on deaf ears.

Researchers have found that younger drivers rate potentially hazardous situations as less hazardous than older drivers do, mainly because they lack knowledge and experience (Hunter 2002). In order to help drivers improve their risk assessment skills, one would think that education could do the trick. The study also found, however, that young drivers do not believe that the "dangers" associated with driving apply to them. Recent research is discovering that the portion of the brain involved with risk assessment is not even fully developed until the age of 25. Thus, while young (male especially) drivers are able to rattle off abstract statistical numbers regarding driving dangers and fatality rates, they have not personalized the risks. In order to reach this group, educators must improve how they deliver their messages, and the use of experiential education methods might be of particular value.

Despite the advent of the Internet and other 10-second news sources, storytelling is still strong in many societies. The fishing industry, in fact, is rich with anecdotes. Not only is it fun to hear about people who engage in similar work, but when the accounts are relevant and applicable, they can be educational as well. In the case study that was used to introduce this chapter, fishermen in the area related well to the story of the two young crew members. The two were widely known. The fact that an immersion suit had saved someone under the harshest conditions made an impact. Because they were able to personalize the event, local fishermen modified their own behaviors long before they were forced to do so.

Marine safety instructors from the area began using the case study in their classes and were able to gain credibility with even the most skeptical audiences. Not only did these "teachers" have practical information, but they were able to convey an important message: With some training, with the right survival equipment, and with the right attitude, you do not need to become a lost-at-sea statistic. One no longer had to go down with the ship. Survival was no longer simply a matter of fate, but it was in a fisherman's own hands. Because the woman lived through a worst-case scenario, fishermen were forced to acknowledge that injury and death were not necessarily job requirements. Instead, equipment and education could mitigate the hazards. No preaching was necessary; the story spoke for itself.

No preaching was necessary; the story spoke for itself.

The use of videos showing actual casualties at sea with fishing vessels also has been a very valuable tool in safety education classes. This methodology has affected people whose risk behavior is described under the Zero Risk Theory (Hunter 2002). By watching a vessel capsize and sink quickly, viewers are able to improve their understanding of the hazard—as well as the immediacy of the situation. Commonly, viewers are heard to say, "I didn't know a boat could sink so fast!" This visual aid was particularly effective for new fishermen who had little at-sea experience. In fact, on at least two occasions, prospective fishermen were so impressed by the footage that they decided to go into a different profession.

Through the use of applicable case studies and close calls, fishermen and outdoor users can become more educated regarding the real hazards of their respective industries. Not only will their risk assessment skills improve, but the message that "stuff happens" hits home. As one fisherman stated recently during a discussion on this topic, “Look at the people we can see in the harbor right now. Three-quarters of the guys have lost boats and survived!” When reality is so close at hand, it becomes very difficult to maintain the belief that “It can’t happen to me.”

Training. In the 1970s, a group of Alaskan safety trainers conducted a series of workshops for fishermen. Each of the trainers had a background in commercial fishing. Their hope was to educate fishermen in the use of survival equipment in an effort to help reduce the rate of marine fatalities. Even the way the workshops were promoted—they were called “survival” classes, not “safety” classes—was done to appeal to the membership of a risk-tolerant culture. The facilitators were credible, and through the use of hands-on trainings, they were able to modify behaviors in the commercial fleet. The way the safety message was delivered was not condescending, nor was it out of touch with the real world of fishing.

Practical, hands-on trainings can play an important role in behavior modification. While cognitive ideas and concepts can be successfully presented in a lecture or discussion format, performance-based skills are best learned through kinesthetic techniques. Most fishermen and other outdoor enthusiasts are very practical. Not only do they work with their hands, but hands-on techniques typically are conducive to their learning styles.

During the hands-on safety trainings, fishermen made several discoveries that probably would have been missed had the same information been offered in a lecture or brochure. During pool and harbor sessions, for example, they learned how important it was to have a properly fitting immersion suit because they *experienced* getting cold and wet if the suit was not well fitted or maintained. There were no written tests used to assess student progress. Rather, participants were required to perform certain skills, such as donning an immersion suit in a given time (60 seconds). The experiential portions of the training are always the most highly rated in course evaluations.

To determine if this training made a difference in safety, Ron Perkins of the Alaska Native Health Service did a follow-up study (1995). Perkins found that 1,500 fishermen had been trained between 1991 and 1995. One hundred fourteen fishermen died in Alaska during this same time frame, but no trained fishermen were included on the fatality list. The study was able to show a high correlation between training and survival rates. Also revealing were the numerous statements that had been collected from workshop graduates. They said that, as the result of the training, their risk perception had been raised, and they were able to avoid some previously unanticipated problems.

Improved Technology. In the 1990s, significant improvements were made in marine safety equipment, and a number of survival equipment requirements were implemented. Not surprisingly, a decrease in the number of fatalities followed. Although life rafts, immersion suits, and emergency position indicating radio beacons (EPIRBs) have helped save hundreds of lives through the years, it is interesting to note that these changes in technology have not had an effect on how many vessels are lost at sea. In other words, improved technologies have not modified the mariners' risky behaviors. Fishermen apparently are exposing themselves to the same risks on the ocean; the number of sinkings has not changed. But because "survival" equipment is now engineered better and is required, mariners are surviving events that previously would have killed them.

A key in the fatality rate drop had to do with the fact that fishermen began believing that the equipment could make a difference to them and to their outcomes. Acting as credible spokesmen, the survivors (some of whom were leaders of their "communities") told their stories to others. Fishermen became aware of friends and colleagues who had lived through harrowing incidents. And the equipment, which had previously been "suspect," became trusted. As it became obvious that these tools were saving more and more fishermen, the equipment gained acceptance in the fleet.

Regulations. In the 1950s, a man named Leon Festinger began studying what he described as the *Cognitive Dissonance Theory* (Festinger and Carlsmith 1959). According to Festinger, cognitive dissonance is a state of internal tension that results when there is an inconsistency between one's knowledge or attitude and one's behavior. This incongruity creates psychological discomfort. Festinger believed that in order to minimize this discomfort, people tend to 1) avoid situations that create or increase dissonance, 2) pass the experience off as an exception to the rule, or 3) change their values or belief systems so that they match the behaviors. In other words, if a person, for whatever reason, is forced to adopt certain behaviors, he or she will begin to believe that that behavior is the right thing to do.

If a person ... is forced to adopt certain behaviors, he or she will begin to believe that that behavior is the right thing to do.

The following is an excerpt from one of Festinger's papers on the topic:

> *When there is an inconsistency between attitudes and behaviors (dissonance), something must change to eliminate the dissonance. ... It is most likely that the attitude will change to accommodate the behavior.*

Regulations often are used to force a change in behaviors. While many people in the outdoor industry tend to fight rules, especially if the rules go against their values, according to Festinger's theory, this type of forced change in behavior ultimately should have a correlative effect on attitudes

(Festinger and Carlsmith 1959). Although this theory, as it applies to the use of regulations, does have its naysayers, there are examples within the fishing industry of its viability and success.

In the 1980s, the U.S. Coast Guard (USCG) began a program to try to convince fishermen to voluntarily purchase immersion suits, life rafts, and EPIRBs. The effort resulted in a negligible improvement in the overall safety of the fishing fleet. By contrast, 10 years later, the USCG began requiring that vessels carry the equipment. In addition, crew members were expected to be trained in its use. Although some fishermen balked at the imposed rules, eventually the regulations were accepted and fatality rates fell. In the 1980s, a few hundred fishermen became educated in survival equipment use and procedures. Under the required training of the 1990s, thousands were trained.

Going back to Festinger's theory, rule makers might be interested to know that, if rewards or punishments are used, the size and type of reward or punishment can make a difference in the effectiveness of a behavior modification program (Festinger and Carlsmith 1959). If a reward or a punishment is small but effective, a person will be more likely to change his or her attitude about a behavior. But if a reward or punishment is excessive, it then can be used to justify a temporary change in behavior. In other words, a person may change his behavior if he thinks there is a chance he will be punished, but the same person actually will be less likely to feel the need to modify his values.

Obviously, regulations are not always going to be effective in changing attitudes toward safety. People might change their behaviors, for instance, only when there is a significant threat of "getting caught." In fact, this strategy (regulations) requires that enforcement take place, which can be difficult, at best, in most outdoor industries.

As a case in point regarding how the likelihood of negative consequences plays into things, consider the F/V

Lasseigne. The vessel sank in 1985 with the loss of all three crew members. There was only one immersion suit onboard for the three crew members. Although the laws at the time did not require vessels to carry suits, the surviving family members filed a civil suit against the boat owner. In that case, the judge declared the vessel unseaworthy because not enough suits were carried, and a large settlement was awarded.

Despite the finding, fishermen in the area did not modify their behaviors. Few went out and purchased suits. Fishermen did not see the risk of being sued as likely. However, once the USCG began requiring the suits and began conducting spot checks, the threat of penalty for noncompliance became an effective motivator.

Well-designed regulations ultimately can "raise the bar" in a safety culture. However, if a regulation's imposers have any hope that a new rule will be accepted, they must make sure that it is carefully considered and the need for it made clear. They also should make sure that the people who will be most affected are allowed to provide input on the rule as well as its implementation. They should have a realistic phase-in period. And above all, regulation imposers should be certain that the rule will be seen as a practical solution to the problem at hand.

If these steps are overlooked, regulations can have an opposite effect that can actually detract from the safety culture that the leaders hope to establish. A backlash can occur that will make enforcement difficult. It is very helpful to remember that the "velvet glove" of education about the need for regulations should precede the "leather fist" of enforcement. For the most part, the USCG followed this formula, and this helped moderate the angst among fishermen who had to make significant outlays of cash to comply with the new equipment and training requirements.

Making Safety Matter. Before any behavior change becomes permanent, the person who is asked to do the changing must believe that the change matters. If mariners believe equipment can save their lives, then they will be more likely to use it. If people believe there is a good chance they will be punished for not doing something, then their behaviors might change as well. Another way to convince people that safety matters is to show them how their behaviors affect the ones they love.

The role of families can make a difference in risky behaviors, and the fishing industry has tried to take advantage of that fact. Wives and children can influence behavior by helping fishermen recognize how an injury or fatality would affect the whole family. Further, by making safety a family issue, it is hoped that there will be improved motivation and greater buy-in from all involved. Family nights have been used to get people to the pool, to don immersion suits, and to introduce all family members to the equipment that is now available.

Changing a safety culture is a complicated enterprise that defies a simple formula.

Besides targeting the present generation of fishermen, much effort has been placed on training the next generation as well. As a result, groups around the country are offering safety education in the schools. The hope is to teach youngsters good habits early on and influence their tolerance for risk while they are in a more open state of personality and behavior development.

Dramatic changes have occurred in the fishing industry over the past 20 years. It is no longer the nation's most dangerous profession. And although the industry can in no way be considered "safe," it has seen steady improvements and will continue to do so. These changes did not take place overnight; the evolution took place over a generation and is still taking place today.

Changing a safety culture is a complicated enterprise that defies a simple formula. Thus, holistic and multiple-layered approaches must be tried. The factors that influence risky behaviors deal with personality, societies, and perhaps even genetics. Some people argue that the key lies in education. Others advocate for regulation. Still others believe that people will always take chances. But the fact is that behaviors and values can be changed. By recognizing what it takes to modify behaviors that are deemed "too risky," safety educators and risk managers can begin to create risk management systems that can move with, instead of against, the tide. They can create an atmosphere that encourages safe behaviors and reinforces the fact that nothing stays the same.

Lessons Learned Across Industries

By Vicki Cornish © 2005

The National Oceanic and Atmospheric Administration (NOAA) Fisheries (referred to here as the National Marine Fisheries Service, or NMFS) deploys observers to collect data from U.S. commercial fishing and processing vessels. Despite the fact that many observers had never even been to sea prior to their employment, during the first 10 to 15 years that the observer program existed, nearly all observer training focused on requisite biology; very little training was conducted in the name of safety. In the 1990s, however, NMFS observer trainers began incorporating greater amounts of safety related topics into the two- to three-week observer-training workshops.

By 2000, this effort had grown significantly as NMFS trainers from around the country (not all of whom were employed by NMFS) worked cooperatively to coordinate their efforts. Today, not only do the various observer training sites have standardized curriculum, but they also use standardized experiential methodologies and have worked to coordinate their crisis response plans.

The information presented here is intended to remind readers that, not only are there lessons to be learned from case studies and history, but there is value in sharing experiences across risk-related industries.

Some would call us lucky. In the last 25 years, the National Marine Fisheries Service (NMFS) has deployed thousands of fisheries observers on fishing vessels, with only one loss of life. On March 22, 1990, the fishing vessel *Aleutian Enterprise*, a medium-sized factory trawler operating in the Bering Sea, was topping off its fish catch before heading home. Upon retrieval of the gear, the lines snapped and the net broke, spilling fish suddenly on deck and causing the vessel to list severely to one side. The fisheries observer working on the vessel at the time was presumably in the factory when water started flooding in through an opening in the hull. The vessel capsized and sank within 10 minutes. Twenty people were recovered; nine people, including the observer, were reported missing and presumed dead.

This event happened at a time when the hazards of fishing were well known, and the fishing industry was working hard to implement improvements in safety. NMFS was acutely aware of the risks of placing observers on fishing vessels and already had a strong safety training program in place in the North Pacific. However, this incident led to a renewed commitment to safety training, with an emphasis placed during training on risk awareness and emergency preparedness. Observers were taught that regardless of how safe a vessel might be and how well the captain and crew might be trained in emergency response, the observer on that vessel also needed to be aware of the hazards of working on fishing vessels and of how to respond quickly in the event of an emergency. Unfortunately, NMFS had not yet realized the value of sharing the lessons learned from this event with other NMFS observer programs around the country.

Fishing is and always has been a dangerous occupation. The U.S. Department of Labor ranks fishing as the second most dangerous occupation in America, with 71 fatalities per 100,000 workers. NMFS deploys over 500 observers on fishing vessels each year. These observers collected over 50,000 days worth of data in 2003. Trained primarily by NMFS, fisheries observers collect data on the fish catch, as well as any marine mammals, sea turtles, and other marine species that may be taken as bycatch (discarded or unintentional catch). While observers are not involved with the deployment or retrieval of fishing gear, they are exposed to many of the other same hazards as fishermen. The nature of these hazards may vary from vessel to vessel, but all vessels are subject to the effects of weather, difficult working conditions, heavy machinery, and long hours.

NMFS operates its observer programs out of 10 different locations around the country. Each observer program has been established independently to meet the unique demands for data collection in one or more regional fisheries. However, without a formal mechanism for communication between programs, each program has had to develop its safety training program largely independently. That, coupled with the fact that training was largely the responsibility of fisheries biologists with little or no background in fishing vessel safety, resulted in a fair amount of variability between programs in the quality of safety training and emergency preparedness among observers.

As the observer program began to grow in the early 1990s, it was apparent that NMFS needed a better process for ensuring the safety of fisheries observers. In 1996, Congress directed NMFS to develop regulations based on nationally applicable guidelines for determining when a vessel is not required to carry an observer due to safety concerns or lack of adequate accommodations. It also required that these guidelines identify actions that vessel owners or operators would reasonably be required to take to render their vessels adequate and safe. These mandates were incorporated in the Sustainable Fisheries Act[2] of 1996, legislation that reauthorized the Magnuson-Stevens Fishery Conservation and Management Act.

The development of observer health and safety regulations that would apply to all NMFS observer programs required coordination at the national level. And it was then that it first became apparent just how differently each of NMFS's regional observer programs approached observer safety. Some programs had well-established procedures for observer safety training and required that observed vessels had emergency response equipment, such as life rafts, fire extinguishers, and

[2] P.L. 104–297, Oct. 11, 1996

emergency position indicating radio beacons (EPIRBs) before an observer could be deployed. Other programs provided observers with only a minimum of training and had no procedures for checking whether a vessel had any emergency response equipment, let alone for preventing observers from being deployed on inadequately equipped vessels.

In the development of the observer health and safety regulations, NMFS drew on the considerable leadership and experience of the U.S. Coast Guard (USCG) in fishing vessel safety. NMFS adopted the USCG voluntary commercial fishing vessel safety examination program as the key indicator of whether a vessel was suitable for the deployment of observers. Although the USCG vessel examination program was voluntary, and only checked for the presence and proper functioning of emergency response equipment, NMFS made having the "safety" decal a federal requirement for all observed vessels.

This new federal requirement was the beginning of a cultural shift in recognizing NMFS's responsibility for the safety of observers. In its 1996 amendments, the Magnuson-Stevens Act also required that NMFS ensure that observers were provided with adequate training. A survey of observer program managers identified safety training as one of the most important areas that needed to be considered in the development of observer competency standards (ASMFC 1999). However, the development of safety training standards would prove to be quite a challenge.

Two events helped kick-start the development of the safety training standards. In June 2000, an international workshop on observer programs brought to light a disconnect between our (i.e., the National Observer Program, [NOP]) safety regulations and our working procedures. Observers at the workshop noted that while the health and safety regulations stated that observers were not required to board, nor stay aboard, unsafe or inadequate vessels (i.e., vessels without the required emergency response equipment), in practice, an observer's refusal to board a vessel could be grounds for dismissal. Observers questioned whether NMFS really supported the observer's right to refuse an unsafe vessel. NOP working practices seemed to suggest that getting the data took priority over ensuring the safety of the observer. The workshop also publicly highlighted inconsistencies in safety training from region to region.

Shortly afterward, in October 2000, several of NMFS's regional observer program managers attended the first International Fishing Industry Safety and Health (IFISH) conference. At the conference, NMFS observer trainers met with the world's leading authorities on fishing vessel safety. The trainers realized that since they were responsible for training observers, it was incumbent on them to improve NMFS safety training and develop minimum national safety training standards. They also realized that there was a group of extremely knowledgeable experts in fishing vessel safety to whom they could turn for help.

The first step was to train the trainers. NMFS contracted with Jerry Dzugan of the Alaska Marine Safety Education Association (AMSEA), whom the trainers had met at IFISH, and asked him to customize his Marine Safety Instructor Training course for the observer trainers. The training emphasized the unique working environment and hazards associated with commercial fishing vessels, and addressed proper emergency response procedures. The course syllabus included not only what to teach, but how to teach it so that emergency response would be instinctive. The trainers received instruction in all aspects of emergency response at sea, as well as effective teaching methods. The observer trainers were taught to prepare lesson plans that emphasized hands-on, student-directed teaching.

In some programs, NMFS needed to place a greater emphasis on training observers to demonstrate competency in the use of survival equipment. Studies have shown that the proper use of safety equipment by fishermen could greatly reduce water exposure fatalities due to vessel loss and falling overboard. The USCG reports that of the 218 fatalities resulting from vessel loss, the usage rates of survival equipment were very low (2000). For PFDs/immersion suits, life rafts, and EPIRBs, the usage rates were only 18 percent, 16 percent, and 24 percent, respectively. The USCG analyses indicate that fishermen survive nearly twice as often when survival equipment is used.

After the initial weeklong course in April 2001, the trainers met to discuss which safety topics were being covered by each regional program and which "core" topics should ideally be covered in every program's safety training. But they were a long way off from being able to cover these topics in all regions. Questions were raised as to what benefits would be provided by developing standards for safety training. Would these standards be limiting for regions that already had well-developed curricula? Would smaller programs be able to meet these standards as well? Despite these questions, NMFS forged ahead with the development of training standards. For these fisheries biologists turned safety trainers, the change would take time and additional training materials. AMSEA helped provide the tools and access to the resources, but it was up to the trainers to apply them.

It was about this time that several of the trainers read the book *Lessons Learned: A Guide to Accident Prevention and Crisis Response* (Ajango 2000). Jerry Dzugan recommended it, suggesting that there might be some parallels between the observer program and the University of Alaska's mountaineering program. Individuals were attracted to the activities offered by both programs because of the adventure promised, with little awareness or regard for the associated risks. The University of Alaska had a solid training and emergency response program but was still unprepared for the backlash that occurred when lives were lost. NMFS had a solid program in most regions, yet realized that little had been done to prepare for what might happen if another observer were seriously injured or killed.

The first area of focus was the development of better documentation of safety training procedures and trainer qualifications in every regional program. Although NMFS fisheries observers are contracted employees, NMFS always has maintained that it is the government's responsibility to conduct or oversee all aspects of training. Because the data that observers collect is fundamental to the agency's ability to effectively manage the nation's fisheries resources, the quality of the data is paramount and can only be guaranteed if NMFS keeps the training in-house. But had our emphasis on training-the-trainers resulted in actual improvements in safety training? Were training procedures adequately documented? Would this documentation hold up to the kind of scrutiny that the University of Alaska went through? Despite how thorough the training might be, would NMFS be seen as negligent if something went wrong because of the lack of national standards identifying minimal training requirements and trainer qualifications? In such a situation, NMFS might be perceived as responsible for not preparing observers adequately for the risks they faced at sea, especially with the increasing deployments of observers on smaller and less well-maintained vessels.

In 2002, NMFS initiated a comprehensive evaluation of its regional safety training procedures and the effectiveness of its trainers, and also set out to more fully document its safety training curriculum (Ajango, Cullenberg, and Dzugan 2004a). The evaluation of each program's safety training procedures was concluded in 2004 and has provided a starting point for making improvements to the observer training program. The safety trainers from each program met to review the results of this evaluation and have used it to develop draft minimum national standards for safety training of observers in all programs. The standards have been adopted and are now in place for all of NMFS's observer programs.

The second area of vulnerability was the lack of a crisis response plan. This point was driven home in October 2002, when an observer was nearly lost after a fire on the fishing vessel *Galaxy*. The observer was well-trained in safety response, had access to her survival gear, and acted quickly and responsibly in treating other injured crew men. In the end, however, she was forced to abandon ship with neither a life raft nor an immersion suit. Supported by a crew man, she was able to survive for several hours in the frigid waters of the North Pacific before being rescued. Had this event turned out otherwise, how would NMFS have responded? Would the agency have been counseled to avoid communicating with the observer's family and to deny any responsibility for the event? How might the agency's response be viewed by other observers? How should the agency balance the need to minimize exposure to liability with the desire to show compassion for a fallen observer?

In 2003, we contracted out for assistance with the development of an agency crisis response plan (Ajango, Cullenberg, and Dzugan 2004b). The recommendations of that report are helping to clarify the agency's crisis response philosophy and identify what procedures will be most appropriate to follow at both the regional and national levels in the event of a crisis.

So what has NMFS learned so far? We have learned that by working together and sharing experiences, we can develop better programs that build on best practices while avoiding common pitfalls. We also have learned that change in large organizations is slow and must take into account all perspectives in order to be successful. We have learned that the majority of work must be done by a core group of committed individuals who can place a high priority on steady progress. And we have learned that progress can be greatly enhanced if there is a commitment to safety at every level.

Within the National Oceanic and Atmospheric Administration (NOAA), NMFS's parent agency, there is a commitment to safety at the highest level. Vice Admiral Conrad Lautenbacher, NOAA's Administrator, has identified safety as one of his top priorities for the agency. The establishment of a safety culture within NOAA is apparent in efforts to develop safety standards for chartered aircraft and fishing vessels to complement standards already in place for NOAA research vessels.

The lessons NMFS has learned along the way are many, and there are many improvements that must still be made. NMFS needs to increase opportunities for sharing information between our regional programs and with other similar programs operated by public and private organizations. We need to strengthen our alliance with the USCG and forge new alliances with the National Institute for Occupational Safety and Health and other groups that are working to enhance fishing vessel safety. We need to be actively involved in internal and external forums that encourage an exchange of ideas and a sharing of experiences. We need to revise our observer health and safety regulations to clarify fishermen's responsibilities when they are selected to carry an observer. We need to encourage full disclosure in the recruitment of new observers, to ensure that they are fully aware of the hazards of working as observers on fishing vessels. We need to fully document the kinds of injuries that observers suffer, and start documenting close calls in all regions as well. We need to place a stronger emphasis on risk awareness and accident prevention. We need to proactively engage the NMFS leadership in thinking about how an observer tragedy might test the agency's resolve. And we need to push ourselves to strive to provide the best program that we can, engaging the fishing industry, observers, and observer provider companies in helping us to improve the safety of observers.

No entity can achieve its safety goals independently. Sharing information with others who have been through the process is critical. Programs that routinely put people at risk must be open to learning from both the successes as well the mistakes of others. They must build alliances with other safety professionals and incorporate the best practices of others into their own procedures. And they must be open to criticisms of their own programs in order to improve them. No program should rely on luck. Instead, there must be a willingness to learn from the experiences of others and share experiences openly to promote a safety culture. Lives depend on it.

Chapter One: Adam's Story

AWA (American Whitewater Affiliation). 1998. "Safety Code of American Whitewater." International Scale of River Difficulty. U.S. Standard Rated Rapids: Class I to Class III+. Revised. Web site: http://www.americanwhitewater.org.

Battaglia, J. 1998 (October 29). *Chronology of Events and Background Information on the July 24, 1998, Accident on the Deerfield River Involving the Near Drowning of Adam Dzialo, a Participant in the Team Adventure Program.* Prepared for Greenfield Community College.

Boston Globe. 2001 (July 26). "A Son's Honor: 3 Years After Tragic Accident, Family Still Seeks Apology from School." Author Patrick Healy, Globe staff.

Dilorenzo, J. 2001 (September 6). "Who's Afraid of Adam Dzialo?" *The Valley Advocate.* Web site: http://old.valleyadvocate.com.

Douglas, K. 2004 (July) to 2005 (August). E-mail messages and personal interviews with Deb Ajango (ed.).

Dzialo, P. 2004 (July) to 2005 (August). E-mail messages and personal interviews with Deb Ajango (ed.).

GCC (Greenfield Community College). 1998 (October 7). Letter to Charles Walbridge. Investigation Scope of Work letter from Charles Wall, president.

Greenfield Health Director. 1998 (August). Letter to GCC. Cease-and-desist letter.

Mooney, F. 2005 (March 15). E-mail message to Deb Ajango (ed.).

Wade, I. 1998 (December 4). *Risk Management Review of Adventures Unlimited, Greenfield Community College.*

Walbridge, C. 1998 (November 2). *Report on Adam Dzialo's Near Drowning.*

Chapter Two: Chuck's Story

Bonning, C. 2004 (July) to 2005 (August). E-mail messages and personal interviews with Deb Ajango.

Bonning, R. 2004 (July) to 2005 (August). E-mail messages and personal interviews with Deb Ajango.

International Express. 1998 (June 30). "Death Climb Mountaineer to Sue Army." Author Greg Swift.

Mills, W. J. 1993. *Frostbite*. Alaska State Medical Association.

Packer, S. 2002 (February). *A Highpointer's Journal.* Self-published.

Chapter Three: Risk Management Planning: A Closer Look

Ajango, D. 2000. *Lessons Learned: A Guide to Accident Prevention and Crisis Response.* Anchorage, Alaska: University of Alaska Anchorage.

Ewert, A. 1989. *Outdoor Adventure Pursuits: Foundations, Models, and Theories*. Scottsdale, Ariz.: Publishing Horizons, Inc.

Gawande, A. 2002. *Complications: A Surgeon's Notes on an Imperfect Science*. New York: Picador.

NHTSA (National Highway and Transportation Safety Administration). 2005. "15-Passenger Vans: High Riding Death Traps." Web site: http://www.safetyforum.com.

Beaufort Gazette. 2005 (June 12). "Insurers, Others Recognizing Passenger Van Safety Concerns." Web site: BeaufortGazette.com.

Williamson, J. 2000 (September). "Serious incident (accident) review process." From the proceedings of the 2000 Wilderness Risk Management Conference, Anchorage, Alaska.

Chapter Four: Creating a Workable Emergency Action Plan

Ajango, D. 2002 (October). "The Ultimate Goal of Crisis Response." From the proceedings of the 2002 Wilderness Risk Management Conference, Reno, Nev.

Anchorage Daily News. 1997a (December 10). "Truth Months Too Late: Report Puts Blame Where it Belongs."

Anchorage Daily News. 1997b (December 14). "Climbing Deaths; The Facts Revealed."

Anchorage Daily News. 1997c (December 19). "It's Time to Get Rid of the Wilderness Studies Program at UAA."

Behar, R. 1990 (March 26). "Exxon Strikes Back." *Time*.

Boston Globe. 2005 (July 24). "Hospitals Study When to Apologize to Patients." Author Liz Kowalczyk, Globe staff.

Caponigro, J. R. 2000. *The Crisis Counselor: A Step-by-Step Guide to Managing a Business Crisis*. Chicago: Contemporary Books.

Exxon Valdez Oil Spill Trustee Council. 2002 (July 19). Web site: http://www.oilspill.state.ak.us.

Gregg, C. 2002 (July 23). Personal interview with Deb Ajango.

J.R. O'Dwyer Company, Inc. 1997 (June 18). *Jack O'Dwyer's Newsletter*. Web site: http://www.odwyerpr.com.

Henry, R. A. 2000. *You'd Better Have a Hose if You Want to Put Out the Fire*. Windsor, Calif.: Gollywobbler Productions.

Lukaszewski, J. E., & D. A. Cooper. 1992 (April/May/June). "You're Courting Disaster … Without a Litigation Communications Strategy." *Executive Action*. The Lukaszewski Group. White Plaines, N.Y.

Mitchell, J., and G. Every. 2001. *Critical Incident Stress Debriefing: An Operations Manual for CISD, Defusing and Other Group Crisis Intervention Services*. Ellicott City, Md: Chevron Publishing.

Mitroff, I. I., C. M. Pearson, and L. K. Harrington. 1996. *The Essential Guide to Managing Corporate Crisis: A Step-by-Step Handbook for Surviving Major Catastrophes.* New York: Oxford University Press.

Susskind, L., and P. Field. 1996. *Dealing With an Angry Public*. New York: The Free Press, a division of Simon & Schuster Inc.

University of Alaska Anchorage. 1997 (July 1). "Information Update on Mountaineering Accident." *University Bulletin*. University Relations.

Vanderbilt Medical Center, 2005. "Why People Sue Their Health Professionals." Web site: http://www.mc.vanderbilt.edu.

Williamson, J., J. Ratz, and D. Miller. 1997 (December 9). *Review Team Report: Alaska Wilderness Studies Program—Ptarmigan Peak Incident of June 29, 1997*. Anchorage, Alaska: Chancellor's Office, University of Alaska.

Williamson, J. 2000 (September). "Serious incident (accident) review process." From the proceedings of the 2000 Wilderness Risk Management Conference, Anchorage, Alaska.

Chapter Five: In the Path of the Ripple: The Effect of a Tragedy on a Program's Employees

Ajango, D. 2000. *Lessons Learned: A Guide to Accident Prevention and Crisis Response.* Anchorage, Alaska: University of Alaska Anchorage.

Allen, J. 2005. *Coping with Trauma: Hope through Understanding*. Arlington, Va.: American Psychiatric Publishing, Inc.

Bolin, R. 1993. "Natural and Technological Disasters: Evidence of Psychopathology." *Environment and Psychopathology*. New York.

Chodron, P. 1997. *When Things Fall Apart: Heart Advice for Difficult Times.* Boston: Shambhala Publications, Inc.

Everly, G., and J. Mitchell. 1998. *Assisting Individuals in Crisis: A Workbook*. Ellicott City, Md.: International Critical Incident Stress Foundation, Inc.

Everly, G., and J. Mitchell. 2000. *Critical Incident Stress Management: Advanced Group Crisis Interventions, A Workbook*. Ellicott City, Md: International Critical Incident Stress Foundation, Inc.

Garvey, D., and J. D. Spencer. 2005. "Improving the Moral Reasoning of our Staff." Prescott College.

Haidt, J. 2003. "The Moral Emotions." In *Handbook of Affective Sciences*. Edited by R. J. Davidson, K. R. Scherer, and H. H. Goldsmith. New York: Oxford University Press.

Leach, J. 1994. *Survival Psychology*. New York: New York University Press.

Mitchell, J., and G. Every. 2001. *Critical Incident Stress Debriefing: An Operations Manual for CISD, Defusing and Other Group Crisis Intervention Services*. Ellicott City, Md: Chevron Publishing.

Naparstek, B. 2004. *Invisible Heroes: Survivors of Trauma and How They Heal*. Bantam.

National Institute for Occupational Safety and Health. 2005. Web site: http://www.cdc.gov/niosh.

Chapter Six: Managing the Risks of a Lawsuit

No references.

Chapter Seven: Understanding How Accidents Happen in Outdoor Pursuits

AEE (Association for Experiential Education). 1998. *Adventure Program Risk Management Report: Volume II.* Incident Data and Narratives from 1991–1997.

AEE and NOLS (National Outdoor Leadership School). 2002. *Adventure Program Risk Management Report: Volume III.* Data and Narratives from 1998–2000.

Ajango, D. 2000. *Lessons Learned: A Guide to Accident Prevention and Crisis Response.* Anchorage, Alaska: University of Alaska Anchorage.

Ajango, D., P. Cullenberg, and J. Dzugan. 2004 (June). *Review & Evaluation of NMFS Observer Safety Training*. Final Report. Prepared for the National Marine Fisheries Service.

American Alpine Club and Alpine Club of Canada. *Accidents in North American Mountaineering.* Accident data. Published annually. Golden, Colo.: American Alpine Club.

Geis, C. 1984. "Human Factors Investigation." University of Southern California.

Gookin, J. 1998 (October). "Defining and Developing Judgment." From the proceedings of the 1998 Wilderness Risk Management Conference, Black Mountain, N.C.

Green, R., and M. Doran. 1998 (October). "Decision-Making for Students." Wilderness Risk Management Conference. From the proceedings of the Wilderness Risk Management Conference. Black Mountain, N.C.

Haddock, C. 1999 (October). "Epics, Lies and Hero Stories; The Folklore of Near Misses in the Outdoors." From the proceedings of the 1999 Wilderness Risk Management Conference, Sierra Vista, Ariz.

Hale, A. 1983. *The Dynamics of Accidents Theory.*

Hawkins, F. 1987. *Human Factors in Flight*. Gower Technical Press.

Leemon, D. 1999 (May). *NOLS Newsletter*. Special Edition Highlighting Risk Management.

Patton, B. C. 1992. "Health, Safety and Risk in Outward Bound." *Journal of Wilderness Medicine 3*.

Perrow, C. 1984. *Normal Accidents; Living with High Risk Technologies*. Princeton University Press.

Reason, J. 1991. "Identifying the Latent Causes of Aircraft Accidents Before and After the Event." ISASI Forum Proceedings.

Sagan, S. D. 1995. *The Limits of Safety: Organizations, Accidents, and Nuclear Weapons*. Princeton University Press.

Schimelpfenig, T. 1995. "Teaching Safety Awareness." *NOLS Newsletter*. Special Edition Highlighting Risk Management.

Thompson, D. 1999. *Operational Risk Management*. Southern California Safety Institute.

Williamson, J. 1997 (October). "Understanding the Meaning of Risk." From the proceedings of the 1997 Wilderness Risk Management Conference, Snowbird, Utah.

Williamson, J. 1999 (October). "Potential Causes of Accidents in Outdoor Education." From the proceedings of the 1999 Wilderness Risk Management Conference, Sierra Vista, Ariz.

Wood, R. 1988. "The Definition of Aircraft Accident Causes." ISASI Forum Proceedings.

Chapter Eight: The Loss of Leadership in the Outdoor Industry

Ewert, A. 1998. "Decision Making in the Outdoor Pursuits Setting." *Journal of Environmental Education*. Washington, D.C.: Heldref Publications.

Gawande, A. 2002. *Complications: A Surgeon's Notes on an Imperfect Science*. New York: Picador.

Graham, J. 1997. *Outdoor Leadership: Technique, Common Sense & Self-Confidence.* Seattle, Wash.: The Mountaineers.

Kohn, L. T., J. M. Corrigan, and M. S. Donaldson, eds. 2000. *To Err Is Human: Building a Safer Health System*. Committee on Quality of Health Care in America, Institute of Medicine. Washington, D.C.: National Academy Press.

Leape, L. L., D. M. Berwick, and D. W. Bates. 2002. "What Practices Will Most Improve Safety? Evidence-Based Medicine Meets Patient Safety." *JAMA*: 288.

Pisano, G., R. Bohmer, and A. Edmonson. 2001. "Organizational Differences in Rates of Learning Evidence from the Adoption of Minimally Invasive Cardiac Surgery." *Management Science*.

Priest, S. and M. A. Gass. 1998. *Effective Leadership in Adventure Programming*. Champaign, Ill.: Human Kinetics.

Wilde, G. 1997 (October). "Risk Homeostasis Theory: An Overview." From the proceedings of the 1997 Wilderness Risk Management Conference, Snowbird, Utah.

Chapter Nine: The Role of Perception, Genes, and Culture on Risky Behaviors

Alvear, M. 2005. "Risky Business." Web site: http://www.salon.com.

Festinger, L., and J. Carlsmith. 1959. "Cognitive Consequences of Forced Compliance." First published in *Journal of Abnormal and Social Psychology*: 58.

Hunter, D. R. 2002 (September). "Risk Perception and Risk Tolerance in Aircraft Pilots." Prepared for the Federal Aviation Administration (FAA), Office of Aerospace Medicine. Washington, D.C. Web site: http://www.hf.faa.gov/docs/508/docs/cami/0217.pdf.

Perkins, R. 1995 (November/December). "Evaluation of An Alaskan Marine Safety Training Program." *Public Health Reports*: 110.

Temple University. 2003. "Reaching The Type T Summit: Temple Prof Heads To Mt. Everest." Tip Sheet: Tips for May 16 to 23. Office of News and Media Relations. Web site: http://www.temple.edu.

Wiegmann, D., H. Zhang, T. von Thaden, G. Sharma, and A. Mitchell. 2002 (June). A Synthesis of Safety Culture and Safety Climate Research. Prepared for the FAA. Aviation Research Lab. Web site: http://www.humanfactors.uiuc.edu.

Wilde, G. 1997 (October). "Risk Homeostasis Theory: An Overview." From the proceedings of the 1997 Wilderness Risk Management Conference, Snowbird, Utah.

Afterword: Lessons Learned Across Industries

Ajango, D. 2000. *Lessons Learned: A Guide to Accident Prevention and Crisis Response.* Anchorage, Alaska: University of Alaska Anchorage.

Ajango, D., P. Cullenberg, and J. Dzugan. 2004a (June). *Review & Evaluation of NMFS Observer Safety Training*. Final Report. Prepared for the National Marine Fisheries Service.

Ajango, D., P. Cullenberg, and J. Dzugan. 2004b (October). *Development of a Comprehensive and Effective Emergency Action Plan for NMFS Observer Programs.* Final Report–Phase II. Prepared for the National Marine Fisheries Service.

ASMFC (Atlantic States Marine Fisheries Commission). 1999 (December 27). *National Fisheries Observer Competency Standard: Summary Evaluation of Training Needs Assessment Survey Responses.* Contract report. Washington, D.C.

USCG (U.S. Coast Guard). 2000. "A Review of Lost Fishing Vessels & Crew Fatalities, 1994 to 2000." Office of Investigation and Analysis.

Chapter One: Adam's Story
By Kay Landis, with assistance from Phil Dzialo

Kay Landis is a staff writer and editor for the Office of Community Partnerships at the University of Alaska Anchorage (UAA). She has a Master of Fine Arts degree in Creative Nonfiction from UAA, and has served as assistant editor for *Alaska Quarterly Review*, the university's literary magazine. She was an associate editor on *Lessons Learned: A Guide to Accident Prevention and Crisis Response.* Some of Kay's original work has been published in *Alaskan Passages* and *Under the Sun.*

Phil Dzialo has a Bachelor of Art in Psychology from Providence College. He also has a Master of Education in Counseling from Salem State, and has completed work toward his Doctorate of Education at Northeastern University (Boston) and the University of Massachusetts in Amherst. Phil has been a high school principal at Mohawk Trail Regional High School in Shelburne Falls, Massachusetts, since 1982, and has been involved in education as a teacher, counselor, and administrator since 1972. He currently sits on the Board of Directors of MASSArc (a statewide disabilities advocacy group) as well as the United Hampshire-Franklin Arc (a disabilities advocacy group in western Massachusetts). Phil is the father of Adam Dzialo.

Chapter Two: Chuck's Story
By Deb Ajango, with assistance from Chuck Bonning

Deb Ajango is the owner and director of SafetyEd: Safety Education for Outdoor and Remote Work Environments. In her work with SafetyEd, Deb has provided consultation as well as conducted safety audits around the United States and overseas. She has spent more than 15 years working in outdoor education and has more than 2,000 days of field experience. Deb has presented at a variety of national symposiums and conferences. From 1997 to 2003, she was coordinator of the University of Alaska Anchorage's academic outdoor education department. She is currently a member of the Association for Experiential Education's Accreditation Council and is one of the coeditors of the *2005 Manual of Accreditation Standards for Adventure Programs*. Deb is also editor and coauthor of *Lessons Learned: A Guide to Accident Prevention and Crisis Response*. She has a Bachelor's degree in Psychology and a Master's degree in Clinical Psychology, both from the University of Wisconsin Madison.

Chuck Bonning retired as an automotive technology professor from Ferris State University in 2004. He has enjoyed a lifetime of outdoor adventure, including bicycling, canoeing, backpacking, and mountain climbing. Chuck was the 84th person to achieve the goal of climbing to the highest point of all 50 states. He presently resides in Big Rapids, Michigan, with his wife, Rachel, and their two Labradors, Denali and Joy.

Chapter Three: Risk Management Planning: A Closer Look
By Deb Ajango

Chapter Four: Creating a Workable Emergency Action Plan
By Deb Ajango

Chapter Five: In the Path of the Ripple: The Effect of Tragedies on Programs and Their Employees
By Deb Ajango

Chapter Six: Managing the Risks of a Lawsuit
By Charles "Reb" Gregg

Charles (Reb) Gregg is an attorney who specializes in outdoor recreation and general litigation. He has served as legal counsel to the National Outdoor Leadership School since the late 1970s. Reb is a frequent speaker in the outdoor recreation industry and has authored a number of articles. He is a former coeditor of the *Outdoor Education & Recreation Law Quarterly*. Reb is currently a member of the Association for Experiential Education's Accreditation Council. He also serves on the Board of Directors for Friends of Big Bend National Park, the Student Conservation Association, and the Wilderness Risk Managers Committee. He is a former president of the Houston Bar Association.

Chapter Seven: Understanding "How Accidents Happen" in Outdoor Pursuits
By Drew Leemon

During his 28 years with the National Outdoor Leadership School (NOLS), *Drew Leemon* has served as instructor, branch director, and, since 1996, Risk Management Director. As Risk Management Director, Drew is responsible for directing all aspects of adventure program risk management systems for NOLS worldwide. Drew developed and implemented the NOLS Accepted Field Practices, one of the cornerstones of NOLS's risk management plan. He is a past chairman and a current member of the Wilderness Risk Managers Committee. He also is the leader of the Adventure Program Incident Data Reporting Project, the editor of the *Adventure Program Risk Management Report*, a member of the Association for Experiential Education (AEE) Accreditation Council, and a coeditor of AEE's *2005 Manual of Accreditation Standards for Adventure Programs*. Drew has presented at an array of professional conferences on risk management issues and provided numerous internal and external program audits, incident reviews, consultations, and expert opinions. He is also coauthor of the recently released book, *Risk Management for Outdoor Leaders*.

Chapter Eight: The Loss of Leadership in the Outdoor Industry
By Blaine Smith

Blaine Smith is an avalanche expert and educator for the Alaska Avalanche School. He has spent more than 2,000 days traveling throughout Alaska and around the world and has worked as a guide for more than two decades. Blaine received his Bachelor's degree in Wildland Recreation Management from the University of Idaho in Moscow. On an ongoing basis, he offers consultation and instruction in technical rescue and avalanche safety to private groups as well as governmental agencies.

Chapter Nine: The Role of Perception, Genes, and Culture on Risky Behaviors
By Jerry Dzugan

Jerry Dzugan has been the executive director of the Alaska Marine Safety Education Association (AMSEA) since 1987. As part of his work with AMSEA, Jerry has developed outdoor survival curriculum and videos, taught marine safety instructor training courses, and developed a number of U.S. Coast Guard-approved workshops. He has written many publications on outdoor safety and survival and has received numerous state, regional, and national awards for work in marine safety education and training. Jerry has a Bachelor's degree in Secondary Education and a Master's degree in Marine Education and Training from the United Nations school in Sweden. He is a member of the Commercial Fishing Vessel Safety Advisory Committee.

Jerry has kayaked in Alaska, Mexico, and Central America; sailed on vessels 16 to 44 feet in length; captained a charter boat; and worked as a commercial fisherman. He has visited and studied in 28 countries in Europe, Asia, South America, and North America. His hobbies include hiking, maritime history, river rafting, and boating.

Afterword: Lessons Learned Across Industries
By Vicki Cornish

Vicki Cornish is a fisheries biologist with the National Oceanic and Atmospheric Administration's National Marine Fisheries Service (NMFS), a federal agency charged with conserving the nation's living marine resources. She began her career with NMFS in 1989 in its Office of Protected Resources, working with commercial fishermen nationally to reduce incidental captures of marine mammals and other protected species in fishing gear. Ms. Cornish went on to lead the NMFS National Observer Program, where she helped coordinate improvements in safety training for fisheries observers, as well as other efforts in support of the agency's regional fishery observer programs. She recently returned to working on marine mammal conservation issues as the Marine Mammal Branch Chief for the agency's Southeast Regional Office in St. Petersburg, Florida, but continues to stay involved in the development of safety policies for both the observer program as well as chartered aircraft and fishing vessels.

Printed in the United States
214204BV00005B/10/A

9 781929 148547